# Praise for *The Twelve*

"Danielle has beautifully woven a book ... ir journey into the feminine and the myste ... .t the goddesses and the feminine found in ... ..gy, mythology, ritual, and the magical, it is not a bo. ... ..umen only. It is a book for all on the seeking path—to the realms of their own inner space; all the types are familiar to us, but now we have the language."

—Erin Sullivan, author, astrologer, and teacher

"Danielle Blackwood has crafted a beautiful and smart zodiacal tribute to the Goddess. All too frequently when astrologers present archetypal descriptions of the twelve Sun signs, the signs are unconsciously framed in terms of the masculine psyche and its agenda. In order to eliminate this habit as astrologers, we need the Goddess to speak first, we need her to speak more often, and we need her to speak from her own authority. To this end, Blackwood has contributed something powerful to the field of archetypal astrology."

—Adam Elenbaas, astrologer, author of
*Fishers of Men: The Gospel of an Ayahuasca Vision Quest*

"Although we've never met, Danielle Blackwood is a kindred spirit. As I read her poetic prose, she beckoned me to join her at that moonlit crossroads where magick and the sacred feminine intersect with astrology. That is where it all began and that is where it will wind up, as the patriarchal spell unravels and we remember who we are. Let *The Twelve Faces of the Goddess* be a lantern for you on that homeward path."

—Steven Forrest, author of *The Inner Sky*

"A refreshing look at astrology from the perspective of the divine feminine. The topic of astrology is often intimidating to learn, but Blackwood presents information about the signs and how to use the magick and power of the goddesses connected to them in an easy-to-understand and relatable way . . . this is a must-read."

—Stephanie Woodfield, author of *Dark Goddess Craft*

"This beautifully written book is a thoroughly uplifting, as well as informative, read and now has a place at the top of my list of favorite astrology books."

—Lisa Tenzin-Dolma, author of
*The Planetary Myths* and *Take Control with Astrology*

"A brilliant melding of the ancient art of astrology with modern depth psychology perspectives, resulting in a partnership that can be used to facilitate personal growth, catalyze spiritual transformation, and deepen one's conscious relationship with the self."

—Jhenah Telyndru, founder of the Sisterhood of Avalon and author of
*Avalon Within: A Sacred Journey of Myth, Mystery, and Inner Wisdom*

"Well and clearly written, this book will please experienced astrologers and take beginners to a higher level of understanding ... Danielle Blackwood's book brings a fresh and useful perspective."
—Ashleen O'Gaea, author of several books on Wicca, including the Celebrating the Season of Life series

"Looking for a book that seamlessly weaves Goddess spirituality, archetypal psychology, and astrology together into a tapestry of love, magic, and (surprise!) real-world wisdom? The Twelve Faces of the Goddess by Danielle Blackwood is the book you are looking for."
—Anne Newkirk Niven, editor of SageWoman magazine

"Danielle Blackwood has created a thoughtful exploration of the reader's personal journey full of empowering aha moments and compassionate wisdom. This is a smart and intuitive guide that connects all the pieces for both the new and seasoned mystical practitioner."
—Mickie Mueller, author of The Witch's Mirror

"With an accessible voice and her distinctive style, Danielle Blackwood brings clarity to the convergence of astrology, archetypes, and Campbell's hero's journey ... all with a deliciously goddess-centric twist! This is a volume to return to again and again."
—Jen McConnel, author of Goddess Spells for Busy Girls

"Danielle Blackwood shares her lifelong study as well as her personal experience of esoteric practices in this friendly, engaging guidebook to self-discovery."
—Donna Henes, author of The Queen of My Self

"Beautifully written and thought-provoking. This book is a clever combination of astrology and magick with some unexpected goddess associations for the twelve zodiac signs."
—Ellen Dugan, author of Natural Witchery

"Danielle Blackwood gives us a unique approach to the sacred feminine by taking her readers on a journey through astrology and magick, joined together in ways both new and ancient. Blackwood's writing is lyrical yet still easily accessible and offers seekers a path to finding their own mystical identities."
—Deborah Blake, author of Everyday Witchcraft

"Danielle offers a mystical yet very practical approach to establishing a personal relationship with the sacred feminine ... With Goddess mythology, hands-on ritual practices, and nods to the stars, the information Danielle presents here is in-depth, highly individualized, and absolutely magickal."
—Priestess Brandi Auset, author of The Goddess Guide

"The Twelve Faces of the Goddess brings new life to the ancient supposition of 'as above, so below.'"
—Kris Waldherr, bestselling author of The Book of Goddesses and creator of the Goddess Tarot

# THE TWELVE FACES OF THE
# GODDESS

## About the Author

Danielle Blackwood is the astrology columnist for *SageWoman* magazine and Banyen Books and Sound and has studied and practiced astrology for more than thirty years. She is certified in the Principles and Practice of Contemporary Psychological Astrology through her teacher, world-renowned astrologer and author Erin Sullivan. Danielle is also a Registered Therapeutic Counselor (RTC) specializing in working with women in the areas of self-esteem, sexuality, body image, life transitions, and cultivating a connection with the sacred feminine through personalized rites of passage ceremony. Danielle encourages clients all over the world to live a life of authenticity and radical self-acceptance, helping them find meaning on their journey and consciously reframe their stories through an archetypal lens. As a priestess, she has been facilitating workshops, classes, ceremonies, and retreats on astrology and women's mysteries since 1994. Danielle lives in an enchanted cottage on magical Salt Spring Island in the Salish Sea with her husband, Jamie, a six-toed cat named Watson, and the newest member of the family, a rescue Staffordshire Terrier named Daisy. You can find her at danielleblackwood.com.

# THE TWELVE FACES OF THE
# GODDESS

## TRANSFORM YOUR LIFE WITH ASTROLOGY, MAGICK, AND THE SACRED FEMININE

## DANIELLE BLACKWOOD

Llewellyn Publications
Woodbury, Minnesota

First Edition
Sixth Printing, 2021

Book design by Donna Burch-Brown
Cover design by Kevin R. Brown
Cover images by Alfons Marie Mucha/Superstock/Fine Art Images

Llewellyn Publications is a registered trademark of Llewellyn Worldwide Ltd.

**Library of Congress Cataloging-in-Publication Data**
Names: Blackwood, Danielle, author.
Title: The twelve faces of the goddess : transform your life with astrology, magick, and the sacred feminine / by Danielle Blackwood.
Description: First Edition. | Woodbury : Llewellyn Worldwide, Ltd., 2018. | Includes bibliographical references and index.
Identifiers: LCCN 2017061506 (print) | LCCN 2018008497 (ebook) | ISBN 9780738756127 (ebook) | ISBN 9780738756035 (alk. paper)
Subjects: LCSH: Goddesses. | Astrology. | Magic. | Goddess religion.
Classification: LCC BL473.5 (ebook) | LCC BL473.5 .B53 2018 (print) | DDC 202/.114—dc23
LC record available at https://lccn.loc.gov/2017061506

Llewellyn Worldwide Ltd. does not participate in, endorse, or have any authority or responsibility concerning private business transactions between our authors and the public.
All mail addressed to the author is forwarded but the publisher cannot, unless specifically instructed by the author, give out an address or phone number.
Any internet references contained in this work are current at publication time, but the publisher cannot guarantee that a specific location will continue to be maintained. Please refer to the publisher's website for links to authors' websites and other sources.

Llewellyn Publications
A Division of Llewellyn Worldwide Ltd.
2143 Wooddale Drive
Woodbury, MN 55125-2989
www.llewellyn.com

Printed in the United States of America

## Dedication

For my grandmother Anna, who taught me the healing medicine of story, the near magical power of hope, and the inherent wisdom in both strength and kindness—and without whose courage, I would never have been here.

# CONTENTS

### Part Two
### The Heroine's Journey:
### Through the Signs with the
### Guiding Goddess Archetypes   63

## Gemini ♊  97

## Cancer ♋  111

## Leo ♌  129

## Virgo ♍  145

## Aquarius ≈ 227

## Pisces ♓ 243

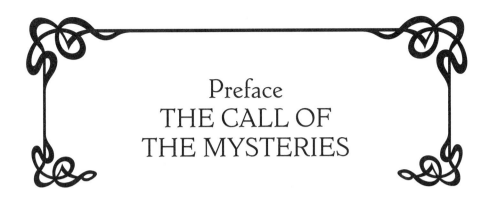

# Preface
# THE CALL OF
# THE MYSTERIES

The Mysteries have always called to me. I grew up in a small West Coast island village, and they whispered from the shadows of the deep green forest I had to pass through on my way to school. I could hear them from my bed at night, crashing up on the wild Pacific shore with a cadence that made my heart ache. Starting in fifth grade, while other kids played at recess, I could be found hidden in the school library, spellbound by tales of mythology and enchanted by books on world religions. When I was thirteen, I happened upon a paperback copy of Waite's *The Pictorial Key to the Tarot* in a free-book bin in the library. I was entranced by the enigmatic images, and I knew intuitively I had opened a door that would lead to the path I didn't even know I was searching for. We were not lucky enough in our small town to have anywhere that sold actual tarot cards, so I carefully cut the black-and-white illustrations out of the book one by one and created my very first deck. I studied the pictures for hours, locked in my room, mesmerized by the mysterious symbols and the flood of impressions that arose from them. Whenever I left my room, I would hide my makeshift cards under a corner of rug I pulled up from the floor of my closet, carefully positioning a pair of shoes on top. Instinctively, I knew my conservative parents would not approve.

Thus began my lifelong study of the esoteric. When I ran away from home to the big city at seventeen, I found to my absolute amazement that there was much more to be discovered. Soon after landing in Vancouver,

British Columbia, I found my way to Banyen Books, a veritable wonderland of books, crystals, tarot cards, and all manner of magickal talismans waiting to be revealed. Wide-eyed and breathless, I put my money on the counter and, feeling like an initiate come to the foot of the temple, reverently purchased my first metaphysical books: *The Inner Sky, The Spiral Dance*, and *Positive Magic*. And, as luck would have it, while leaving the shop laden with my new treasures, I noticed a community bulletin board advertising astrology classes. I was home.

Although it's an understatement, life in the Big Smoke as a teenage runaway was less than idyllic. I ate, slept, and breathed astrology and tarot and spent whatever extra money I could conjure on books. I did tarot readings for friends and cast my first astrology charts the old-fashioned way—without a computer. I did them by hand, doing mathematical calculations armed with a protractor, an ephemeris, and an old atlas. I committed to studying as an apprentice under a local astrologer, Nikiah Jaguar. I wanted more than anything to make a living as an astrologer, but that would not come to pass for some time.

Coming back to my apartment late one evening after a Prince concert, I curled up in an armchair, opened my journal, and began to write. Although I often ended my day jotting down my thoughts, that night I scribbled in my notebook past the wee hours and into the sunrise. Call it automatic writing, call it channeling; what emerged was life changing. There are intermittent phrases peppering this forty-page epiphany, such as "I don't know what's happening, I seem to be on some kind of roll!" In the still of that night, I unwittingly stumbled onto something much bigger than myself. As the sun crept in and illuminated the new day, I held in my hands a curious sheaf of papers—many of which I had no recollection of writing—that was a veritable table of correspondences and explanations as to how magick, tarot, and astrology were all interwoven with the same threads. I felt as though I had stumbled upon nothing less than the meaning of the universe, and the way I saw the world would never be the same.

Fast-forward thirteen years later. I was in Glastonbury, England, at the tail end of my Saturn return and searching for clues to my next chapter. Got my first tattoo—the mystical vesica piscis symbol—on the back of my neck. I climbed Glastonbury Tor in the cold December night and tried to sit vigil there to watch the sun come up, but it was freezing and my flight back to Canada was the next day. I vowed I would return in the spring.

I arrived on Lunar Beltane 1999. And I decided to stay for a while. It was like I had stepped into the land of Faery; it could have been a thousand years ago. The memories of that time are elusive, ephemeral, and numinous. Scenes dance through my head: climbing up the back of the Tor in the dark, laughing, falling into a patch of stinging nettle, and, finally, tucked in under the Full Moon, sitting atop the mystical Eggstone with the faery tree looking on. Cupping my hands and drinking the healing waters from the Red and White Springs. Studying for hours in the Library of Avalon. Sitting before sunrise on the side of Glastonbury Tor, to turn around and see that the tower had disappeared ("Just like before the Christians got here!"). Initiation. Betrayal that shook me to my foundations. Spherical twin rainbows over the Chalice Well. Tying ribbons on an ancient tree at a baby-naming ceremony on Solstice Eve. Falling on my knees in the abandoned abbey. Straying into the Otherworld.

Somehow, I eventually extricated myself from this land where time ran so differently. I went back to my world, but I left a piece of myself there and brought a little bit of Faery back with me, tucked in a hidden corner of my big red backpack. And as many do if they find their way out of the realm of the Fae, I returned with a slight touch of madness. I began writing, painting, creating ritual—anything to try to translate that mystical rite of passage. I picked up my academic career, which had been interrupted all those years ago as a teenage runaway, and enrolled in university. It has been years since I last set foot on that distant shore, and it has taken many moons, many pathworkings, and endless conversations to integrate the experience. I still dream of it.

And so here I am, 2018. I have realized my dream: I make my living as a full-time archetypal astrologer and registered counseling therapist. The journey took a while, but there is no substitution for the initiation of hard-won wisdom and a life well lived.

## Part One
# ASTROLOGY AND MAGICK
## A Sacred Marriage
## between Heaven and Earth

Astrology and magick are woven from the same threads. The more you learn about one, the more you will intuitively understand about the other. The elements used in astrology—fire, earth, air, and water—are the same elements used in most magickal traditions. This is because they are the basic building blocks of all life, the substance of the known universe.

Astrology is a symbolic language of energy, and when we realize how its patterns are so artfully aligned with the turning of the seasons and the rhythms of the earth, it becomes an evocative vocabulary that can empower us to find our own sacred connection to the immanent divinity in nature and ourselves. Astrology can illuminate our personal myths, helping us see the deeper meaning of events, relationships, trials, and victories that unfold in our lives.

The twelve astrological signs contain a virtual treasure trove of potential and possibility, with a seemingly endless array of expression. As a whole, these twelve archetypes reflect the entire spectrum of life and all the lessons on the path. They include everything in the collective unconscious and reflect the stories, mythos, and truths of every culture through every time. They are the twelve faces of the Goddess.

I wrote this book with my clients in mind: people who identify as women who want to explore astrology, magick, and the sacred feminine in a practical way that will help them understand themselves better and enhance their everyday lives. These women don't necessarily want to give up their day jobs to become astrologers or magickal adepts, but they do crave insight about why they're here and are curious about what gifts, talents, and life lessons they brought with them into this lifetime. Many are often self-described seekers and have already done much personal work through therapy, yoga, meditation, self-help books, workshops, and retreats. Others have recently begun taking their first steps toward spiritual exploration and self-discovery. Some are going through significant personal transition and are looking for guidance, inspiration, and meaning.

Many are understandably feeling frustrated with the state of the world and the ongoing race, class, and gender injustice that is the hallmark of a patriarchal society. They want to know that there is an alternative perspective. While many women are familiar with the term *sacred feminine*, some are hearing it for the first time, and it strikes a chord—they are intrigued and want to learn more. All have in common a longing for the numinous and wish for a deeper, more visceral connection with the sacred. Perhaps most importantly, all these women have heard the call of the Mysteries and feel compelled to follow that call.

While this book focuses on the sacred feminine and the lives of women, all are welcome. The Goddess is present in all of us regardless of gender, and her wisdom is needed in the world now perhaps more than ever. I have intentionally focused this book from a feminine perspective for two reasons. The first is that in my practice I specialize in working with women. The second is that I believe that traditional astrology has always been very male-centric. For example, all ten planets with the exception of the Moon and Venus are traditionally considered masculine. I think this reflects a long history of patriarchal dominance, whose time has come to be questioned across all disciplines, including astrology. And, while much groundbreaking work has been done in astrology to include the feminine through the exploration of recently discovered asteroids, there is always room for new perspective and further evolution in this ancient science and art.

Perhaps because I am a double Aries, which is known in traditional astrology as a so-called masculine sign, I've always wondered why the Aries traits of courage, bravery, and enthusiasm necessarily had to be labeled masculine. I questioned why most of the traditional planetary rulers were Greek gods and not goddesses. In astrology, Aries is ruled (or associated) with Mars, the warrior god. Why couldn't Aries also be associated with a feminine deity who embodied the archetypal qualities that Mars stands for? I knew these warrior goddesses existed because I spent my childhood immersed in books on Celtic mythology featuring feisty female characters that stirred my blood. My favorite TV shows were *Wonder Woman, The Secrets of Isis,* and *The Bionic Woman,* and while these shows are definitely products of the seventies, they sent the message that it was possible for women to be daring, adventurous, and independent.

After studying the psychology of gender in university, I can now name the bias in astrology for what it is: gender essentialism. In a nutshell, gender essentialism is the attribution of binary essential qualities to the masculine and the feminine. For example, it is apparently a male predisposition to have a penchant for sports and cars. Males also are supposedly more assertive and less nurturing. Females are supposed to be drawn to makeup and clothes and are intuitive and nurturing by nature. I'm sure we all have female friends who love sports and male friends who are compassionate and nurturing. While many of us are now realizing that gender is much more fluid than was culturally accepted even a short time ago, there is still light to be shed on the societally proscribed constructs of gender.

I decided long ago to make it my mission to explore the archetypal feminine face of each sign. My research for this book has been through diverse channels: academic study of psychology and gender; a passionate love affair with myth and archetypal psychology; and of course, years of one-on-one astrological counseling sessions with thousands of women of all ages, races, sexual orientations, and socioeconomic backgrounds. I have worked with women who made their livings as lawyers, executives, entrepreneurs, editors, actors, artists, dancers, and sex workers, and each had a valuable perspective to share.

I also decided that instead of just focusing on deities from the Greek pantheon for this book, I wanted to make space for goddesses from across all cultures. For example, in traditional astrology, Libra is associated with Venus, and while this goddess is still aligned with the Libra archetype, it was the Hindu goddess Lakshmi who stepped to the fore to represent Libra as I was writing that chapter. While I have highlighted one central goddess for each sign, you will find other goddesses who resonate with that sign in the list of correspondences found at the end of each chapter.

In this book, you will learn how to personally connect with the twelve faces of the Goddess through astrology, story, ritual, and guided meditation. As you read about the myths associated with each goddess, you may notice parallels in your own life, which will lead to a deeper and more profound understanding of the archetypal motifs unfolding on your path. It is my hope that in recognizing the mythological themes in your story, you will be inspired to new levels of self-awareness and personal empowerment as well as gain a renewed sense of realization that your life is a sacred journey, with you as the protagonist.

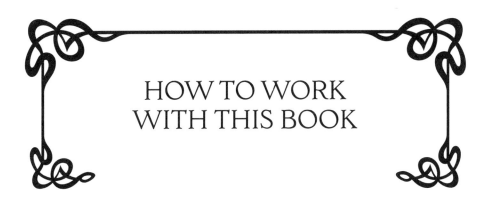

# HOW TO WORK
# WITH THIS BOOK

First, if you don't already have a copy of your birth chart, I highly recommend getting one so you can get to know yourself at a deeper level than you ever imagined possible. Your birth chart is absolutely unique to you, like a fingerprint. No two have ever been exactly alike, and no one will ever have the same birth chart again. Your chart is a blueprint of your psyche, a map of your soul, and it contains detailed information about why you're here, your life lessons, and your gifts. It also has a thing or two to say about your past lives and, most importantly, where you should be pointing your ship in this lifetime. It is a map of your unique journey and can show you what steps to take next and what direction to follow when you find yourself at a crossroads. You can think of your birth chart like this: at the moment you took your first breath, from the perspective of the time and place you were born, someone was able to take a picture of the heavens that shows exactly where all the planets were positioned in relation to the earth. As psychologist Carl Jung explained, "The starry vault of heaven is in truth the open book of cosmic projection, in which are reflected the mythologems, i.e., the archetypes. In this vision astrology and alchemy, the two classical functionaries of the psychology of the collective unconscious, join hands." [1]

Luckily, there are some places online that can instantly calculate your chart for you for free. Do a quick Google search for "online birth chart."

---

1. C. G. Jung, *Collected Works of C.G. Jung, Volume 8: Structure & Dynamics of the Psyche* (Princeton, NJ: Princeton University Press, 2014), 195.

All you need to get started is your date, time, and place of birth. Birth time is very important, as it sets up your chart from the moment you arrived in this world and makes your chart specific to you. If you don't know your birth time, you can contact the hospital where you were born—they will usually have it on record. If you absolutely cannot find your birth time, not to worry; you can still glean lots of insight from your chart.

There are several ways you can work with this book. Many readers will want to start by reading about their Sun sign and the guiding goddess associated with it. From there I recommend exploring your Moon sign and ascendant, or rising sign. Together these three can point to clues about the themes emerging in your chart. Take note of the element and mode of each sign and reflect on the deeper qualities found therein. It's all connected and makes up your personal energy signature. From there I suggest moving outward, starting with the personal planets (Mercury, Venus, and Mars) and then on to the rest of the planets in your chart (Jupiter, Saturn, Uranus, Neptune, and Pluto).

Another way you can use this book is by working with the goddesses, rituals, and pathworkings for each sign in accordance with the New and Full Moons that occur each month. Essentially, New Moons are a natural time to reset. The New Moon is the most potent time to get crystal clear about your goals, set intentions, and plant the seeds for something new. Full Moons are a time of fruition. They often coincide with something in your life coming to light, or they reveal the answer to an important question. Full Moons are also a good time for divination and celebration. A powerful way to align with the energy of either the New or Full Moon is to find out what sign and degree the Moon will be in, and then find that point in your chart. To find out what sign or phase the Moon is in on a given day, consult an astrological day planner such as *Llewellyn's Astrological Pocket Planner*. Let's say you see that the next New Moon will be at 2 degrees Virgo. First, look at the outer circle of your chart and find the Virgo symbol (many charts include a legend so you can easily find the symbols for each sign if you are new to astrology). Starting at your rising sign, which will be on the left (nine if you were looking at a clock), and moving in a counterclockwise direction, find 2 degrees of Virgo in your chart. The house you find at 2 degrees of Virgo is where the next New Moon will fall in your chart, thus highlighting the themes of that house, or life area, and showing you where you can best focus your seedling intentions.

Although the energy of the Moon is most potent when it is in either its new or full phase, you can still align with the energies of the Moon when it is in each sign, regardless of what phase it's in. The Moon changes signs approximately every two and a half days and goes through all twelve signs in one month. For example, you may feel the need to work on setting stronger personal boundaries and want to do the Aries pathworking, Standing Your Ground, but the Moon will be neither new nor full in Aries for months. You don't have to wait. You can give your ritual or pathworking an extra boost by checking when the Moon will next be in Aries this month.

An additional way to work with this book any time you need some insight is to take a deep, grounding breath and ask, "What do I need to know right now?" Open the book to whatever page it falls on, and tune in from there by reflecting on how this information currently pertains to your life. If you feel intuitively that any of the rituals or pathworkings will be of benefit to you now, you may proceed regardless of the sign the Moon is currently in. Trust your intuition.

## What Exactly Is an Archetype?

The term *archetype* originated in ancient Greece, but psychologist Carl Jung pioneered the contemporary concept of archetypes in his work on the human psyche. He posited that mythic patterns, images, or characters symbolically exist in the collective unconscious, and an understanding of how these patterns arise in our lives can bring personal insight, empowerment, and self-knowledge. Archetypes are recurring symbols found in dreams, literature, art, mythology, religion, and story. Some common examples include the Queen, the Great Mother, the Hero, the Warrior, the Trickster, the Wise Elder, and the Wild Woman. However, while these are some of the more well-known archetypal symbols, it is important to note that there is no finite or exhaustive list of archetypes.

Cross-cultural deities and characters of folk and fairy tales are also often archetypal figures. The elements fire, earth, air, and water have archetypal dimensions, as do the River, the Ocean, and the World Tree. The Shaman, the Witch, the Wise Woman, and the Sacred Prostitute are all archetypes, as are the twelve signs of the zodiac.[2]

Throughout this book I mention the *hero's journey*, an archetypal motif that originates in *The Hero with a Thousand Faces*, the seminal work on comparative mythology by Joseph Campbell. In his highly influential book, Campbell illustrates the archetypal journey of the hero and posits that all major world myths throughout history follow a basic structure, which he calls the *monomyth*. Since its first publication in 1949, the stages of the hero's journey in *The Hero with a Thousand Faces* have influenced the works of countless authors, artists, poets, screenwriters, and therapists.

There are seventeen stages in Campbell's hero's journey, which are broken down into three main sections: departure, initiation, and return. Not all myths include all seventeen stages, and they are not always in the order Campbell lays out. Correspondingly, our personal individuation does not always contain all seventeen stages, or necessarily follow them in sequential order. However, the basic structural motif of departure, initiation, and return does seem to play out through the stories of our lives. In the *departure* part of the story, the hero receives a call to go on a quest of some sort (*the call to adventure*). The hero is often reluctant at first, but a mentor figure usually appears to help him get his foot out the door. In the *initiation*, the hero leaves his known world and faces trials, tasks, and obstacles (*the road of trials*). The hero may go this part of the journey alone or receive the assistance of helpers along the way. Eventually, the hero reaches the pinnacle or main crisis of the story and must overcome the ultimate enemy or obstacle. In doing so, he receives the reward, treasure, or, as Campbell calls it, the "boon." The hero must once again cross back into the previously known world with treasure in

2. If you'd like to read more about Greek goddess archetypes, I recommend Jean Shinoda Bolen's *Goddesses in Everywoman* (New York: Harper & Row, 1984).

hand. The hero may be reluctant or challenged in crossing the threshold and may need assistance to make it back to the ordinary world. In this *return* part of the story, the hero returns to the ordinary world (*the crossing of the return threshold*) with the treasure that will be of use to his community. The hero is transformed by the adventure and has gained hard-won spiritual wisdom of himself and the nature of both worlds (*master of the two worlds*). Here are the seventeen stages of Campbell's hero's journey:

DEPARTURE

1. The Call to Adventure

2. Refusal of the Call

3. Supernatural Aid

4. The Crossing of the First Threshold

5. The Belly of the Whale

INITIATION

1. The Road of Trials

2. The Meeting with the Goddess

3. Woman as the Temptress

4. Atonement with the Father

5. Apotheosis

6. The Ultimate Boon

RETURN

1. Refusal of the Return

2. The Magic Flight

3. Rescue from Without

4. The Crossing of the Return Threshold

5. Master of the Two Worlds

6. Freedom to Live

Just as the stages of Campbell's hero's journey echo throughout world myth, they also have correspondences with the soul's spiritual journey through the twelve signs of the zodiac. And, while the stages of the hero's journey do not correspond exactly in order with the twelve signs, they are a useful way of engaging with and understanding the different stages of our own individuation.

## What Is Archetypal Astrology?

Archetypal astrology, also known as psychological astrology, focuses on the archetypes arising from your birth chart. In archetypal astrology, we dive into your birth chart and see the mythic perspectives that illuminate your potential, shine light on your unconscious patterns, and help you gain deeper wisdom on your journey. I like to blend archetypal astrology with evolutionary astrology, which focuses on the evolutionary unfolding of the soul throughout myriad lifetimes. I find combining these two approaches focuses on personal growth and is a deeply effective path to embracing the themes of one's life from an archetypal perspective.

## What Is the Shadow?

You will hear me talk about the *shadow* throughout this book. Every sign and every person has a shadow side. According to Jung, the shadow is the part of the unconscious where disowned fragments of the self reside. Any aspects of our personality that we have felt the need to deny get relegated to the shadow. And while this includes suppressed anger, fears, vulnerabilities, and personality quirks we're not particularly proud of, it also encompasses passions, abilities, or interests that we may have had in our formative years that were deemed unacceptable in some way. Our unique sense of self and personal power may also be hidden in the shadow.

Maybe when you were growing up, it wasn't safe for you to speak your truth, stand up for yourself, or express your needs. You may have learned to internalize these feelings as a survival mechanism. Now the threat may be gone, but you're still hesitant to step up and stand in your power. When parts of us are operating from the shadow, they still come out, but in a subconscious way. For example, if it wasn't safe for you to express anger, the feeling of anger will still come up, but you might have trouble accessing it, and it doesn't come out as a clear boundary. It comes out as passive-aggression, which can trigger all kinds of issues in your life. If you are caught in the passive-aggressive resentment loop, you are probably not even aware why you react that way. Shining a light into these places helps us become whole. Accepting, healing, and integrating the shadow is one of the most regenerating things we can do for ourselves.

## Guiding Goddess Archetypes: Which Archetypes Reside in Your Birth Chart?

*Guiding goddess archetype* is a term I've developed to describe which particular goddesses come to life in your birth chart and are therefore recurring themes and sources of guidance in your everyday life. Every birth chart is unique and will resonate with specific mythic and archetypal energies of the sacred feminine from every culture. Connecting with your guiding goddesses will reignite a sense of mystery in your life and help you forge a connection with the Divine. In addition, aligning with your personal guiding goddess archetypes will help you reframe challenges and consciously design your life in a way that defines your soul purpose. Getting to know the myths and stories of your guiding goddesses will also provide reassurance and comfort when shaking off the self-doubt that plagues us all from time to time. Although the Goddess has an almost infinite variety of faces, each one resonates with a core archetype, and every aspect of the sacred feminine is embodied and reflected in the twelve astrological signs.

Recognizing and aligning ourselves with the sacred feminine is an empowering and radical act that can guide us on every step of our journey. Seeing our own initiations in the myriad stories of the Goddess reminds us that we are connected to an amazing wealth of magic and meaning. Our lives are unfolding stories, and for every circumstance we face, the Goddess provides a tale, which comes down to us across time and through every culture to provide insight and illumination when we most need it. Although I have intuitively assigned a main goddess to each sign, along with corresponding rituals and pathworkings, I have provided a list of other goddesses that also resonate with a particular sign. If you are drawn to another goddess connected with any sign, I encourage you to explore that further. There is something that this goddess wants to impart to you, and as always, you should follow your intuition.

Perhaps you look at your chart and see, through the positions of the planets and the signs that are highlighted, that you have a special affinity for Aphrodite—you are a sensual woman driven by your passions who loves to create and immerse herself in beauty. Or maybe you find Kali is an important guide for you in this lifetime—you have a thirst for social justice and often find yourself in a series of transformational rites of passage followed by profound personal rebirths. Or it could be the goddess Rhiannon who steps to the fore: you are confident and independent and know in your bones that sovereignty is your birthright.

Knowing which goddesses reside in your birth chart can go a long way in moving you toward your goals with clarity and confidence, while helping you circumnavigate the detours. You can cultivate a deeper connection with the qualities of the goddesses you want to draw into your life through ritual and pathworking. Each goddess you find in your birth chart is a personal guide and a source of wisdom and inspiration. Once you delve in and uncover the central goddess archetypes in your chart, you can connect with them to find everyday guidance, increased self-awareness, and new and cathartic ways to be your most authentic self.

## You Are Every Sign

While we all find central themes and archetypes highlighted in our lives, all of us also have every sign in our birth chart. Most of us are familiar with our Sun signs because every newspaper, magazine, and e-zine has a Sun sign column. But your Sun sign describes only a portion of who you are and who you came here to be.

Because every birth chart contains every sign, we can therefore draw on every archetype in the cosmos as we will. We can consciously choose to focus on any area to become empowered in any way we need at any time. How often have I heard a friend lament, "If only I had some Virgo in my chart, maybe I could get a handle on organizing my life." Or "I'm such a Scorpio! I wish I could just detach and not be so suspicious." Or "I'm a double Pisces; why can't I be more like a Capricorn and get my career up and running?" These are all examples of a little astrology knowledge limiting your potential. The fact is, everyone *does* have Virgo, Capricorn, and Pisces somewhere in their chart. All the astrological archetypes are awaiting your discovery, like a hidden wellspring.

You can tap into the qualities of any sign you are drawn to by reading about the sign and finding what house it's in your chart. If you look at your chart and find that you don't have any planets in a given sign, look at the outer wheel. You will see the symbols for all twelve signs positioned around the outer circle. The beginning of each house, or *cusp*, will have a sign on it and will color the life area associated with that house with the themes of that sign. For example, you may not have a planet in the sign of Pisces, but you find that the symbol for Pisces is on your fifth house cusp. That means you are likely to experience fifth house matters (creative drive, romance, passion, etc.) through a Piscean lens. You could make a list of the houses, first through twelfth, and beside each write in the sign you have on the cusp of each house. Refer to "The Houses: Areas of Experience" beginning on page 26 for an explanation of the meanings of each.

# THE BASICS
# OF ASTROLOGY

What makes a sign what it is? Why is Aries regarded as courageous and daring while Capricorn is known for being practical and cautious? Although astrology is a complex art and science and exploring its intricacies can be a lifelong study, at its heart are the elements and modes.

## The Elements

The *elements* we refer to in astrology are the classical Greek elements: fire, earth, air, and water. Numerous astrologers have compared the elements to Jung's *cognitive functions*: thinking, sensing, feeling, and intuition. Traditional astrology also assigns a polarity to the elements as masculine or feminine. I find it more useful to see fire and air as the extroverted signs and earth and water as the introverted signs. In other words, the energy of fire and air is outward moving, focused on other people and things outside the self, whereas earth and water energy is more of a subjective, inner experience, focused on feelings and perceptions.

Here's a brief description of each of the elements to help you get a feel for the energy connected with them. Take a moment to meditate on each, and reflect on any other associations that come up for you.

### Fire

The fire element is dynamic, ardent, and creative. Fire provides inspiration, courage, and vision. Its flames cleanse and transform, clearing away the outworn habits, patterns, and relationships that no longer serve us, making way for new forms to emerge from the ashes. Fire gives us energy, light, warmth, and passion. It is what fuels our dreams and motivates us to act. Fire is the antidote for depression. When the fire element is out of balance or expressing from its shadow, it can be reckless, arrogant, or destructive in its all-encompassing fervor. In most magickal traditions, fire is associated with the direction south. The fire signs are Aries, Leo, and Sagittarius.

### Earth

The earth element is fertile and sustaining. Earth provides foundation and stability. Earth is our home, *terra firma*. Earth steadies us, provides for us, and grounds us. It is the principle behind knowing how to live in a body on this planet and therefore is associated with work, money, status, food, shelter, and sensual pleasure. When the earth element is out of balance or expressing through its shadow, it can be stuck in the mud, dogmatic, or overly cautious. In most magickal traditions, earth is associated with the direction north. The earth signs are Taurus, Virgo, and Capricorn.

### Air

The air element is the realm of the mind. As Descartes famously wrote, "I think, therefore I am." Air provides ideas and an objective perspective. Air is intellect, communication, thoughts, and the gathering and spreading of information. Air is associated with the internet, social media, writing, speaking, teaching, and languages. When air is out of balance or expressing its shadow, it can be scattered, abstract, or detached. In many magickal traditions, air is associated with the direction east. The air signs are Gemini, Libra, and Aquarius.

### Water

The water element is the realm of emotions, feelings, relationships, love, and deep internal currents. Water provides intuition, empathy, and inner knowing. Water resonates with ancestral memory, genetic wisdom, the unfathomable depths of the psyche, and the collective unconscious. When water is out of balance or acting from its shadow, it can be smothering, maudlin, or depressive. In most magickal traditions, water is associated with the direction west. The water signs are Cancer, Scorpio, and Pisces.

# The Modes

The next thing we look at in determining what makes up a given astrological sign is the *mode*, or *modality*. There are three modes: cardinal, fixed, and mutable. These correspond with the part of the season in which a sign occurs.

## Cardinal

The cardinal signs begin a season. They can be considered gateways into the journey of a new chapter. Cardinal energy is the outgoing thrust—initiating, spontaneous, and leading the way. When cardinal energy is out of balance or expressing its shadow, it can be impulsive, rash, or headstrong. The cardinal signs correspond with the solstices and equinoxes and include Aries (spring equinox), Cancer (summer solstice), Libra (autumn equinox), and Capricorn (winter solstice).

## Fixed

The fixed signs are the heart of a season. The fixed modality is sustaining, enduring, and committed. When fixed energy is out of balance or expressing its shadow, it can manifest as rigidity, stubbornness, or the inability to see other perspectives. The fixed signs are Taurus, Leo, Scorpio, and Aquarius. The fixed signs correspond with the ancient Celtic agricultural festivals, otherwise known as the *cross-quarter days*: Samhain, Imbolc, Beltane, and Lughnasadh (or Lammas). The cross-quarter days are the midpoints between the astronomical gateways.

## Mutable

The mutable signs are the thresholds that bridge one season into the next. Mutable energy is connecting, fluid, versatile, and flexible. Although the mutable signs are not directly associated with any astronomical turning points or cross-quarter days, they correspond with transition times that have their own subtle magic. The mutable signs are the shape-shifters. Gemini and Virgo share an association with the planet Mercury, the Romanized version of the Greek god Hermes. As psychcopomp, the messenger god could move freely between the world of the mortal, the world of the divine, and also the realm of the dead. Sagittarius is a centaur, half animal and half human. And Pisces connects the collective unconscious with the conscious world. When mutable energy is out of balance or expressing its shadow, it can be inconsistent, scattered, or noncommittal. The mutable signs are Gemini, Virgo, Sagittarius, and Pisces.

## The Signs

In their most basic sense, the twelve signs of the zodiac are each made up of an element, and a mode. If you consider the part of the season in which each sign occurs, it all starts to come together. There is both a rhyme and a reason. Eight of the astrological signs correspond with the points on the Wheel of the Year, with the threshold signs bridging each of these significant days to the next. Please note: the exact dates for the equinoxes and solstices can vary slightly from year to year. If you are born on the cusp of a sign, you'll need to know your time of birth to find out exactly what sign the Sun was in when you were born. Please check your astrological date planner to ascertain the exact date changes for the current year.

| Sign | Element | Mode | Point on the Wheel of the Year |
|------|---------|------|-------------------------------|
| Aries | Fire | Cardinal | Spring equinox (March 20) |
| Taurus | Earth | Fixed | Beltane (April 30–May 1) |
| Gemini | Air | Mutable | Threshold between spring and summer |
| Cancer | Water | Cardinal | Summer solstice (June 21) |
| Leo | Fire | Fixed | Lughnasadh (August 1 or 2) |
| Virgo | Earth | Mutable | Threshold between summer and autumn |
| Libra | Air | Cardinal | Autumn equinox (September 21) |

| Scorpio | Water | Fixed | Samhain (October 31) |
|---|---|---|---|
| Sagittarius | Fire | Mutable | Threshold between autumn and winter |
| Capricorn | Earth | Cardinal | Winter solstice (December 21) |
| Aquarius | Air | Fixed | Imbolc (February 2) |
| Pisces | Water | Mutable | Threshold between winter and spring |

# The Planets:
## The Ten Archetypes Alive in Your Psyche

There are ten planets in astrology, including the Sun and Moon. Each represents a separate archetype, or psychological drive within your psyche, illuminating a different part of the picture of who you are. Each planet was in a particular sign at the time of your birth, and taken as a whole, this makes up your energy signature. In addition to the planets, we will also be looking at your *ascendant*, or *rising sign*.

The Sun, Moon, Mercury, Venus, and Mars are considered the *personal* or *inner planets*. They symbolically correlate with our personality and inner experience of life in a subjective way. The *outer* planets—Jupiter, Saturn, Uranus, Neptune, and Pluto—also figure into who we are, but in a wider sense. Although Jupiter and Saturn are technically outer planets, they have often been termed the *social planets* because their sphere of influence in the birth chart is associated with less personal areas than the inner planets. They tend to relate more with growth, expansion, culture, and our place in society than with the subjectivity of our moods, feelings, desires, or sexual nature. They represent our urge to move beyond our immediate environment.

In ancient times, Saturn was the farthest planet that could be seen with the naked eye. It was considered the last planet in the solar system, which is why it is associated with endings and boundaries. The twelve signs shared what was then a system of seven planets up to and including Saturn. Aries and Scorpio shared Mars as their ruling planet. Sagittarius and Pisces shared Jupiter's rulership, and Capricorn and

Aquarius both shared Saturn. This brings us to the outer three planets, or *transpersonal* planets—Uranus, Neptune, and Pluto, which were discovered in 1781, 1846, and 1930 respectively. Because of the strong affinity they seem to have with the signs they are paired with (Uranus with Aquarius, Neptune with Pisces, and Pluto with Scorpio), many contemporary astrologers use them in their practice. However, while many astrologers use the modern rulerships for Aquarius, Pisces, and Scorpio, there are still some astrologers who prefer to use only the seven classical planets in their work. It is all a matter of personal resonance. Astrology, much like psychology, has many different schools of thought, with proponents for each.

The outer planets move very slowly around the Sun and therefore are considered generational influences, as they are in each sign for a long time. For example, it takes Pluto 248 years to revolve around the Sun, and it spends approximately between thirteen and thirty years in each sign. For example, anyone born between 1971 and 1984 will have Pluto in Libra, because that's when Pluto was navigating through that part of the sky. The following generation has Pluto in Scorpio and was born between 1983 (1984) and 1995. The transpersonal planets represent both higher consciousness and the collective unconscious, describing our evolutionary calling toward liberation and individuation (Uranus), direct experience of the numinous (Neptune), and capacity for deep transformation (Pluto).

### The Sun

While technically the Sun is a star and not a planet, the Sun and Moon (the luminaries) are considered planets in astrology. As such, the Sun represents your core self and central identity in this lifetime, as well as your drive and vital force. In Jungian parlance, the Sun is connected to the *animus*, or inner masculine principle, as well as the conscious self. While many cultures throughout antiquity have indeed viewed the Sun as masculine, author Stephanie Woodfield has brought us a wealth of examples of cross-cultural solar goddesses in her trailblazing book, *Drawing Down the Sun: Rekindle the Magick of the Solar Goddesses.*

While the Sun is related to the conscious self, light, logic, and reason, it is also connected to passion, creativity, growth, strength, and vitality. Its sign and position in your chart determines what makes you a separate individual and shows where you naturally shine. Although you are more than just your Sun sign, consciously cultivating the positive qualities of your Sun will align you with a meaningful sense of purpose, and exploring the guiding goddess archetypes associated with your Sun sign will reignite your spark. The Sun's position comes from the yearly cycle of the earth's rotation, and it changes signs approximately every thirty days. The Sun is associated with the sign Leo.

### The Moon

The Moon is connected to our emotions, instincts, and intuition. It represents the subconscious self and shows what we need to feel comfortable, safe, and taken care of—what we need in order to feel "fed" on an emotional level. The Moon is related to Jung's *anima,* the feminine, receptive principle, and her changing faces have been represented as the Triple Goddess in her Maiden, Mother, and Crone aspects. The Moon is associated with genetic memory and ancestral wisdom and governs the waxing and waning of our personal cycles. The Moon often provides clues to how we may have experienced our own mother (and other important women in our early life) and to our perception of ourselves as women. The sign the Moon was in at our birth comes from the monthly cycle, and the Moon changes signs approximately every two and a half days. The Moon is associated with the sign Cancer.

### Mercury

Mercury is the Roman equivalent of the Greek messenger god Hermes, the youthful, androgynous trickster god who presides over expression, communication, boundaries, thieves, writing, and poetry. He is the psychopomp and the divine messenger, able to move unimpeded between the worlds. Mercury represents the principle of communication: how we take in and convey information. It is connected to language, speaking, writing, the internet, thought processes, reasoning, learning style, and perception. Mercury's placement in the chart shows our ability to conceptualize and to use rational thought and logic, and describes our communication style. Although all the planets go retrograde (the apparent backward motion as perceived from our vantage point on earth), the phrase *Mercury retrograde* has hit the mainstream vernacular, and when the planet reverses course (usually three times a year), it is cause for widespread complaint. All manner of missed appointments and misunderstandings are attributed to the retrograde motion of the closest planet to the Sun. Mercury is associated with the signs Gemini and Virgo.

### Venus

Venus is the Roman counterpart of the Greek goddess Aphrodite, the quintessential goddess of love. Mythologically, there are two aspects of Aphrodite: Aphrodite Urania and Aphrodite Pandemos. The former relates to the so-called higher principles of love and relationships (affection, beauty, proportion, and the arts) and is aligned with the sign Libra. The second is associated with pleasure, comfort, and sensuality and is aligned with the sign Taurus. The astrological Venus is the principle of attraction and represents interconnection, love, and what we value. Venus is associated with the arts, culture, luxury, beauty, harmony, and resources. Venus in our chart points to what we are drawn to and find pleasing or beautiful. Look to Venus's placement in your chart to learn more about your needs in relationships and what you need to surround yourself with to feel rich, abundant, and beautiful.

### Mars

Mars is the Roman equivalent to the Greek god Ares, god of war, who is often depicted in myth as a lover of Aphrodite. Mars is the principle of action and motivation. Mars is the Warrior and is connected to confidence and willpower in our chart. It represents how we experience sexual desire, the way we tend to assert ourselves, and how we express ourselves when we're angry. When channeled positively, it's the principle that helps us stand up for our beliefs, defend our loved ones, and get what we want in life. It is the stuff of both basic survival and strategy. Mars's placement in our chart shows how we manage conflict and the way we go after what's important to us. Mars is associated with the sign Aries and is the traditional ruler of Scorpio.

## Jupiter

Jupiter is the largest planet in the solar system and is named for the god Jupiter, the Roman counterpart to the Greek Zeus, king of the gods. Zeus is the son of Kronos (Saturn) and Rhea. Kronos swallows all seven of the children he sired to avert the prophecy that his own son would supersede him, as he did his own father, Ouranos. However, just before Zeus is born, Rhea formulates a plan to save him and gives birth to him on the island of Crete. She wraps a stone in swaddling clothes, which she gives to Kronos, and he promptly swallows it. Rhea hides Zeus in a cave, and although there are many versions of how he is raised, he does grow to manhood and eventually overthrows his father, becoming king of the gods. Ever since, Jupiter has been known as the Great Benefic and is cognate with opportunity, blessings, and good luck. In astrology, Jupiter is also connected to the principle of growth and expansion. Jupiter relates to belief systems, faith, meaning, the higher mind, wisdom, philosophy, culture, metaphysics, travel, world religion, and the quest. Jupiter's placement in our chart also shows where things come easily to us, or where we tend to receive outside support. Jupiter is further connected to abundance, benevolence, generosity, and good humor. It is associated with the sign Sagittarius and is the traditional ruler of Pisces.

## Saturn

Because Saturn was the last planet that the ancients could clearly see with the naked eye and because of its unique appearance, being the only planet surrounded by rings, it came to be associated with structure, restriction, and boundaries. Saturn's predecessor is the earlier Greek god Kronos, the son of Ouranos the sky god and Gaia the earth mother. According to myth, on his mother's advice, Kronos castrates his father with a sickle, throwing his testicles into the sea, which causes the separation of earth from sky. Kronos later came to be identified with the Roman agricultural god Saturn or Saturnus, who presides over the concepts of order and time. Astrologically, Saturn is the reality principle. It is associated with responsibility, definition, boundaries, and hard work. Saturn's placement in our birth chart often shows us where we are apt to experience key life lessons. And, while Saturn's position in our chart sometimes highlights life areas where we may initially feel some restriction, it also points to the things we view as serious or important. For example, having Saturn in the seventh house of partnership may indicate someone who has life lessons to learn about relationships. But far from dire old-school astrological predictions about being perennially challenged in love, it can mean instead that a relationship is so important to this individual that they will take their time in finding the right person to commit to. Commitment is serious business to them and something they do not take lightly. Saturn is also related to how we can manifest achievement and results in the outer world through hard work and accountability. Saturn teaches us about the importance of accepting what something actually is and how to work with that reality to manifest something of worth. Although Saturn brings lessons of perseverance, self-discipline, and delayed gratification, it is also aligned with the harvest. If we accept Saturn's teachings willingly and work hard, it will provide rewards and recognition for our efforts. Saturn is associated with the sign Capricorn and is the traditional ruler of Aquarius.

### Uranus

Uranus was discovered by surprise in 1781 by Sir William Herschel and was the first planet discovered with a telescope. Its discovery pushed the boundaries of the known universe and opened new paradigms. Uranus is named for the Greek sky god Ouranos, the father of Kronos (Saturn), and has the distinction of being the only planet with a Greek name instead of a Romanized version. Uranus is unique in its rotation and is tilted so far that it appears to orbit the Sun on its side. It also rotates in a retrograde direction, opposite the direction that most other planets turn. Often referred to in astrology as the Great Awakener, Uranus represents the principles of liberation and individuation. Uranus is associated with rebellion, revolution, social change, radical honesty, and breaking the rules of the status quo. It also rules science and technology, the future, community, tribe, independence, and change. Wherever Uranus is placed in our chart is where we tend to chafe at restrictions and push for the freedom to express ourselves in a unique way. Uranus is associated with the sign Aquarius.

## Neptune

Neptune was discovered in 1846, during the Romantic movement, and has the distinction of being the only planet in the solar system found by mathematical prediction before being observed by empirical means. Neptune is the Roman counterpart of Poseidon, the Greek god of the sea, and brother of Jupiter and Pluto. Neptune is the most ethereal, subtle, and otherworldly of all the planetary archetypes. It is the principle of transcendence and the "urge to merge." Wherever Neptune is placed in our chart is where we tend to want to dissolve boundaries and where we yearn for mystical experience and union with something greater than our own ego. It may also be where we tend to see things through rose-colored glasses or where we need to be more conscious of creating healthy boundaries. It may also point to where we have the tendency to want to escape, through fantasy, denial, or addiction. However, Neptune is also associated with the numinous, inspiration, imagination, dreams, the collective unconscious, creativity, idealism, faith, the Mysteries, and intuition. Neptune is associated with the sign Pisces.

## Pluto

Pluto was discovered in 1930 and is the Roman equivalent to Hades, the Greek god of the underworld. Although it was reclassified as a dwarf planet in 2006, in astrology it is recognized as a compelling and cathartic energy, both in the birth chart and in the cosmos. Pluto is the principle of deep transformation and evolution. Pluto relates to anything that is secret, undercover, or hidden and represents the mysterious dimensions of sex, death, and rebirth. Its placement in our chart shows where we can go through the fire and rise from our own ashes. Pluto's place-ment in the chart can also show us a wealth of information about our soul's evolutionary journey. Pluto is connected to the concept of power, including our personal sense of power. It also represents our psychic depths—the "basement" of our psyche. Although there are shadows in the basement, there are also hidden treasures, abilities, wisdom, and strengths on which we must shine the light of consciousness so we can make use of our hidden riches. Pluto is associated with the sign Scorpio.

### The Ascendant, or Rising Sign

Although the ascendant is not a planet but an important angle in the birth chart, it is one of the main things we look at in astrology in determining your personality. The rising sign is literally the sign that was ascending on the eastern horizon at the moment you were born, and it changes approx-imately every two hours. It is the cusp of the first house in your chart: it would be nine if you were looking at a clock and is the beginning point of the twelve houses in your chart, which follow in a counterclockwise direction. The sign and degree of the rising sign sets up the whole wheel of your chart and determines which of the twelve houses the planets will fall into, which is why an accurate time of birth is important. The ascen-dant, or rising sign, is your persona. In a sense, it is like a filter that the Sun, Moon, and other planets shine through. It is how you show up in the world, the way you choose to present yourself, and how others perceive you. It influences your personal style and appearance. The ascendant also often shows something of the circumstances and environment around the time of your birth into early childhood.

## The Houses: Areas of Experience

If you look at your chart, you will see it is divided into twelve sections. These are the *houses* of your birth chart. Each house signifies a particu-lar area of life. Depending on the degree of the sign that was rising on the eastern horizon at the time of your birth (your rising sign), each of the ten planets will fall into a house in your chart, highlighting that area and underlining certain themes in your life. For example, you may have

Sun in Cancer, but your Cancerian Sun will shine through a completely different lens depending on what house it is in. Yes, you will likely resonate with the qualities associated with Cancer, but in a unique way that differentiates you from another person with Sun in Cancer who has their Sun in a different house.

In some birth charts, we see a cluster of four or more planets in a particular house or sign. This is called a *stellium,* and it means there will be a concentration of energy in the life area denoted by that house or sign. It is also very common to have some houses empty, as it all depends on where in the sky the planets were at the time you were born. As well as noting any planets that fall into each house, check to see what sign you have on each house cusp, particularly if a house has no planets in it. This will give you further insight into how you experience different life areas. Note that every house is related to its opposite on the chart wheel, as they form two polarities of the same energy line, or *axis*. Understanding the meaning of one house will give clues to its opposite for a holistic picture that will illuminate both.

### First House

The sign on the cusp of your first house is your rising sign, or ascendant. Medieval astrology had it that you could ascertain a person's rising sign by their physical appearance. Although we now know genetics and other factors play a big part in what we look like, the ascendant can still affect the way you choose to present yourself—the kind of clothes you like, the way you wear your hair, or whether you opt for tattoos and piercings. The first house also relates to early childhood factors and our basic approach to the world, as well as personality, leadership, beginnings, assertion, courage, and the self. It is connected to Aries and the planet Mars.

### Second House

The second house is about living in a body in the material world. On one hand, it's connected to tangible assets like money, real estate, and possessions. On the other, it's also about some of those less tangible things that nevertheless support us, such as self-esteem, self-respect, and core values. Themes relating to body image, beauty, comfort, and sensual pleasure live here. The second house is associated with Aphrodite Pandemos, the goddess of love in her sensual, earthy aspect. This is an earth house, encompassing gardening, building, making things with one's hands, wildcrafting, and the enjoyment of earthly delights. This is also where you will find an appreciation for the finer things in life. The second house is connected to Taurus and the planet Venus.

### Third House

The third house is about communication—writing, language, education, study, social media, and interspecies communication. This is where we think globally and act locally. Networking, socializing, short trips, workshops, webinars, conferences, weekend retreats, and catching up over coffee all fall under the third house. Siblings and neighbors are associated with the third house, and it is where we maintain connections with those immediately around us, although "immediately around us" in this era can mean chatting online to friends on the other side of the world. The third house is the place where we learn a new skill or refresh our resume. It is connected to Gemini and the planet Mercury.

### Fourth House

This house's cusp—called the IC, or *Imum Coeli* (Latin for "bottom of the sky")—is one of the four important angles on the chart: it shows us where midnight was at the time of our birth. The fourth house is the deep well of our psyche. The sign on its cusp tells us something about our family of origin, roots, ancestral inheritance, influences during childhood, and our psychological underpinnings. It is the foundation of our personal subconscious and contains subjective undercurrents that we may or may not be aware of. This is where our memories live. The fourth house is also related to the home and family we create for ourselves. It is connected to the sign Cancer and the Moon.

## Fifth House

The fifth house is about love affairs and romance, whether it be with a person, a creative project, or a way of being that sweeps you off your feet and seduces you into that heady feeling of being in love. This is the house where self-confidence is developed and where creative self-expression is an urge that cannot be denied. Creativity, pleasure, and play all come under the fifth. Children and childlike wonder live here as well. The fifth house is connected to the sign Leo and the Sun.

## Sixth House

The sixth house is about everyday life, organization, work environment, diet, health, the body-mind connection, and ways of being of service. It's also connected to healing through naturopathic medicine, aroma-therapy, acupuncture, traditional Chinese medicine, and Ayurveda. This is the house that has you obsessively reading labels on everything in the grocery store and where you commit to a regular yoga practice and make sure your clothes are made from sustainable natural fibers. The sixth is connected to the craftsperson or artisan and to making practical, durable things. It is connected to Virgo and the planet Mercury.

## Seventh House

The seventh house is about partnership and relationships and relates to marriage and other one-on-one relationships, such as business partnerships and client-therapist relationships. The sign on the cusp of this house, the *descendant*, tells us something about the type of partners we are subconsciously attracted to. On the chart wheel, this house is opposite to the ascendant, or first house, which describes the self. The seventh house can show us where we may find ourselves projecting on someone, either with rose-colored glasses or our shadow selves. This is a Venus-ruled house, so Aphrodite holds court here, but the seventh is associated with Aphrodite Urania, or "heavenly Aphrodite," the aspect of the goddess related to the higher, more lofty vibrations, as opposed to the earthy and sensual attributes of Aphrodite Pandemos and the second house. Beauty, love, relationships, marriage, and the arts are all encompassed by this house, but sometimes so is the shadow side of the goddess of love: jealousy, unconscious patterns of manipulation, and disowned abandonment issues. The seventh house is connected to Libra and the planet Venus.

## Eighth House

The eighth house is saturated in the deep, shadowy waters of secrecy. This is the house connected to the mysteries of birth, death, rebirth, and sex. It also relates to intimacy and shared resources, as well as debt, taxes, and inheritance. It is the place we look in our chart to see where our deepest transformations can occur and where we may descend into the underworld to come up reborn and tempered. Our psyche's hidden elements live in this house, not only the unwanted parts of ourselves relegated to the shadow but also disowned fragments that contain forgotten treasure. Taboo subjects also live here, as do unspoken undercurrents. The eighth is also related to depth psychology, magick, healing, medicine, and shamanism. It is associated with Scorpio and the planet Pluto.

## Ninth House

The ninth house is about worldview, philosophy, higher education, metaphysics, and travel to faraway places, both inner and outer. It is related to the Quest and taking a leap of faith. Other concepts connected to the ninth house are publishing, religion, law, cultural exploration, and pilgrimage. Imagine setting foot on a new shore and allowing yourself to be alchemized by the sights, scents, inhabitants, and customs of a completely fresh perspective that broadens your experience of life. Wanderlust lives in this house. It's the house associated with setting off for India. It is the feeling you get when you arrive at the foot of a temple in Nepal. It's startling insights deep in conversation with strangers at a campfire on the West Coast Trail. It is also related to deciding to go back to university and finish your degree. This is the house where we are compelled to seek truth, ultimate meaning, and the courage to play with possibilities. The ninth house is connected to the sign Sagittarius and the planet Jupiter.

### Tenth House

The tenth house is the highest point in the chart—high noon in relation to our birth. It shows you something about your calling in life, your vocation. The cusp of the tenth house is one of the four important angles in the birth chart, the *Midheaven*, which often points toward clues about finding a fulfilling career and right livelihood. The tenth house relates to themes of mastery, public image, success, reputation, and achievement. Along with the sign on the Midheaven, any planets in this house can also color your career choices. Venus in the tenth? A career in the arts might call. Uranus? You may be drawn to what others consider an unconventional career. Sun or Moon in the tenth? Without getting into clichés about fame, you may have the potential to achieve a public position of prestige or notoriety, or you may become a subject matter expert in your field. This house is connected to Capricorn and the planet Saturn.

### Eleventh House

The eleventh house is connected to tribe, community, and friends. It is also where you may express your individuality in a way that is different from the status quo. The eleventh is related to the themes of social justice, causes, and politics. Feminism and gender fluidity are encompassed by this house, as well as the potential desire to explore alternative social structures, including nontraditional relationships, polyamory, unconventional family systems, and intentional communities. The eleventh house is also connected to visionary ideals, game plans, and setting goals. It is connected to the sign Aquarius and the planet Uranus.

### Twelfth House

The twelfth house is the last on the wheel of the chart and often gets a bad rap in old-school astrology, being associated with such things as prisons, institutions, and hospitals. However, we are not living in the

Middle Ages anymore, and it's time to update this misunderstood house. The twelfth is connected to spirituality, the numinous, and the sense that there is more than the everyday world we live in. It is associated with the collective unconscious, esoteric symbolism, and ancestral memory. It resonates with consciousness-expanding ayahuasca ceremonies and meditation retreats. The twelfth house also correlates with devotion to a spiritual path, communing with the gods, and channeling spiritual wisdom. It is that space between breaths in a yoga pose.

However, the twelfth house also represents the urge to merge, and the shadow side of that can be addiction, escapism, or the tendency to hide in illusion (all of which, of course, can arguably be like a prison). Because the twelfth is the last house in the wheel of the chart, it is sometimes associated with the ending of a cycle, particularly when an outer planet transits this house. Natal planets in the twelfth may indicate difficulty in accessing what that planet symbolizes. For example, if one has Mars in the twelfth, it may be challenging for the individual to get in touch with their assertive side. The twelfth house can also suggest where we need to develop critical thinking and be vigilant around creating healthy boundaries. At the same time, poetry, creative inspiration, intuition, and a visceral sense of the Mysteries are found in the twelfth house. The muse lives here. The twelfth house is connected to the sign Pisces and the planet Neptune.

# MAGICK AND THE
# WHEEL OF THE YEAR

The Wheel of the Year is a cyclical, ever-turning seasonal "calendar" marked in eight places: the astronomical turning points of the solstices and equinoxes and four Celtic agricultural fire festivals, or *cross-quarter days*—Samhain (October 31), Imbolc (February 2), Beltane (May 1), and Lughnasadh or Lammas (August 1 or 2). The cross-quarter days are also the midpoints between the seasons. Again, the solstices and equinoxes correspond to the cardinal signs (Aries, Cancer, Libra, and Capricorn), whereas the cross-quarter days correspond to the fixed signs (Taurus, Leo, Scorpio, and Aquarius).

In many traditions, the Wheel begins with Samhain, also known as the Celtic New Year. Samhain is considered both the end and the beginning of the cycle. In some magickal traditions, the places on the Wheel of the Year also correspond mythopoeically to the courtship of the Goddess and the God, with many variations depending on which tradition is being observed. Although no culture in antiquity has ever observed the Wheel of the Year as a whole, the way many Pagans view it today, it is a synthesis of ancient Celtic and Teutonic observances that make sense on both seasonal and intuitive levels. Observing and celebrating the turning points on the Wheel is a reminder to live in the moment, to align oneself with the cycles of the seasons, and to tap into the energies of a given space and time. To better understand each of the points on the Wheel, turn to the section of the sign that corresponds with it, which will give you a deeper awareness of the archetype of the season.

# Samhain (October 31): The Heart of Autumn
## Cross-Quarter Day • Scorpio • Fixed • Water

The shadows are growing longer, and darkness falls a little earlier each night. Already passed into memory are the long golden days of summer, and in their place are the deeply evocative, earthy smells of ripe apples, turning leaves, and wood fires. The Goddess is now the Crone, and the God waits in the underworld until his resurrection at Yule. Samhain is the third and final Harvest, at the midpoint between the autumn equinox and the winter solstice. It is both the first and last of the cross-quarter festivals, and the roots of today's Halloween are firmly embedded in and nourished by ancient Celtic soil. Samhain was traditionally celebrated between sunset on October 31 and sunset on November 1.

The ancient peoples of northern Europe were much more attuned to the cycles of the year because their survival was tied inextricably to the land. To them, it was apparent that Samhain was the end of one cycle and therefore naturally the beginning of the next. The ancients observed that by Samhain the once green and fertile fields were becoming barren, and the very last of the crops would be brought in to see the people through the cold winter ahead. Cattle were brought down from the high summer pastures, and some were sacrificed for the harvest feast while others were smoked and dried for the coming dark months. Burnished red apples and earthy root vegetables were stored for future suppers on nights when the winter wind would howl fiercely and the abundant bounty of summer was but a distant dream of another time.

Samhain was thought to be liminal space, and the veil between the worlds was at its thinnest, facilitating communication with the ancestors, but also opening the door to those of the Otherworld, such as nature spirits and faeries. People would put out offerings of food and drink for the spirits of the dead, which may be where the tradition of trick-or-treating originates. Alternatively, trick-or-treating could also have come from the practice of mumming, in which folk would dress in costume and recite verses for food. Ceremonial bonfires were lit, and from this sacred fire all other fires were lit. Divination was also commonly practiced on the Eve of Samhain, as was the custom of setting a place at the table for those who had gone before.[3]

## Tuning In

Samhain occurs during Scorpio season, and there are many parallels between the symbolism of the two. Scorpio is intimately connected with the cycles of death and rebirth, and transformation is at the core of its archetype. Today many still celebrate Samhain by remembering their beloved dead. This time of year is liminal space, a between-the-worlds moment in the fabric of the seasonal year when we can connect with those who have gone before. This is also the time to honor the Crone, or Wise Woman, aspect of the Goddess. In the youth-worshipping culture we live in, it is all too seldom that the learned wisdom of the Wise Woman is venerated.

Samhain is a time to look fearlessly into our shadow selves and own what we find. Only then are we able to shine light into those hidden places and begin the process of healing. Samhain is not only a time for reflection, it is also a powerful time to release outworn personas, relationships, and phases of our lives that are no longer serving us. Samhain invites us to step across the threshold toward regeneration and personal rebirth through storytelling, guided meditation, and personal ceremony, as we shed our old skins and prepare to begin our next chapter.

## Seasonal Altar

Because almost all the leaves are gone and it is the time of the dying of the year, you may wish to decorate your altar in deep or somber colors to reflect the tone of the season, such as black, deep red, muted purple, or shades of gray. Other symbols of death, such as skulls or skeletons, are also appropriate, as they speak to honoring the ancestors. And, of course, you may also want to include pictures of your own beloved dead, as the veils between the worlds are now at their thinnest, and it

---

3. James George Frazer, *The Golden Bough* (London: Macmillan, 1890; Old Saybrook, CT: Konecky & Konecky, 2010), 606–10.

is a good time to connect with loved ones who have passed to the other side. You may want to set up your altar with the last of the fallen leaves, apples, pumpkins, root vegetables, and corn sheaves to align with the season. Because Samhain has always been a time for divination, you can charge your tarot cards or runes by placing them on your altar. Remember that Samhain is Scorpio season, so for more ideas turn to the Scorpio chapter and table of correspondences. With all the sabbats there are alternate ways to honor each season, and you may wish to focus on one of the goddesses connected with Scorpio, such as Inanna or Cerridwen.

## Yule (December 21): Gateway to Winter

### Winter Solstice • Capricorn • Cardinal • Earth

Winter solstice marks the astronomical turning point that is the beginning of winter. It is the longest night of the year and ushers in the beginning of Capricorn season, which is cognate with the rebirth of the Sun. It was an important event for the ancient peoples of the Northern Hemisphere because it symbolized the miraculous continuation of life itself and provided hope at the darkest time of the year. Occurring on or around December 21, megalithic structures were built to honor and mark the return of the Sun, including Stonehenge in England and Newgrange in Ireland. This is the time of year when the God is reborn as an infant and the Goddess is seen in her phase of *an cailleach*, the old woman, or crone, of winter. The motif of rebirth is also reflected in Christian tradition, as Christmas marks the birth of the Christ Child within days of the winter solstice. The old tale of the Holly King and the Oak King describes the endless battle between the light and dark halves of the year that takes place at each solstice. At the winter solstice, the strapping young Oak King defeats the aged Holly King and grows in power until he in turn is vanquished once again by the Holly King at the summer solstice.

In many places in northern Europe, a Yule log, often oak, would be placed in the fire and the ashes scattered over the fields to ensure a good growing season. There were many folk customs and stories associated with the Yule log. Some believed keeping it under the bed would protect the house from fire and lightning for the ensuing year, while others attested that steeping a piece of the Yule log in water would help cows calve easier. Still others asserted that the ashes would protect the wheat from mildew.[4] All in all, it seems that the Yule log was strongly associated with both protective and curative magick.

### Tuning In

Winter solstice is a time for reflection. It is a time to pause (the word *solstice* means "Sun stands still" in Latin), and, indeed, it appears for a few days that the Sun sets in the same place around the solstice, giving us the illusion that it is standing still. And, just as the trees have long shed the last of their leaves to preserve their energy through the cold season and certain animals have gone into hibernation, we too have a chance to rest. The longer nights have given us an opportunity to nest, to curl up with a good book, and to dream. Although it's not always possible with our busy schedules, a wonderful way to attune ourselves with the rebirth of the Sun is to keep vigil through the night and watch the sunrise in the morning. While the winter solstice heralds the beginning of winter, paradoxically it also marks the time that the days will soon be getting incrementally longer. If the solstice happens to be on a weekend, consider having a "rebirth of the Sun" gathering, so you can watch the sunrise with loved ones. Of course, mulled wine and comfort food would be part of the celebration, as would singing songs featuring the Sun. A backyard bonfire would be ideal to encourage the return of the Sun, but an indoor fire (with a Yule log) would also work well. In a pinch, a small brazier or even candles call the Sun back. Alternatively, you may wish to stay up and watch the newborn Sun rise on your own, so you can use this deeply introspective time to reflect and align yourself with the turning of the Wheel.

---

4. Frazer, *The Golden Bough*, 611–13.

*Seasonal Altar*

Since this is a solar festival that celebrates the rebirth of the God, it makes sense to include solar symbols as well as symbols of the sacred masculine. Because winter solstice marks the time of the return of the Oak King, you could include acorns, a small fallen oak branch, dried oak leaves, or an oak Yule log if you have a fireplace. Sun wheels, small Sun objects, and yellow or gold candles can represent the Sun. Alternatively, you can decorate your altar in icy colors that reflect nature: winter white, silver, or silver-blue. Another color scheme that echoes this time of year is deep green, blood red, and white. Include fresh boughs of evergreens as well as holly and mistletoe, as these are all associated with this time of year and each has symbolic properties that resonate with different aspects of this day. Holly and oak represent the Holly King and the Oak King, while mistletoe was sacred to the Druids and is tied to masculine fertility.[5] Because this festival marks the beginning of Capricorn season, check the Capricorn chapter and table of correspondences for alternative ways to honor the winter solstice.

# Imbolc (February 2): The Heart of Winter
## Cross-Quarter Day • Aquarius • Fixed • Air

Imbolc is the harbinger of spring, the time when the Goddess is celebrated in her Maiden aspect. It is the second of the cross-quarter festivals and sits midway between Yule and the spring equinox. Imbolc is a time of renewed hope and increasing optimism as the days grow visibly longer and the sunlight begins to warm the earth once again. Life is beginning in the quiet darkness of the earth's womb, and our spark of inspiration is rekindled. This is a time to plant seeds of all kinds and to have faith that although we cannot yet see what they will grow into, there is life brewing, and spring is on its way. In Irish Gaelic, *Imbolc* means "ewe's milk" or "in the belly" and heralds the start of lambing

---

5. Robert Graves, *The White Goddess* (1948; repr., New York: Farrar, Straus and Giroux, 1999), 57, 65.

season in the Celtic countries. It is sacred to Brigit, goddess of poetry, healing, inspiration, and smithcraft.

## Tuning In

Make sure you find the time to go for a meditative walk in nature today. You may be surprised to see that most ubiquitous symbol of Imbolc, the snowdrop, has returned. Its delicate spears of green against gently nodding pure white blossoms remind us that spring is just a turn of the Wheel away. If you can, pick a spot toward the west and check it at five in the evening a week or so before this sabbat, and then look again on Imbolc. Prepare yourself for a numinous moment: there will now be a glimmer of light on the western horizon revealing that the days are already becoming noticeably longer. There is a palpable quickening that stirs us on Imbolc, a spark of inspiration that becomes a quiet sense of hope that infuses our spirit and lets us know that winter is almost past.

## Seasonal Altar

As Imbolc is especially connected to the goddess Brigit, it makes sense to honor her on this day. There are many folk customs associated with Brigit that you can incorporate into your Imbolc altar. Some like to weave a Brigit's cross or make a "Bride's Bed" and place it by the fire to welcome her. Another popular way to align with Brigit is by making a Brigit corn dolly. One year just before Imbolc I came upon a Christmas angel in a thrift store. She was made of corn sheaves, with long braided corn hair. I took one look at her, and all I could see was the goddess Brigit hiding beneath the angel's smock and glued-on wings. I took her home and carefully deconstructed the Christmas overlay, removing the cross and the wings. Next, I took off the angel smock and dressed her in a green velvet cape I fashioned from an old scrap of material, tied red silk ribbons in her braids, and placed a Celtic knotwork necklace around her neck. And behold! I had the most beautiful Brigit dolly just in time for Imbolc. I couldn't help but see the symbolic irony in all of this, for part of Brigit's lore is that the people of Ireland loved their goddess so much that when Christianity came, they turned her into a saint so they could keep honoring her. With my Brigit dolly, I feel like I simply uncovered the goddess who was hiding beneath the angel the whole time.

Other ways to set up your altar for Imbolc are to include potted early spring bulbs that are readily available at most grocery stores. Be sure to add lots of candles, as Imbolc is also known as Candlemas. Colors for your altar can be colors associated with Brigit: white, green, and red. White is for the snow that still lies on the ground in many places in the Northern Hemisphere as well as for her aspect as the Maiden. Green is for the renewal of life, and red is for her connection to the fire element. I have also always associated Imbolc with pale blue gray, which echoes both the water element and the color of the sky at this time of year in the Celtic lands. As Brigit presided over sacred wells, you may wish to add a chalice of spring water. She is also connected to the fire element, so apart from candles you might want to burn some incense or light a fire in a small cauldron. Other offerings appropriate for Brigit are milk, cheese, honey, and wool. Turn to the Aquarius chapter to learn more about the goddess Brigit and for more altar suggestions.

## Ostara (March 20): Gateway to Spring
### Spring Equinox • Aries • Cardinal • Fire

We feel the anticipation of the growing light rise within us, just as the sap rises in the trees. The Wheel turns again and we are at Ostara, when all of nature celebrates the mystery of rebirth. The vernal equinox occurs on or around March 20 (depending on the year—check your astrological date planner), and light and dark, masculine and feminine are balanced. Spring equinox marks the time when the God and Goddess are equal in strength, with the God gaining power as the light increases. Young and spirited, the Goddess and God are courting. Buds burst from their cases, birds awaken us with their own courting music, and there is an undeniable feeling of unfurling optimism deep within the very rhythm of life itself.

Spring equinox has been celebrated in many cultures throughout history as a time of rebirth. In ancient Greece, Persephone rose from the underworld to be reunited with her mother, Demeter. In her joy,

Demeter restored fertility and abundance to the land, causing the renewal of the earth. In the West Country of England, Ostara is sometimes referred to as "Lady Day," a celebration of the Goddess and the reawakening of the land. Because all life is interconnected, we too feel the resurgence of energy, the exhale after the constriction of winter's darkness. Now is the time to make new beginnings, to cast off any remaining hindrances that might be holding us back. As all of nature is in the throes of new growth, the time is ripe to embrace that flow and make positive changes in our own lives. Now is one of the most potent times of the year to embark on bold new beginnings.

### Tuning In

At spring equinox, we get the opportunity to hit the reset button and begin again. It is the gateway into a new cycle, a time for planting seeds, envisioning possibilities, and stepping forward with courage and fresh optimism. Where do you wish you could start over? Align yourself with the energy of renewal and resurrection by taking a walk outside and mindfully noticing the signs of spring everywhere. Do you see the buds on every branch? The tender green shoots poking through the earth? Is there a change in the scent of the air? These are the signs that winter is finally over, and the magic of rebirth is tangible, immediate, and alive. Depending on where you live, try to find spring foods that only come out at this time of year, such as early asparagus, kale, nettles, or my absolute favorite, fiddleheads. Another powerful way to connect with this time of year is to plant something. If it is still too cold to plant outside, plant some herbs and place them in your kitchen window. The creative impulse of new life is everywhere. Spring equinox gives us a push and empowers us toward self-actualization, daring us to take a leap of faith and show up for our own initiation. Give some consideration to the role of creativity in your life. Do you make space for it, or is it something that you continually push to the back burner? This is an ideal time to reclaim the creative aspects of yourself and conjure something new.

*Seasonal Altar*

Although the weather may not be cooperative, an outdoor altar for Ostara is ideal. If the warmer days haven't quite started yet, consider going for a walk before you set up your indoor altar, and collect some tokens of spring on your way. A fallen branch covered in new buds or some early spring flowers like daffodils or crocus bring the symbolism of this sacred time into your home. Alternatively, you can buy a living pot of spring flowers and place it on your altar. You may wish to include symbolism of the God and Goddess to signify the balance at this time of year. You can find iconography in the form of statues or images, or you can use a red candle to symbolize the Goddess and a white one to symbolize the God. Eggs are also a time-honored symbol of spring, as they suggest the potential of new life and fertility. Spring equinox is also the beginning of Aries season, so be sure to check the Aries chapter as well as the table of correspondences for more suggestions. You may want to celebrate the season by honoring a goddess connected with Aries.

# Beltane (April 30–May 1): The Heart of Spring
Cross-Quarter Day • Taurus • Fixed • Earth

The first of May marks the third of the ancient cross-quarter festivals, known as Beltane or *Beltaine*. Beltane is an ancient Irish fertility festival and the midpoint between the seasonal gateways of the spring equinox and the summer solstice. It represents the consummation of the sacred marriage of the Goddess and the God. Flowers open, tempting bees and butterflies with their seductive colors and intoxicating perfumes, and the air is fragrant and warm, calling us to play outside or spend time in the garden.

In ancient times, bonfires were lit and the cattle driven between them to ensure good luck for the growing season before they were led to the bounty of their summer pastures. Another custom was to extinguish the hearth fires of each household, and then relight them from the village bonfire, or *needfire*.[6] Echoing the sensual dance of nature,

---

6. Frazer, *The Golden Bough*, 593–94.

men and women would stray into the woods on May Eve to partake in the joyous celebration of earthly pleasures. However, it's been long said that on Beltane the veils between this world and the Otherworld are thin, and if you happen to be wandering in the woods after dusk, chances are good that you may encounter one of the Fae. You never knew if the handsome lad or enchanting woman beckoning you into the forest was of this world or the other. Irish lore has it that the faery race evolved from the *Tuatha Dé Danann*, "the people of the goddess Danu," and there are countless stories of humans straying into the Otherworld through a magickal portal, staying what seemed like a few hours, only to emerge and find a hundred years or more had passed.

We are left with one familiar vestige of Beltane, the maypole. Apart from its obvious phallic symbolism, in the traditional dance, which can still be seen in some places, an equal number of males and females entwine ribbons joyfully around a wooden pole planted in the ground. The dance symbolizes the intertwining, spiraling energy of yin and yang, or God and Goddess. Beltane occurs during Taurus season, and there are many parallels between this ancient fertility festival and the archetype of Taurus. Both are intimately concerned with the embodiment of pleasure, creativity, and the things of the body and of the earth.

### Tuning In

You can align with the full-bodied energy of Beltane to reconnect with yourself as a sensual being. This is the time to give yourself permission to enjoy the skin you're in and cultivate not only desire but also pleasure. This is the perfect time to reflect on any body image issues you might be struggling with and to embrace yourself as the manifestation of the goddess that you are. Take a moment to check in with yourself and ask yourself who you are as a sensual and sexual being. What are your needs? There are no right or wrong answers.

As Beltane and Taurus season is connected to the body, it's a great time to indulge in the simple but ecstatic pleasure of dance. Whether you go out to dance or put on music in your own living room, feel the music right down to your core and let it align you with your sacral chakra, your center of sensuality, emotional stability, intimacy, and creativity. If you are a yoga person, it is also a fitting time for some deep, succulent stretches to get you out of your head and back into your body. Sensual pleasure comes in many forms. Beltane is the time to embrace what you love and fully give yourself to the moment. Eat your favorite foods, gift yourself some luxurious new bedding, or get out into the garden and feel the sensual satisfaction of getting your hands into the dirt. Make sure you find a moment to be outside, and go on a walking meditation around your yard, a neighborhood park, or forest. Give yourself over to the flow and realize you are a part of it.

### Seasonal Altar

If the weather permits, setting up your Beltane altar outside is preferable, although you can bring the outside in and decorate your altar with seasonal flowers, some local organic honey, or a found branch with glossy green leaves. Because of Beltane's association with the Fae, you might want to include an offering for them on your altar. Honey or a bowl of milk are traditional, but I've left them small crystals as a token in my garden. It appears the Fae appreciate creativity, so use your intuition. As Beltane is Taurus time, refer to the Taurus chapter and list of correspondences for more altar ideas. You may wish to dedicate your altar to the union of the Goddess and the God, the goddess of love Aphrodite, or any of the other Taurean goddesses you're drawn to. Appropriate themes to embrace and celebrate now are creativity, sexuality, and abundance (including cultivating meaningful work and prosperity).

## Summer Solstice (June 21): Gateway to Summer
### Summer Solstice • Cancer • Cardinal • Water

Summer solstice marks the astronomical turning point that is the beginning of summer. It is the longest day of the year and heralds the beginning of Cancer season, when life is at its most fertile. Usually on or around June 21, depending on the year, everything is at its full flowering peak—a final thrust before the gradual drift into the long exhale that is the dark half of the year. This is the time on the Wheel when we once again celebrate the sacred masculine. The God has grown steadily in power and strength to reach the point when he is at the peak of his vitality and everything in nature is bursting with life. Just like the Goddess, the God also has many faces, and at this time of year, he is especially attuned with his aspects of Cernunnos, the Greenman, and the Horned God. He channels the wild joy of the outward directed energy of the summer solstice. This is the time of the Oak King at his zenith of power. The Oak King presides over the waxing half of the year, from the rebirth of the Sun at winter solstice until the pinnacle of his strength at summer solstice, when the Holly King once again takes his crown. Although the summer solstice has been celebrated for thousands of years throughout many places in the world, it is especially remarkable at the ancient monument of Stonehenge in Wiltshire, England. On the morning of summer solstice, the Sun rises dramatically over the heel stone, which is outside the circle, heralding the longest day of the year.

## Tuning In

You can tap into the potent energy of summer solstice to reinvigorate yourself and strengthen your core. Since this is the time of the sacred masculine, it is the perfect time to reflect on your own animus, which, according to Jung, is the inner masculine that resides in all women. However, while this is a definitive Jungian meaning of the term, author and Jungian analyst Dr. Clarissa Pinkola Estés writes, "Animus can best be understood as a force that assists women in acting in their own behalves in the outer world."[7] She further illustrates that "the role of the *hidalgo*, king or mentor, in a woman's psyche is supposed to be to help her realize her possibilities and goals, to make manifest the ideas and ideals she holds dear, to weigh the justice of things, take care of the

7. Clarissa Pinkola Estés, *Women Who Run with the Wolves: Myths and Stories of the Wild Woman Archetype* (New York: Ballentine Books, 1992), 311.

armaments, strategize when she is threatened, to help her unite all her psychic territories."[8]

Is your animus healthy, alive, potent? Is it doing its job of helping you stand your ground? Draw healthy boundaries? Go after the things that are important to you? If your animus seems less effectual than you'd like it to be, now's the time to reawaken it. Estés explains that "the dreams of women strong in outer manifesting ability often feature a strong male figure who consistently appears in various guises."[9] I once had a dream of a beautiful golden child who I understood to be my animus. He was a child because he was still developing, and I was still in the process of learning to stand up for myself and act on my own behalf. Years later, he showed up again in a dream, but this time he was a strapping adolescent. Around the time of the second dream, I had just made the monumental step of going back to school as a single parent. I was learning to take care of myself and move toward my goals with more courage. Who is your animus? What does he look like? If you have never given much thought to such questions before, now's the time. One way you can get a glimpse of your animus is by reflecting on characters in myth or story that you admire. Perhaps you have an inner Gandalf, or maybe you resonate more with Luke Skywalker or a literary hero like Lord Byron. Your animus can even be represented by someone you know, perhaps a beloved grandfather who embodies characteristics you admire. I have always thought of the animus as the archetypal wise inner king, the counselor who offers sage advice but can show his fierce side when necessary.

Summer solstice is a celebratory time, and we are called outside to revel in the fecundity of the season. Try to find some time to go outdoors and connect with this turning point. Use all your senses, and reflect on the fullness of nature. Spend at least ten minutes really seeing what's happening around you. Breathe this enlivening energy deep into your core, and allow it to replenish your vitality.

8. Estés, *Women Who Run with the Wolves*, 313.

9. Estés, *Women Who Run with the Wolves*, 310–11.

## *Seasonal Altar*

If possible, try to set up your altar outside so you can make the most of the revitalizing spirit of this time of year. A balcony or even a spot by a window can also work. Choose what aspect of the summer solstice you are intuitively drawn to when setting up your seasonal altar. Like many of the sabbats on the Wheel of the Year, the summer solstice is rich with symbolism that can seem paradoxical but nevertheless is appropriate. For example, you may wish to focus on the power of the Sun or the sacred masculine and decorate your altar with an image of your animus, the Greenman, antlers, acorns (for the Oak King), or any other manifestation of the masculine that resonates with you. You can use Sun colors: yellow, orange, and red. Be sure to light a candle in one of these colors to honor the sacred masculine. Alternatively, as summer solstice is also the beginning of Cancer season, you can also refer to the Cancer chapter and table of correspondences for altar suggestions for this aspect of the sabbat. You can also honor this time of year by connecting with the water element and placing a chalice of sea or spring water on your altar. Seashells, driftwood, and sea salt are also good additions to a water element altar. On the other hand, you may feel called to celebrate several of the aspects of summer solstice. In that case, feel free to intuitively include any or all the correspondences, reflecting on the underlying mystery that ties it all together.

# Lughnasadh/Lammas (August 1 or 2):
## The Heart of Summer

Cross-Quarter Day • Leo • Fixed • Fire

Celebrated either August 1 or 2, the next cross-quarter festival on the ancient Celtic calendar is Lammas, or Lughnasadh. This day also marks the first of the three harvest celebrations, followed by the Second Harvest (autumn equinox) and the Final Harvest (Samhain), and is the midpoint between the summer solstice and the autumn equinox. This is the time when the God, having reached his peak at the summer solstice, now becomes the Lord of the Harvest, who is symbolically sacrificed as the grain so life may continue. It is a celebration of the transformation of the grain into life-sustaining food for the community. Although the God symbolically dies at this time of year, we know that he will be reborn again at Yule. The motif of eating the body of the sacrificed god echoes the Christian rite of the Eucharist, taking into oneself the body and blood of Christ. As with the other sabbats, Lammas is about the mystery of the cycles of birth, growth, death, and rebirth.

In Ireland, this day is known as *Lughnasadh*, after the god Lugh, meaning "the commemoration of Lugh." Lugh was honored in Ireland and throughout Britain as well as continental Europe, and it is of note that this day happens to occur in the middle of Leo season, as Lugh was a god of light, a Sun deity, and went under such epithets as "Lugh the Long Handed" or "Lugh of the Many Skills." In *The White Goddess*, scholar Robert Graves describes Lughnasadh as a time celebrated with games, athletic competitions, feasting, and merriment. Trial marriages, which lasted for a year and a day, also occurred on Lughnasadh.[10] This was traditionally a time of great feasting and gratitude for the abundance of the earth, as well as the harvest of the first crops: wheat, corn, and barley. In England, this day was known as Lammas, from Old English *hlaf-mas*, or "loaf mass," and people would bake special loaves decorated with symbols of protection, fertility, and prosperity.[11]

### Tuning In

Although it is the heart of summer, the power of the Sun is now visibly beginning to wane. The seeds we planted in the spring are now ripening, and we look back at what we visualized six months ago at Imbolc and give thanks for what we are now bringing into manifestation. Take a walking meditation outside and make note of any impressions that arise. If you are able to go to a field, farm, or orchard where first fruits are being harvested, even better. Farmer's markets are overflowing with early apples, blackberries, blueberries, and luscious grapes. Take a mo-

10. Graves, *The White Goddess*, 301–2.

11. Graves, *The White Goddess*, 178.

ment to reflect on the underlying mystery of this sacred time. What is coming to fruition in your own life that was once just a seed? How did you nurture that seed into what it is today? What sacrifices did you make? Time? Effort? Resources? Although this is a time of gratitude and celebration, there is also a slightly bittersweet undertone to Lughnasadh. If we look closely, we will see that there is a slight glimmer of gold now beneath the green. On an intuitive level we know that summer is fleeting and that harvest time will soon begin in earnest.

### Seasonal Altar

Decorate your altar in the rich colors of the season: reds, gold, orange, yellow, and amber. Sunflowers are coming into their own now, as are ripe blackberries. Baked goods, especially bread, hold pride of place on a Lammas altar, reminding us of the transformation of seed into grain. As Lugh was also considered a god of crafts, or "many skills," you can also add symbols of your own creative endeavors to your altar. And, as Lughnasadh falls right in the heart of Leo season, turn to the Leo chapter and table of correspondences for more ideas.

# Autumn Equinox (September 21): Gateway to Autumn

## Autumn Equinox • Libra • Cardinal • Air

The Wheel of the Year continues to turn, and the shadows are growing ever longer as the light graciously gives way to the approaching dark. On or around September 21, depending on the year, light and dark are balanced once again. The Sun enters the sign of Libra, and the Goddess now wears the face of wisdom. What are we reaping in our lives? What can we bring to the table after all the work we have done in the past year? Although we will be bringing in some bountiful crops, there will be some cherished plans and ideas we'll have to let die on the vine. This is the Second Harvest, and it feels right to take stock of our lives and make sure our energies are balanced.

The autumn equinox is a natural, earth-centered time for giving thanks. The ancestors in the Northern Hemisphere would have celebrated this time of year with a harvest feast, complete with crackling bonfires and general merriment. Conversely, it was also a time for weighing and assessment, a time for reflection and rest after a long, active season of planting and tending. It marked the place on the Wheel to ready the nest for the approaching longer nights by putting up preserves, smoking meats, and ensuring all was sound for the coming winter. The balance of equal day and equal night was reflected in the celebration of the abundance of the passing summer while preparing for the coming dark. This is the time of year when Persephone leaves the topside world and descends into Hades to take her place as queen of the underworld, while her mother, Demeter, grieves her daughter's absence and nothing grows again until her return in the spring.

### Tuning In

At this liminal moment that hovers between light and dark, we have a chance to pause and reflect on the passing of the year. Try to find some time to be in nature and situate yourself with this important turning point. The days are now noticeably shorter, and the temperatures are cooler. The leaves are a riot of color, as the trees themselves are tuned in to the declining daylight as they prepare for winter. The green chlorophyll breaks down, and the trees will rest throughout the coming cold season, conserving their energy and living off the food they have stored throughout summer. Given the fact that the school year has just started and many people are back to work after summer vacations, we don't often have the opportunity to rest at autumn equinox. But, even taking an hour to align yourself with the symbolism of this time of year can be beneficial for your natural rhythms and prepare you for a smooth and soulful transition into the dark half of the year. Consider planning a harvest feast in gratitude of the abundance of the season. Invite your loved ones and have everyone bring something that is freshly harvested and local. Each person can take a moment to express appreciation for what the passing year has brought them, thus creating an opportunity to build community, share stories, and cultivate a sense of belonging that will see them through the coming winter.

*Seasonal Altar*

Decorate your seasonal altar with colorful leaves and acorns, nuts, seeds, ears of corn, and root vegetables. In the Northern Hemisphere many varieties of grapes are now being harvested, and it's a perfect time to visit a winery and experience the excitement of the harvest directly. You can bring home a bottle or two and place a cup of wine on your altar as an offering to the season. Honor Demeter and her daughter Persephone by placing a ripe red pomegranate on your altar, as a symbol of her cyclical return to the underworld. And, because the energies are balanced once again, you may choose to honor both the God and the Goddess on your altar, using iconography of each. Use the colors of nature to guide your color choices for altar cloths and such, or turn to the Libra chapter and table of correspondences for alternate ideas on celebrating this time of year.

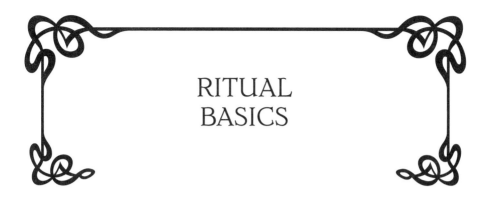

# RITUAL
# BASICS

Creating ritual is an intuitive art, not an exact science, and while many Pagans incorporate ritual as a part of a specific spiritual path, you don't have to identify as such to benefit from engaging with it. Ritual helps us mark important times in our lives and often accompanies significant rites of passage. For example, most weddings involve ritual of some kind, from reciting vows to exchanging rings. Another common form of ritual is used to help alleviate grief. Whether we are grieving the loss of a loved one or the end of a relationship, it can be therapeutic to create ritual to say goodbye and gain closure. Ritual can be simple or elaborate. You can personalize and create your own rituals, making them more meaningful to you and tailored to your specific needs. And while there are many time-honored elements of ritual that derive from various Pagan traditions that are beneficial (e.g., casting a circle), the most important thing is your intent.

All the chapters in this book conclude with a pathworking and ritual specific to each astrological archetype and associated goddess. Essentially, a ritual usually contains a set of actions, words, and visualizations that help us focus our energy to connect with our personal subconscious, as well as the collective unconscious, the universe, or deity. Some rituals enable us to direct our energy toward attaining a specific goal, while others facilitate a deeper experience of the specific energies we choose to work with. For example, many of the rituals in this book help us align with the archetypal energies of a particular goddess because we want to bring the qualities she embodies into our lives.

For the rituals in this book, you may want to take the time to prepare yourself and your space or to gather certain items to help you focus your intentions. See the following sections for some basic elements that you may want to incorporate for beginning and concluding your ritual. For a simple ritual, you may feel that clearing your space and grounding and centering are sufficient. In fact, I suggest clearing, grounding, and centering for any ritual or ceremony. Please use your intuition as a guideline and feel free to experiment. What works for one person doesn't always work for another.

## A Note on Pathworkings in This Book

Although the term *pathworking* originates from working with the pathways of the Kabbalistic Tree of Life, it has more recently become cognate with guided meditation that is designed to take you on a spiritual journey or visualization. This is how I intend the use of the term in this book.

For the pathworkings in this book, it is to your benefit to be in a safe and quiet space where you know you won't be interrupted for at least fifteen to twenty minutes. Remember to turn off your phone. Wear loose, unrestrictive clothing, and sit comfortably or lie down. If you need extra physical support, use cushions or bolsters. Clear your space with sage or incense or by burning essential oils before you begin. (Some chapters include a particular incense or oil blend for a pathworking that aligns with a certain goddess, which will deepen your connection to her attributes. However, if you do not have that specific incense or oil, you can still do the pathworking, but do use sage to clear your space instead.) Several Savitri breaths will help to calm any mind chatter and prepare you to relax into a receptive state. *Savitri Pranayama* is a simple rhythmic breathing technique that is useful for calming, concentration, and focus. You can engage with this yogic breathing technique in sequences of four-two-four-two, six-three-six-three, or eight-four-eight-four. For example, breathe in to the count of four. Hold for the count of two. Breathe out to the count of four. Hold for the count of two. If you are interested in learning more about this or other beneficial breathing techniques, consult a local yoga teacher. My sister Vaysha taught me this very useful technique when she was going through yoga teacher training and I was cramming for exams in my first year of college.

There are several ways you can engage with a pathworking: you can read it aloud, you can record yourself reading it and then play the recording, or you can memorize it. If you are working with a friend, one of you can read the pathworking aloud while the other journeys. When you finish your pathworking, take your time to get up, stretch, and come back into waking consciousness. Because you will likely be in a fully relaxed state, it's a good time to write down anything that came up for you during your pathworking, including thoughts, feelings, sensations, images, and impressions. You may wish to get a special journal that you use for this purpose. You may also choose to draw what came up for you. Realizations, answers, and new insights often arise from pathworking.

## Clearing Space and Grounding and Centering

Some of you may already have your own way of preparing for ritual or magickal work, and there are as many different ways as there are practitioners. The following are some helpful basic techniques drawn from various practices. There are many great resources available if you wish to learn about any of the following in more detail.

### Clearing Space

Before grounding and centering, it is wise to clear the space you'll be working in. This can be as simple as just burning some incense or essential oil or lighting some sage to smudge the area. Not only does clearing the space you're about to work in reset and banish negative energy, but it also gives your subconscious a cue that something special or out of the ordinary is about to take place. Sage, cedar, and palo santo are all excellent smudges that you can purchase in most natural-food or metaphysical stores.

Light your smudge wand and walk counterclockwise around the circumference of the space where you'll be performing your ritual. Visualize the smoke carrying away any unwanted energy. If you are working indoors, open a window so the smoke can escape. You might want to say a few words to affirm your intention, such as "This space is now clear and clean of any and all unwanted energies. I am protected and safe." I also like ringing a bell three times or once at each corner of the room after I smudge. Ringing a bell is an ancient practice used by many cultures to clear the air. Additionally, I find that physically tidying up the area first helps me concentrate better, so the laundry in the corner or the pile of dishes that need to be washed doesn't distract me.

### Grounding and Centering

Grounding and centering before ritual helps focus our intent, subtly shifting our awareness toward the work we're about to do. After grounding and centering, you will likely feel a sense of deep calm and focused awareness as you begin your ritual. When the ritual is finished, it is helpful to repeat your grounding and centering process, as you always want to come back to center. Think of energy as just that—*energy*. For example, electricity is a form of energy that helps us do all kinds of things when channeled and focused for specific purposes, but you wouldn't want too much of it coursing through the air or through your body! Likewise, excess energy that isn't properly grounded after a ritual can make you feel scattered, irritated, amped up like you've had too much coffee, or worse. Drinking water or eating something after ritual work can help you ground. Avoid sugar and stimulants like caffeine, and opt for protein instead, such as cheese, tofu, nut butter, or eggs. Going for a walk or a bike ride or doing some yoga can also bring you back into your body. Another great way to ground yourself after a ritual is to take a bath in Epsom or sea salts. You want to leave your ritual feeling relaxed yet invigorated, confident that you directed the energy toward your goal.

## Music, Drumming, and Movement

Once you have cleared your space and grounded and centered, you may wish to further shift your awareness by listening to meditative drumming music or playing a drum (if you have one) to achieve a light trance state in which you are still alert but operating from a slightly different level of consciousness. Movement and ecstatic dance are other useful ways to shift awareness and raise energy. Ecstatic dance is essentially a moving meditation that can help shift your awareness. It is also known as trance dance and is a freeform body-mind practice with no structured steps and no need for prior experience. While there are ecstatic dance centers in virtually every city and town, it is something that you can easily do in your own living room. Ecstatic dance brings you into a place where you can access the essential wisdom of the body, leaving you feeling a sense of release, peace, and heightened awareness. Do an internet search for *trance dance* or *ecstatic dance music* to find a playlist that works for you. One of the best-known teachers in this field is the late Gabrielle Roth, who founded the 5Rhythms movement system in the late seventies.

## Casting a Circle

Most magickal traditions include the casting of a protective circle before doing ritual work. The purpose of the circle is twofold: the first part is to concentrate and contain your energy while letting your subconscious know this is liminal and sacred space "between the worlds," and the second part is protection. Working with energy is very real. The energy you raise is dynamic and immensely attractive, not only for aligning yourself with your chosen deities and purposes but also to other energies that you might not want joining in the festivities.

Different traditions have various methods for circle casting, but the most important thing is to define your area and firmly declare that your space is sacred and contained. You can do this by walking clockwise around your space while using your pointing finger or the intention of your gaze to delineate the circle. I sprinkle salt around the circumference of my circle, salt being a time-honored substance used for protection and purification. However, sometimes it's just not feasible to do all of this. Sometimes you need to do a quick ritual or cast a circle of protection around yourself on the fly in a public place. In this case, visualize yourself surrounded by a circle or sphere of glowing white light. Affirm silently that you are protected and safe.

# Creating an Altar

An altar is an intentional space, a place to connect with aspects of your deeper self and also with deity. An altar can be as simple—a treasured raven feather found at the beach, some handmade incense, and a special stone—or as elaborate as you wish. There are many different kinds of altars and no right or wrong way to do them. You can have one altar or many throughout your home or property. Some altars are seasonal, changing to reflect points on the Wheel of the Year. Others are perma- nent, and dedicated to a certain deity. There are altars devoted to the ancestors and altars created to invoke a particular element. Whatever you choose to place upon your altar aligns you with deeper meaning and specific energy. You can dedicate an altar to one or all of the guid- ing goddess archetypes you will find throughout this book, as you feel drawn. For help designing your altar, look in the tables of correspon- dences at the end of each chapter for everything from crystals to colors associated with each sign.

I have several altars, both indoor and outdoor. The one in the studio where I see clients is seasonal, but there are some things on it that hold pride of place throughout the year. This particular altar also has some- thing to represent each element: a barnacle-encrusted abalone shell found on the west coast of Vancouver Island represents water, a feather found on a kayaking trip summons air, a very special black moonstone sphere stands for earth, and a handmade candle infused with cedar and vanilla calls in fire.

I also have altar boxes where I store beautiful remnants of cloth in different colors for draping my altars, as well as objects, photographs, pieces of driftwood, crystals, statues, and special mementos discovered while traveling. As the seasons change, or as I feel inspired, I can go to my altar boxes and choose from a treasure trove of shimmering silks and sumptuous velvets in a myriad of colors to create a new feeling and channel a particular energy. Near Samhain, for instance, I might use a burgundy velvet shawl as a base and layer it with a length of antique black lace. On top of this I might add some acorns, autumn leaves, and a bell on a piece of aged ribbon brought from the old country by my grandmother.

An altar can be a secret corner in a bookshelf or a grand display in your foyer that greets each person who visits your home. A dresser top, an old table, an interesting piece of driftwood dragged home from the beach, or a flat-topped rock all work well as bases. Be creative! Here are some tips to create a visually striking altar:

- Place the tallest objects at the back or on each side of a center piece.
- Employ the design rule of three or five main objects.
- Use a riser to elevate small objects or little statues. Purchase plexiglass risers in any size from a retail-supply shop or get creative and use another object instead (for instance, I currently have a bronze statue of the goddess Danu perched on top of a small cauldron on my altar).
- If you can't find an appropriate object to use as a riser, cover the makeshift riser with a small square of silk fabric.
- Make an interesting backdrop by placing a book with an evocative cover against the wall behind your altar.

## A Note on Recipes in This Book

Many of the chapters include recipes for handcrafting incense and essential oil blends related to the Sun signs and corresponding guiding goddess archetypes. Here you'll find some guidelines and instructions that will assist you in preparing the recipes.

Aromatherapy uses the properties of certain scents from the essential oils of trees, barks, resins, herbs, and flowers to heal, promote well-being, and create a desired physiological effect. Scent molecules can be inhaled from a single oil or combined to create a synergistic blend that is more than the sum of its parts. The scent infuses the air you breathe and connects with the olfactory system, the brain, and the limbic system, which can produce therapeutic and psychological effects, such as stress relief, focus and clarity, balancing hormones, and soothing anxiety. Scents can also be used to attune with magickal correspondences and for meditation, ritual and ceremony, healing, and spiritual cleansing.

## Mixing Essential Oils

Glass blending bottles: ½- to ¼-ounce containers with lids

Other types of containers, depending on what you're making: e.g., spritz bottle for face or room spray

Glass dropper or toothpicks for transferring oil

Cotton balls for testing blend

Gloves

## Basic Ratio Guide for Various Purposes

Face spritzer: 4-ounce bottle, 20 to 24 drops with purified water (1%)

Room spray, body spray, or anointment: 4-ounce bottle, 40 to 48 drops in purified water (2%)

Oil burner, diffuser, or vaporizer: can be used neat

You can play with the ratios to get a scent exactly where you want it. Sense of smell is subjective, and everyone will have different preferences.

You can burn the oil in an essential oil burner or vaporizer, put it in a tub, or add purified water to turn it into a spritzer.

You may wish to use a carrier oil if using as anointing oil; sweet almond, jojoba, grapeseed, and olive oil are good choices. Let the newly created oil rest for a day or two in a dark place so the oils can harmonize and deepen.

## Making Incense

Charcoal tablets

Tweezers

Measuring spoons

Metal or glass bowl for mixing

Mortar and pestle

Large seashell or incense burner

Incense sand if using a shell (easily obtained in most metaphysical supply shops or online)

Small glass jar with lid, or small sealable plastic bags

Mix your ingredients together in a metal or glass bowl or directly into your mortar and pestle. Grind until the larger pieces of resin have broken down into tiny bits. You can grind them to a powder or create a coarser blend if you prefer. Many ingredients are available already ground. If you wish, you may consecrate your incense to the goddess of your choice by stating your intention in your own words: for example, "I hereby consecrate this incense to Inanna, Queen of Heaven and Earth." You can state this before you begin or when you are finished. It also helps to focus your intent by having iconography of the goddess you wish to work with nearby, on an altar, or on the counter beside your workspace.

You may wish to start with a very small batch to test, using a quarter teaspoon for each part. This way you can test the incense and adjust it to your preference.

Most incense is ready to use immediately. Put the remainder into your jar or bag. Label the container and store it in a dark, cool place.

To burn, place the charcoal tablet on the incense burner; if using a shell or other heatproof dish, fill the dish with sand and then place charcoal tablet on the sand. Light the charcoal and allow it to burn for a few minutes, until it begins to turn whitish-gray. Use the tweezers if you need to handle or reposition the charcoal tablet, as it gets very hot. Place a pinch of incense on top of the charcoal.

## A Bath to Ground and Center
### after a Ritual or Divination

After a particularly busy day of counseling and astrological consultations, I find this bath just the cure for energy overload. I highly recommend it after a ritual, divination, or just a long day of inadvertently absorbing other people's energy. The salt is both purifying and protective, drawing out and cleansing. It's also helpful for soothing aching muscles, which can be a side effect of carrying stuff that doesn't belong to you. The essential oils work on a subtle level, adding their therapeutic benefits to calm and reset. Make sure you use good-quality, therapeutic-grade oils. Above all, you don't want to use synthetic oils, as they don't have any real benefits. Add one or two cups of bath salt to running water. Make a batch ahead of time and store it in labeled jars for any time you need an extra boost to ground or cleanse your energy.

### Grounding and Purifying Bath

5 cups Epsom salts
Approximately 60 drops essential oils
    For grounding: sandalwood, patchouli, cedar, clary sage
    For purifying: cypress, juniper berry, rosemary, ginger
1 cup baking soda

Choose at least one oil from each category (e.g., cedar and rosemary). Use your judgment in terms of how much scent you want. Start with a small amount like 4 to 5 drops per 1 cup of salt and add more according to your preference. I usually go with at least 10 drops total for each cup, for a more aromatic experience.

Mix oils into Epsom salts thoroughly in a large metal or glass mixing bowl. Stir in baking soda. Scoop into mason jars and cover. The oils keep best if stored in a dark place. Feel free to mix and match the scents using your nose and your intuition. You might even want to make a few different blends to have on hand. Remember to label each jar so you know which essential oils are in each batch. Makes 6 cups.

# Part Two

# THE HEROINE'S JOURNEY
## Through the Signs with the Guiding Goddess Archetypes

A s I have written this book for women, I have chosen to refer to the journey through the twelve signs as the *heroine's journey*: the quest toward individuation from a feminine perspective. Each of us is the heroine of our own life story, and we can see the motifs of departure, initiation, and return play out time and time again throughout our lives. Whether we choose to attend university, write a book, have a child, or start a business, every time we step out onto the road and heed the call to adventure, we are moving toward becoming whole. Every time we take up the challenge and step out of our comfort zone to do something that has meaning for us, we are accruing wisdom that can be shared with others.

While ritual, magick, and astrology are multilayered knowledge systems that can take a whole lifetime—or many lifetimes—to master, you have gone over some of the basics and now have everything you need to dive into the next section and take part in the rituals and pathworkings associated with each goddess and sign. You also have enough knowledge to set out on your path with confidence as you explore the archetypes that make up who you are and who you came here to be. I encourage you to keep studying and to continue on your path to self-knowledge through the infinite resources on astrology and magick. Remember that you have every sign in your chart and therefore can draw on any of the astrological energies or guiding goddesses you need at any time.

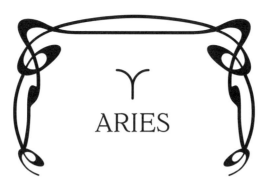

# ARIES

For all of Aries's legendary bravado, it is often not acknowledged that she is, at heart, a sensitive soul. If we think about Aries season—the earliest days of spring—we see that those first brave shoots that poke up triumphantly through the soil are also very vulnerable. All the tender new life that returns at this magical time of beginnings is fragile, precarious, and uncertain. The lingering chill of winter threatens the survival of those brave new sentries of rebirth. Because of this seasonal resonance that is imprinted on the Aries archetype, Aries is often associated with the qualities of courage, forward motion, and the instinct to survive. Aries is a cardinal fire sign—a gateway into a new season (in this case, spring)—and relates to the spirited, enthusiastic element of fire. The spring equinox heralds the beginning of the Sun's journey through the zodiac and marks the beginning of Aries season. Aries is the first sign, the individuated life force that rises out of the collective. Aries is connected to the call to adventure in mythologist Joseph Campbell's hero's journey. It is the starting point of the soul's individuation at the beginning of the spiritual journey through the lessons of the signs. I also often think of Aries as the Fool in the tarot: the innocent stepping forward without any sense of fear, and a quality of pure childlike exuberance. Look to your chart to see where you have the sign of Aries; this will show you the area of life where you have the ability to assert yourself or get something up and running.

Aries is ruled by Mars, and like Aries, its archetype is often misunderstood. Mars is our drive, our get-up-and-go. It's the way we go after what we want, the forward thrust. Although Mars was later celebrated as the Roman god of battle, he was also originally a fertility deity and vegetation god, as well as protector of farmers, fields, and boundaries.[12] Mars is the planetary archetype that is associated with life force, libido, assertion, and anger. Aries knows that healthy anger over injustice to those who are less empowered is the impetus that can create change. Aries energy is exemplified in our impulse to defend our young, stand up for ourselves, and make a move that can change our life. It is saying no to abusive partners and situations and acting on our own behalf. It is the creative impulse that starts a business, paints a picture, or births a baby. Aries is passion. It is what ignites our imaginations and stirs our embers into crackling hearth fires.

## The Aries Woman

In Celtic and ancient Germanic society, it wasn't only the men who went to battle. Women fought alongside the men with just as much ferocity, courage, and valor. Lagertha, the formidable shieldmaiden made popular on History Channel's *Vikings*, is a female protagonist who embodies the archetype of the Aries woman. According to legend, Lagertha was a Viking warrior and ruler whose story is mentioned in the *Gesta Danorum,* a twelfth-century account of Danish and Scandinavian history by Saxo Grammaticus. As the character in *Vikings,* Lagertha is portrayed as having integrity and a noble spirit. She is fiercely protective of her home and family and eventually reclaims her throne as Queen of Kattegat, echoing the highest principle of Aries, that of wise leadership and sovereignty.

Another historical example of the Aries woman archetype is the legendary Iceni queen Boudicca. Boudicca, whose name means "victorious" in the Brythonic language, was an Iron Age Celtic queen who lived in Roman-occupied Britain in the first century CE. The Iceni, under Boudicca's husband Prasutagus, agreed to live under Roman rule

---

12. Frazer, *The Golden Bough,* 553; Miranda Green, *Symbol and Image in Celtic Religious Art* (London: Routledge, 1992), 111.

in exchange for lasting peace. When Prasutagus died, he left the Iceni kingdom in his will to his wife Boudicca and his two young daughters. However, Rome did not recognize the right of women to rule and marched into the peaceable and prosperous kingdom, making the dubious claim that the kingdom owed Rome taxes that were long overdue. People were beaten, thrown from their homes, and systematically murdered as they tried desperately to protect their children, livestock, and food supply. As the queen of the deceased ruler, Boudicca was whipped almost to the point of death, and her two young daughters were publicly tortured and gang raped by Roman soldiers. The harrowing sight of her desolated tribe and her broken and abused daughters was the catalyst that galvanized her into action. Rome might not have recognized the right of a woman to rule, but the Iceni were no strangers to female champions, and they rallied to their queen's side. In an unprecedented uprising against the status quo, over a hundred thousand Britons marched on Londinium and Verulamium, laying the mighty Roman-occupied cities to waste.

Eventually, the Romans refortified and defeated the Britons at the Battle of Watling Street. Tragically, in the final hours, it is said that Boudicca took her own life rather than surrender to capture by Rome. Her example of courage, passion, and valor in the face of nearly insurmountable odds embodies the archetype of the Aries woman.

Much like her historical counterparts, the contemporary Aries woman often gets a sort of modern-day battle fever that occurs when she is defending her own boundaries or stirred by the plight of those who are marginalized. However, as contemptuous as she can be of the "enemy," the Aries woman can never be accused of being mean-spirited. She is at her happiest when she has a cause, whether that is spearheading an initiative to keep the city from tearing down heritage homes, fighting for water rights, or fighting for religious freedom. Social justice is in Aries's blood. Aries is a born activist, and as impetuous and headstrong as she can sometimes seem, bring an injustice to her attention and she will be preparing her next campaign.

If she doesn't have a cause to champion, Aries can become frustrated and irritable. She needs something to defend. An Aries woman needs to keep her metaphorical sword sharp and will resort to sparring with almost anyone in her path to keep up her chops. This often takes the form of a battle of the wits. She needs to keep her finely tuned and agile mind well honed and will practice by debating almost any subject. *Taking a stance* is a phrase made for Aries. If her wits grow dull from lack of use or she lacks a suitable contestant, she can become depressed, that indomitable and sparkling Aries spirit turned inward. One of the ways she builds her self-esteem and sense of self-worth is through healthy competition. Although this can be an exercise of her physical prowess, she is just as likely to be showing off her verbal skills in an online debate. Aries can wield words like weapons when her passion is ignited.

There is, however, another rarer Aries type who attempts to avoid conflict at almost any cost. Usually, this is the woman who witnessed firsthand early in her life what unbridled anger can lead to. She may have grown up in a climate of rage and emotional tension and now strives to avoid situations that feel potentially unstable. If she is aware of this impulse and doesn't sublimate her true feelings, she can work on developing healthy boundaries and get in touch with her anger and ability to assert herself in a constructive way by consciously focusing on the positive qualities of her Sun sign.

Not all Aries women are bossy and domineering as old-school astrology attests. However, most are very busy and active, manifesting things that are important to them in the outer world. More retiring signs are often surprised, if not secretly envious of the sheer amount Aries gets up to. She is a natural doer and finds it hard, if not impossible, to be still for long. Aries does not usually suffer from procrastination. She is literally compelled to act, as action keeps her flame burning. If you have an Aries friend on Facebook, you might feel exhausted just reading their status updates and wonder how they can possibly manage to fit everything in. One day they're starting yet another exciting project, and the next they are enrolling in summer classes.

But all this constant motion can lead to burnout. Aries women need to be conscious of their physical needs when they have thrown themselves into a project. This is the woman who forgets to eat or sleep when she is passionate about something, the woman who burns the proverbial candle at both ends. The Aries woman can take a cue or two from her opposite sign, Libra, and learn the fine art of balance. She would do well to blend her enthusiastic need for action and accomplishment with some downtime. Aries can benefit from yoga and mindfulness meditation so she can refuel herself. I know that many an Aries is reading this and laughing out loud. "Ha! I can't shut my mind off long enough to meditate—not going to happen!" I'm not talking about sitting still for an hour in silent contemplation, Aries, but *everyone* can meditate for five minutes—even you. The trick for Aries is not to feel overwhelmed. When Aries feels overwhelmed, she tends to throw in the towel and move on, as she has a low threshold for frustration and boredom.

Exercise, whether it be in the gym or regular cycling is also good for managing her considerable energy. Aries would also do well to stay away from too much caffeine and sugar, as her already amped-up nervous system doesn't need it. Lots of clean protein, B vitamins, and iron rich beans and legumes help earth too much fire and can assist Aries in directing her formidable energy in constructive ways.

In the secret heart of many an Aries, she is a bit of a rock star. You can see it in the toss of her head and the slight swagger when she's walking in her favorite pair of boots. And she doesn't just resonate with female rock stars in her heart of hearts; she is equally apt to have an inner Prince or Mick Jagger as her animus. As the first sign of the zodiac, she makes an entrance that cannot be ignored and is highly conscious of the persona she chooses to project. Aries is proud of her carefully cultivated image, as it enhances her personal myth.

In love, the Aries woman is a passionate creature. Vivacious, playful, feisty, and charming, her heart is quick to become engaged, and she's just as likely to be the one doing the courting as the one being courted. Aries is swept away by the grand epic and loves a good story. She is often drawn into relationships in which she must embark on a quest of some kind to consummate union with her intended beloved. She lives in Portland and he lives in Australia? Perfect! The Aries woman must be on guard not to be drawn in by the perennially struggling musician, starving artist, or broody Byronic hero. Aries seems to have the propensity to fall in love with a paramour's potential rather than what is actually right in front of her. Her heart is true, earnest and trusting. Aries is a fiercely loyal sign, and if she loves and respects you, she is not likely to cheat. If she has given her heart, she will also expect the same from you. This is not the kind of woman who takes betrayal in stride and eventually "gets over it." To her, betrayal means you are a coward with a fatal character flaw, and this woman makes no allowances for cowardice.

Sexually, the Aries woman is blessed with a lusty appetite, and she often has a great deal of pride in her sexual prowess. If you think you've got it in the bag when you meet a sexy Aries lady, be forewarned that the easy target is no feather in her cap; she needs a challenge. In fact, there is a particular kind of Aries woman who is a bit of a trophy hunter regarding sexual conquests and sets her sights on big game such as celebrities and the like. Most Aries women will proudly tell you their "number" without batting an eye, and that number can be quite high, depending on the Aries in question. Most Aries women do not take kindly to being part of a stable, and if you are the kind of person who wants to play the field and keep your options open, Aries may not be the sign for you. She might initially go along with being one of a few, but that's only if her sense of competition is roused to the point where she wants to knock any competitors out of the ring. If it turns out that the object of her attention doesn't realize when he or she has encountered "the best" and insists on dating lesser suitors anyway, she will be incredulous (and often terribly hurt) but will then quickly set her sights on a new, worthier target. Aries needs to be proud of her partner, and she is usually confident of what she has to offer.

Being an independent self-starter, Aries is a born entrepreneur and is often happiest as her own boss or at least working with minimal supervision. Although she enjoys the company of others, she works well on her own, where she can fully immerse herself in her visions. Aries needs to be passionately inspired to bring out her best, and as the first sign, she has a propensity to birth new ideas, initiate creativity, and manifest the divine spark. Aries is also the Artist. Starting an endeavor is not something Aries has difficulty with, but finishing it can be a challenge for her. Unless she is sufficiently inspired, she is famous for bold new beginnings but often has trouble staying the course and waiting for her projects to come to fruition. Patience is not Aries's strong suit. She does well partnering with someone who can take her brilliant ideas and handle the practical details. Old-school astrology speaks often of Aries being drawn to occupations like police officer, firefighter, or professional athlete. However, it's time to update that list. You will find Aries championing the rights of the less privileged and leading social-justice initiatives. Aries also makes a good social worker because she truly will go the distance to make a difference. She can be a fierce advocate and a brilliant lawyer. You will also find many Aries women working for environmental issues and animal rights. Remember, she needs a cause, and all the better if she can turn it into a career. Aries women make great entrepreneurs and can thrive on the challenge of being a small business owner. Aries accepts the uncertainty and ups and downs of entrepreneurship with a can-do attitude. And of course, the startup company has Aries's name all over it.

As Aries women mature, they alchemize the fiery bravado of youth into a steady flame that still burns brightly but doesn't burn out. Many retain their sense of enthusiasm and their passion for justice. In fact, her age and experience blended with her unwavering desire to fight for a worthy cause can make an older Aries woman the most formidable warrior of all. Aries tends to stay youthful and vibrant well into her later years, but as she matures, she usually tempers some of the unrestrained bluster of her younger days into an enduring glow. She becomes the wise one who inspires the next generation with a twinkle in her eye and a far-fetched tale at the fireside, which just might be true.

# Guiding Goddess Archetype: Macha

Macha is an ancient Irish goddess usually associated with one of the triple aspects of the great war goddess the Morrigan, whose name means "great queen." Macha is connected to abundance, prosperity, and the fertility of the land, as well as protection, boundaries, and sovereignty. The *Lebor Gabála Érenn* refers to her as "Macha, greatness of wealth."[13] Although there are several distinct stories related to Macha throughout Irish mythology, it is her aspect as *Macha Mong Ruad* ("red mane") that most aligns her with the Aries archetype. As Macha Mong Ruad, she is the only queen named in the List of the High Kings of Ireland.

When Macha's father, Aed Ruad, dies, Macha steps up and claims the kingship. The right of a woman to rule is not recognized, and her father's cousins Dithorba and Cimbaeth subsequently challenge Macha to a battle, which she wins. Dithorba is killed in this battle, and a second battle between Macha and Dithorba's sons ensues. She disguises herself as a leper and pursues the three men through the woods of Connacht, luring each of them in turn to have sex with her. Then she overcomes them, ties them up, and brings them back to Ulster, which speaks not only of Macha's potent sexual aspect but also her ability to shape-shift. Instead of having the sons of Dithorba killed, Macha enslaves them and has them build the Bronze Age fort Emain Macha. Legend has it that she marked out the boundaries of her new stronghold with her brooch. This story illustrates not only Macha's association with battle, but also her keen aptitude for cunning strategy and her connection with creating and maintaining boundaries. It also shows us a goddess who refused to be subjugated by men and instead boldly claimed sovereignty according to her own merits. As Aries is Mars ruled and thus associated with sex, the sexual confidence that Macha employs as a tactic when she seduces the sons of Dithorba further underlines her connection to the Aries archetype. And, also like Aries, Macha is associated with the fire element: she is referred to in the *Dindshenchas* as "Grian," "the sun of

---

13. R. A. Stewart Macalister, trans., *Lebor Gabála Érenn* (Dublin: Irish Text Society, 1956), verse 64, https://archive.org/details/leborgablare00macauoft.

womankind." [14] Ravens, crows, and horses are all important elements in the stories and legends connected to Macha, and therefore are considered sacred to her.

A second story featuring another aspect of Macha that resonates with the Aries archetype is in her guise as the wife of Cruinniuc. In this tale, we see Macha as a Faery woman who arrives on the doorstep of the widower Cruinniuc and takes on the role of his wife. With Macha at his side, the farmer becomes increasingly prosperous, and his life is blessed with further abundance when she becomes pregnant with twins.

Like many Faery lovers, Macha asks her mortal mate not to speak of her otherworldly origin. Macha exhibits several magickal qualities, including supernatural speed. She can run faster than a stallion, and instead of riding out on errands, she comes and goes great distances on foot within minutes. Cruinniuc cannot believe his luck to have such a woman and after a few pints can't help but boast of his talented Faery wife. King Conchobor overhears the farmer's bragging and challenges Cruinniuc to bring his wife to the fair to race against his chariot. Macha, hugely pregnant, protests and asks that she be allowed to give birth first, but the king commands that she race against his horses, pregnant or not, or risk the life of her husband. Macha wins the race, collapsing at the finish line and giving birth to twins. Clutching her babies in her arms, she pronounces a curse on the men of Ulster for nine generations: in their hour of greatest need, they shall be overcome with labor pains and be as weak as a woman in childbirth.

Themes in this story of the goddess Macha center on competition, honor, and boundaries, all of which are hallmarks of the Aries archetype. Although Macha does fiercely protest being pitted in competition against the king's horses, she does win the race, and we know winning against all odds is a recurring motif for Aries. Macha also defends her husband's honor and her own by taking up the challenge. Boundaries are another

14. Edward Gwynn, trans., *The Metrical Dindshenchas* (Electronic reproduction by Dublin Institute for Advanced Studies, 1991), 127, http://www.ucc.ie/celt/published/T106500A/index.html.

concept that resurfaces in this story. Macha draws her boundaries right away by making it clear that her husband cannot discuss her otherworldly status with anyone. She is willing to bestow prosperity and fertility on his home, but only under certain conditions. There are two alternate endings to the story, and each resonates with the archetype of the Aries woman. In one ending, Macha gives birth to her babies and dies after pronouncing her curse on the men of Ulster. In the other ending, Macha gathers up her newborn twins and disappears, which is also in line with an Aries response. Not only does she not suffer fools (her verbose husband), she is perfectly capable of leaving an abusive situation and striking off on her own. Like Macha, Aries embodies a spirit of sovereignty, and she will not tolerate dishonor.

## Pathworking: Standing Your Ground

Setting safe and healthy boundaries is something that takes practice for most of us. Whether it be letting family members know when they're stepping over the line, putting your foot down in a tricky situation at work, or knowing when to draw the line in a relationship, most of us could use a little support when standing up for ourselves in some area of life. Boundaries are important. They let others know how we want to be treated and can actually enhance a relationship. Even though setting healthy boundaries can be difficult if you're not used to drawing the proverbial line in the sand, you can learn with practice. Most of us have had times in our life when we agreed to something that we knew deep down we really didn't want. We may have given our time, resources, energy and consent and been left with the gnawing feeling that we have somehow betrayed ourselves.

Although the need to set clear boundaries is not gender specific, women have historically had a more difficult time of doing so. Generations of teachings that have admonished women to be "nice" and constantly put the needs and desires of others above their own have effectively weakened many women's ability to say no. This is not just an inconvenience—it can be dangerous. Women have been sexually assaulted and murdered because this ingrained trait of being nice and compliant has led them to engage someone in conversation, even when their instincts have screamed, "Walk away *now*." We may not want to offend. We may want to be perceived as friendly, open-minded, cool, or compassionate. Most of us want to be liked. Aries wisdom teaches that we must learn to be confident in asserting what is right for us, and that it's okay not to be liked by everyone. Setting healthy boundaries will not only give you the grounded sense that you are standing in your own power, but it can also keep your rights from being eroded.

*You are standing on a mossy green outcropping of rock overlooking a calm blue sea. Like ancient guardians, tall trees encircle and embrace the clearing you are in. The Sun is shining, and the songs of birds and the stirrings of the small creatures that inhabit this place rustle in the background. A mother deer and her two fawns graze peacefully nearby, unafraid. You look around at this earthly paradise and realize that you are custodian of this land. This is your home, and just as the trees and spirit of the place guard you, you are also part of the fabric of this land and therefore its steward. You feel the warm earth beneath your feet, connecting and grounding you with its deep internal rhythm. You breathe in the scent of blackberry, wild rose, and the sharp tang of salt air. Your heart swells, and you know instinctively that you would fight to protect this sacred place if need be.*

*You turn and see a little thatched-roof cottage nestled halfway up the hill, overlooking the ocean, and you are compelled to walk toward it. Above the door are two black ravens wrought in iron. The door is slightly ajar, and you cannot help but poke your head in. You see a beautiful chestnut-haired woman tending to a little fire in the hearth. She looks up and greets you with a warm smile as though she has been expecting you. She motions for you to come in and have a seat by the fire. She glows with the strength and passion of a woman who has seen and experienced much. There are fine lines around her eyes that let you know this is one who has laughed much but who has also fought hard for the peace and prosperity she now has. You realize that this is the goddess Macha before you, queen of battle, guardian of boundaries, and lady of prophecy.*

*She fixes you with her golden-green eyes and speaks to you with her mind: "Don't ever think that it cannot happen here." All at once your mind is flooded with images of the idyllic land all around you. Then the images shift, and instead of green rolling hills and the peaceful sound of birdsong, you flinch inwardly as you see bulldozers and hear the sound of chainsaws. The land is ravaged, torn, and decimated. There is a sense of heartbreak and utter desolation. Just when you feel that you cannot take another minute of this scene, you are back beside the fire with her again. All is well outside the door—quiet, calm, and beautiful as before.*

*She reaches out and touches your hand. "There are some things worth fighting for. Even now the peace and security of this land may be threatened. You must ask yourself what is truly important to you. What would you pick up the sword to defend?" She gets up and pushes the cottage door open. You follow her to the front porch and look out at the forest and, beyond it, the sparkling sea. You breathe in the peace and the abundance of life all around.*

*She turns to you. "Even now, the forces that will threaten the peace of this land are galvanizing. Will you put your head in the sand and pretend that something you love is not in danger? Find the courage of the Warrior's heart within you and be fierce if you must. Stand your ground and let love and your sense of what's right guide your next steps. There are many ways to resist."*

*You pause for a moment and know without a shadow of a doubt that you would do whatever you could to protect this sacred place. You turn to thank her.*

*She is already gone, but the hearth fire is still burning.*

## Ritual: Rekindling Your Inner Flame

Sometimes we feel as though our fire has burned too low. We feel tired, lethargic, and uninspired. Aries is the spark of life, the individuated life force that magically ignites at the beginning of spring, just when it seems that winter will never end. Light this candle anytime to remind yourself that the spark of life is within you and needs only to be re-kindled. To make it even more potent, make or light the candle during Aries season, spring equinox, or when the Moon is in Aries or new.

## Ignite Your Spark Aries Energy Candle

Hemp or cotton wick

8 oz. beeswax or soy wax (note: beeswax will impart a natural honey scent)

Double boiler

⅓ cup coconut oil

40 drops fire-element essential oils, such as cinnamon, ginger, clove, bergamot, and cardamom

Jar or container for candle

Wooden stick (chopstick, skewer, etc.)

Measure the wick from bottom to top of the container, leaving about 2 inches extra at top. Melt wax in a double boiler until it reaches approximately 150 degrees Fahrenheit. Add coconut oil and essential oils. Cool the mixture a little but not enough for it to harden. Pour about ⅓ into bottom of container and root the wick. Tie the top of the wick to the stick and place the stick across the opening of the container. Let it cool until it's almost solid. Fill in the rest of the jar with the slightly cooled melted wax/oil mixture and let sit for a couple of days before using. This candle is meant to be a jar candle (i.e., keep it and burn it in the jar).

## Rekindling Your Inner Flame

You will need an Ignite Your Spark Aries Energy Candle. When you are ready to light the candle, clear your space and ground yourself first. Visualize a small glowing flame beginning in your solar plexus, its warmth and heat emanating throughout your body. Recognize this as your life spark, that magical essence that animates your life and can never be truly extinguished. Remember that the same light that lights your life is the same energy that lights the stars and the Sun. It is the source of all light, warmth, growth, and the essence of life itself. Feel yourself connect with this energy. Your own life is a divine manifestation of this one life force. When you feel the connection, strike a match to light your candle. Gaze into its flame and inhale the scent of the fire-element essential oils you have created it with. Affirm aloud,

> *The fire that lights the Sun and stars is the same fire that lights my life. I hereby call on this fire, the divine life energy, to kindle, to become a glow that inspires and sustains me. May this sacred light illuminate my path, bring me inspiration, and clarify my passion. I hereby rekindle my flame.*

Place the candle on an altar or in a safe space and allow it to burn a few minutes while you meditate on the flame. When you feel a sense of completion, put out the flame with a candle snuffer.

## Ritual: New Moon Mandala

Aries is connected to the Moon in its new and waxing phase, a time of setting new intentions and having the courage to begin again. The New Moon is a liminal moment in time and, like first sign Aries, is about possibility and potential. Sometimes, without even realizing it, we find we have given up our sense of self. This can happen through an unhealthy relationship, a job that drains us and doesn't let our true talents shine, or just day-to-day living in which we're constantly dealing with the needs of others. The erosion of our sense of self can happen slowly and insidiously. We may realize that we don't even know what our passions are anymore, let alone what we even like. Aries is about reclaiming our passions on our own terms. Aries is connected to individuation, self-actualization, and self-development. It is the knowledge that before we can be of service to anyone or anything else in a meaningful way, we must first support and nurture ourselves. We must show up as who we truly are.

*You Will Need:*

Art supplies: chalk paint pens, pastels, white paint pen, glue, and assorted small, meaningful objects

Major arcana tarot cards

Sage for smudging and purifying

Aries candle (see page 77) or light green candle

Paper

Pen

Mandala: round piece of paper or wood, black or painted black, approx. 16 inches in diameter

Find yourself a comfortable place to sit, either on the floor or at a table or desk. Place the art supplies and cards near you for easy access. Purify and cleanse your space with the sage. Ground and center. Allow yourself to enter a light trance state. Light your candle and place it nearby where you can see it. Take a moment to reflect, and when you are ready, take out the paper and pen and write down three things that fire you up and get you excited. Next, write down three things that you would fight for. Finally, write down one thing you would do if you knew you would succeed.

Close your eyes and ask one of the Aries goddesses for a message (see correspondences on page 80). Put the tarot cards face down in front of you and swish them around with your hands until you feel a sense of completion. Find a card you are drawn to and turn it face up. There is something in this card that will help you begin again, something you need to know that will help you set your seedling intentions. Are there any colors or symbols that you notice? Anything you need to release or bring into your life? Whether you know the tarot or not, begin to free associate with what you see in the card.

When you are ready, choose from your art supplies and draw a symbol on your mandala that stands for the message you receive. You don't have to know how to draw, and if you wish, you can write a word that comes up for you instead. Refer to the paper you have written on, and write or draw any images on your mandala that relate to what you have written. Perhaps something totally surprising or unexpected comes up. Keep going. Try drawing with your nondominant hand. Don't censor or judge whatever you are creating. If you wish, you can incorporate any small objects into your mandala by gluing them on; they are part of your creative supplies. Draw, paint, and create in a meditative state until your mandala feels complete. Take the paper on which you have written and burn it in the flame of the Aries candle safely over a fireproof surface. Take the ashes outside, preferably when there is a wind, and release them to the winds of change. Remember that air feeds fire, and fire is transformation. Take your mandala and place it on your altar as a reminder of your new intentions.

## Aries Correspondences

*Astrological Dates:* March 19 through April 20

*Sabbat:* Spring equinox (Ostara)

*Aries Goddess Archetypes:* Macha, Banu Goshasp, the Morrigan, Freya, Andraste, Pele, Linshui, Tripura Sundari, Scathach, Brynhild, Yevdokia

*House:* First

*Element:* Fire

*Mode:* Cardinal

*Planet:* Mars

*Colors:* Red, light green

*Crystals:* Bloodstone, fire agate, clear quartz, garnet, red spinel, tektite

*Essential Oils:* Cinnamon, ginger, clove, bergamot, cardamom, juniper, peppermint, dragon's blood

*Parts of the Body:* Head, face

# TAURUS

After the riotous fanfare of rebirth that begins with Aries, life now has a foothold and is supported to thrive, prosper, and be cultivated in the warmer days. Taurus is a fixed earth sign, meaning that it embodies the heart of a season (in this case spring) and resonates with the grounded fertile element of earth. Raw survival is no longer the impetus and is replaced with the desire to shape, nurture, and develop. Taurus is aligned with the art of cultivating. The new life that began at spring equinox is strengthening and taking root, and the benevolence of the season now also gives rise to a new concept: pleasure. Taurus is intimately connected to the enjoyment of earthly delights. Taurus takes the lusty sexuality of Aries a step further and cultivates the sensual aspect of sex. And it is not just sex where Taurus's appreciation for the sensual arises. Massage, delicious food, good wine, luxurious fabric, and an almost sublime appreciation of beauty are all encompassed by the Taurus archetype.

Taurus is the builder, the shaper, the gardener, the maker. Worth and value are two ideas exemplified by Taurus—in other words, the riches of the land, which can be translated into resources, including money. Taurus craves security, stability, abundance, and contentment. I cannot help but think of the Empress card in the tarot when I meditate on the archetype of Taurus, particularly the image painted by Pamela Colman Smith in the Rider-Waite deck. The Empress is voluptuous, languorously lounging on a throne of sumptuous pillows, signifying her connection to wealth and beauty. The abundant land she presides over is richly fertile, with ripe wheat in the foreground, deep, wild forest behind her, and a stream nourishing all. A heart-shaped stone that makes up the foundation of her throne is inscribed with the symbol of Venus, the planet associated with Taurus.

The cross-quarter festival of Beltane occurs in the middle of Taurus season, underlining the Taurean themes of abundance, sensuality, and the beauty of nature at her full-flowering peak.

## The Taurus Woman

The way the Taurus woman expresses her ruling planet, Venus, can manifest in a variety of ways. She will usually be connected to beauty, earthly pleasure, comfort, and security, but the way these qualities show up in the individual Taurean can be very different. On one hand, there is the Taurus woman who embodies the Venus archetype in an obvious and expected way. This is the woman who is highly concerned with her physical appearance and will spend a great deal of time and effort indulging herself at the spa. She loves beautiful fabrics and considers expensive labels an investment in quality. To her, high-thread-count sheets, a nice car, and a luxurious home equal stability.

However, she is not flashy or garish in her appreciation for the so-called finer things in life. She values quality and venerable old names that have stood the test of time, whether it be clothing, cars, or a skin-care line. The pursuit of beauty and pleasure is an important part of her lifestyle, which in many ways defines her, and although it might be easy to dismiss her love of luxury as superficial or materialistic, she can explain these tendencies in the most practical and reasonable way. She believes deep down that appearance does count for something in the material world we live in. She knows that beauty can be a commodity, and unlike many women, she has no qualms about this. To her this is just common sense and healthy realism. Although she truly enjoys all the luxurious trappings and beauty rituals, she reasons that if one wants to have a secure and comfortable life, one must work with her goddess-given gifts. She surmises that putting her best foot forward will get her up the career ladder faster. She also rationalizes that it's only sensible that presenting herself in a hyperfeminine, Venusian way will help her find a worthy mate. Both these ambitions, she reasons, will help fulfill her need for security.

Another common incarnation of the Taurus woman may seem to be just the opposite. But we will see upon looking deeper that there are hidden parallels between the two. She is still deeply connected to the idea of the earth and the material plane we live on—Taurus is, after all, an earth sign and is therefore grounded in the tangible. She appreciates comfort, good quality, and solid workmanship, and she also has an intrinsic connection to music, art, and beauty in all its forms.

However, this second type of Taurus woman will often roll her eyes at frivolous status symbols. She is a creature of the earth in a direct and visceral way, and you will often find her with her hands in the dirt tending her garden. This is the woman who might be passionate about plant-based medicine or making her own beeswax candles. It doesn't matter if she lives in the city or the country; this Taurus woman understands the importance of the land and is drawn to the hands-on sensuality of growing and making. If she lives in the city, she likely has dreams of eventually living in rural paradise. Visions of baby goats, building her own cabin, and blessed quiet keep her sane. She might grow herbs in her apartment window box and dream of the day she can have her own garden. She may content herself for now to have a small brood of backyard chickens or to head out of the city whenever she can to camp in the mountains and breathe fresh air. She may be an ecologist or a champion of the healing properties of Ayurvedic medicine. Her senses are highly developed, but instead of gravitating to designer sheets and expensive wine, she will prefer ecoconscious lamb's wool bedding and homemade organic wine from a friend's vineyard. Although both types of Taurus women share a love of creature comforts, the way each propitiates the Goddess is very different.

Beyond their differences, most Taurus women are practical, dependable, and concerned with stability and seek peace and frequent solitude. Because of the fixed nature of the sign, most Taurus women prefer to move slowly when making an important decision or a commitment.

This is not the woman who jumps into anything with both feet, conse-quences be damned. She also is famous for her stubborn tenacity and dislike of sudden change. Although she is slow to anger and may be the model of patience, her temper can be formidable when something does set her off.

It is in love and relationships that we can see many of these Taurean qualities most vividly. After all, her ruler is none other than Venus, the goddess of love herself. The Taurus woman is a romantic soul, and be-cause she is such an innately sensual creature, candlelight, music, wine, flowers, and ambience are like an aphrodisiac to her. She appreciates all the trappings of romance, perhaps because she views them as a symbol of worth. For Taurus, a lover who tries to make things romantic obvi-ously considers her worth the effort, and in turn, the Taurus woman may also see the lover as worth her time. For Taurus, the concepts of worth and value are an underlying theme that show up in many ways. Tokens of love and affection are not wasted on her. As an earth sign, she appreciates actual physical objects that symbolize affection or commit-ment. Depending on the Taurus in question, this can range anywhere from a little antique curio, to a high-powered blender, to a fabulous dia-mond ring. Practical gestures of love are also highly valued, especially if they speak to her sense of security. The gesture that sealed the deal for one Taurus woman was her boyfriend paying off all her debts. To her, this was the ultimate symbol of love: practical and unbelievably roman-tic. It signified that he was serious about her and willing to prove it in a tangible way.

Taurus is, however, notoriously slow when it comes to making a commitment. She wants to be absolutely sure before she makes a choice that could change her life. Remember that Taurus doesn't take to change easily, even when it's potentially positive change. She is pa-tient and prefers to take her time, whether it's having sex with some-one or beginning a relationship. However, once she gives her heart and makes a commitment, Taurus is steadfastly loyal and will be there for her beloved through thick and thin. There really is no more committed partner or mate than a Taurus woman.

Taurus is typically not given to emotional outbursts, with one rare exception. If she perceives a threat to something or someone she considers hers, then her fearsome temper can explode. Taurus does have a possessive streak, and if she finds proof that you are cheating on her, watch out. Yes, of course she loves you, but maybe even more important, how *dare* you do anything that will threaten the peace and stability of her happy home? If your actions imply that her sense of contentment is threatened or that any change in the relationship might ensue, watch out. Because Taurus gets angry so infrequently, it can be shocking and scary to behold. Unlike Aries, whose temper flares up and then calms just as quickly, Taurus's fixed nature can mean she takes a long time to cool down.

Sexually, Taurus is a sensuous, earthy woman who enjoys all the nuances of intimacy. Although typically one wouldn't refer to her as kinky or particularly sexually adventurous, she certainly does not lack passion or subtlety. She engages her five senses completely and revels in the sheer joy of embodying the earthy nature of the goddess Aphrodite. Because she is such a creature of her senses, ambience is especially important for her during sex. For Taurus, sex is a sacrament of the Goddess, and creating sacred space is important. Good lighting (candlelight, salt lamps, or faery lights) set the stage. Soft music. Incense. Comfortable bedding that feels good to the touch. Bonus points for scented massage oil, bedside nibbles, and wine. Although the Taurus woman does appreciate a beautiful bedroom in which to explore her appetites, she also occasionally enjoys an outdoor tryst, in the forest, in a peaceful meadow, or on a blanket on a secluded beach. To her, sex can be steamy, erotic, and languorous but never tawdry or slovenly. When it comes to sex, you can't just phone it in with a Taurus woman.

As a fixed earth sign, Taurus might be considered the most earth-oriented of all the earth signs, and as such, she is deeply connected with resources, the fruits of the earth, and, of course, money. Money, after all, is a symbol for resources. Taurus wouldn't be considered the most ambitious of the signs, but she does tend to be quite astute with financial matters. To her, having enough is practical good sense. She may not have aspirations of being wildly rich, but she is concerned with comfort, stability, and financial security, perhaps more than any other sign. The term *nest egg* was probably coined by a Taurus. And, although Taurus is not usually an ambitious type A, she is both pragmatic and clever. She will carefully choose a job that she knows she can grow in. She might be making minimum wage with an unimpressive title at the start, but she has an astute ability to ascertain whether a job will be worth her while in the long run and will patiently put one foot in front of the other until she is in a secure position with a salary, health insurance, and a solid retirement plan. It's not unusual for Taurus women in their early twenties to be concerned with their retirement. Taurus is drawn to several fields but can often happily work in any area provided their bottom line is secure. However, because of her connection to Aphrodite, many Taurus women are drawn to careers in finance, beauty, fashion, or the arts. She could be a curator at an art gallery, an interior designer, a musician, an artist, a property developer, a realtor, or an esthetician. Another potential career direction is the body and holistic therapies. As Taurus is associated with the body, she can make an excellent massage therapist, acupuncturist, yoga teacher, dance instructor, or naturopath. Her connection with the earth may draw her to an occupation that gives her the opportunity to work closely with it, such as organic farming, making natural products, herbalism, building natural materials, or ecology.

Many Taurus women have an innate association with earth spirituality and are often drawn to explore a Pagan path, Druidry, or shamanic wisdom teachings. Their ability to experience the energies of the earth in a direct way often bypasses layers of dogma. Taurus has an uncomplicated appreciation of the spirituality of nature and the ability to feel it in the body without having to analyze and label the connection she experiences. For Taurus, the simple act of gardening can be a numinous experience. A walk in the woods and listening to the voices of the trees leaves her with a feeling of wonder at the awesome power of Source.

# Guiding Goddess Archetype: Aphrodite Pandemos

Every era has brought a new incarnation of Aphrodite, who embodies the changing feminine sexual ideal of the times. The examples of the goddess of love have been many, from the full-figured curves of the Renaissance woman to the tightly corseted, exaggerated-hourglass, female form of the Victorian age. In the past one hundred years alone, the female sexual ideal has spanned the decades bringing the lithe lines that exemplified the new freedom of the 1920s flapper, epitomized by actress Clara Bow, while the 1950s brought the return of the soft, rounded curves conveyed by Marilyn Monroe. Contemporary times have brought a new female ideal popularized by celebrities such as Kim Kardashian, which features a nearly impossible shape to attain without intervention: large breasts, a cinched waist, and full hips are touted by pop culture and the media as the new "it" shape. Throughout history, the cultural expression of the Aphrodite archetype has always reflected the cultural mores, trends, and politics of the zeitgeist.

Aphrodite is the most beautiful of all the goddesses in the Olympian pantheon and has the ability to make others fall in love with each other, sometimes to their detriment. She presides over sexual attraction and seduction and is connected to the irresistible feeling of falling in love. Although falling in love with another person is an obvious expression of Aphrodite's influence, falling in love with a creative project, an idea, or anything that sweeps us off our feet is also included. Aphrodite's awe-inspiring power can be experienced in the inspiration of looking at a beautiful sunset, beholding a work of art, or being moved deeply by a piece of music.

Although she is married to the lame forge god, Hephaestus, Aphrodite herself indulges in many love affairs, with Ares, Hermes, and the mortal lovers Adonis and Anchises amongst them. She also has many children by her different lovers, underlining her aspect of fertility goddess. Aphrodite enjoys a particular freedom in Olympia that the other goddesses don't share. No male deity suppresses, regulates, or punishes her behavior, which suggests that she fully embraces and owns her power, her individuality, and her sexuality.

While many are familiar with the goddess Aphrodite and her many myths, it is not as widely known that there are actually two distinct (although related) versions of the goddess. The first, which many are familiar with, is the Aphrodite made famous in the painting *The Birth of Venus* by Botticelli. This is *Aphrodite Urania*, or "Heavenly Aphrodite." In the story of her origin, Kronos castrates his father Ouranos and throws his genitals into the sea. Aphrodite is born from the sea foam that arises from the severed genitals and rides to shore in a scallop shell as a fully blossomed goddess. Aphrodite Urania is connected to nonphysical, "higher" abstract forms of love.

The second Aphrodite, and the one that most closely resonates with the Taurus archetype, is the daughter of Zeus and Dione. She is known as *Aphrodite Pandemos*, or "Aphrodite common to all the people." She is the earthy, sensual fertility goddess associated with desire and the pleasure of physical love. Aphrodite Pandemos was the patroness of courtesans, hetaira and hierodule alike. In ancient Greece, women had few rights and were considered the property of men. The highest class of Greek courtesans, *hetairai* or "female companions," were a separate class of women who were paid for their time, rather than specifically for sex. Hetairai attended events with their clients and were versed in the arts of conversation and music. They were set apart from lower classes of sex workers in that they had a measure of choice in who they would engage as a client. Often, instead of receiving direct payment for their services, they would receive gifts and favors. Too, the reciprocity of the client-worker relationship was sometimes unspoken; thus, "by not being obvious...these high-class prostitutes maintained a fiction of respectability that increased the demand for their company."[15] They also kept company with an array of influential lovers and were allowed in spaces where other women were not. The *hierodule*, on the other hand,

15. Debra Hamel, *Trying Neaira: The True Story of a Courtesan's Scandalous Life in Ancient Greece* (New Haven, CT: Yale University Press, 2003), 12–13.

which roughly translates to "sacred slave," was another class of prostitute who did not enjoy the same rights, privileges, and esteem of the hetaera. Although it is tempting to believe in a romanticized ancient world where prostitution was always a sacred communion between priestess and worshipper, it is important to remember that while there may have been a class of women who engaged on this level, there were also many women sold into slavery and brothels who were not there by choice or for spiritual reasons. We must recall that every archetype has its shadow.

Various temples and shrines were dedicated to Aphrodite Pandemos in ancient Greece. Some of the most notable of these were in the city of Corinth, on the island of Cythera, and on the island of Cyprus. In *Worshipping Aphrodite*, author Rachel Rosenzweig writes, "The common theme in her worship was unification: between brides and grooms, between prostitutes and customers."[16] The festival of Aphrodisia was held in honor of Aphrodite Pandemos each summer. The red rose, dove, apple, myrtle, sparrow, and pomegranate are said to be sacred to Aphrodite.

For many women, healthy, self-defined sexuality is an ongoing quest that is fraught with challenges both on a personal level and from the collective. We may have a history of sexual trauma. Perhaps we are recovering from a broken heart. We may be aging and question our validity in an overculture that does not value older women. All women are subjected to a bombardment of cultural expectations and stereotypes that have made us question at some point in our lives whether we are enough or too much. We compare ourselves to impossible airbrushed ideals and contradictory constructs. If a woman embraces her sexual agency, she's a slut. If she isn't drawn to a current sexual trend, she's not only a prude, she's deluding herself, and just needs to be more open— "Come on, everybody's doing it!" Internet porn has damaged women and men alike, offering up a grotesque caricature that often has nothing to do with pleasure and everything to do with the normalization of domination and degradation. We are pressured to be "open-minded" in

---

16. Rachel Rosenzweig, *Worshipping Aphrodite: Art and Culture in Classical Athens* (Ann Arbor: University of Michigan Press, 2004), 4.

the face of what others want and have less space to reflect on what we want.

We must give ourselves the space, time, and permission to heal and discover our sexuality, to reclaim a self-defined relationship to our bodies. Like Aphrodite, we need to claim pleasure as our birthright and open our hearts to self-love and true sexual freedom on our own terms. It is now more important than ever for women to reject the patriarchal stereotypes and expectations that continue to try to shape who we are as sexual beings. It's time to reject those false, misogynistic constructs that would make us small. Say no to slut shaming, body shaming, and homophobia. It is imperative that we celebrate who we are and reclaim joy in our bodies. It is time to forge a radically embodied relationship with our own definition of pleasure and beauty.

## Pathworking: Meeting the Goddess of Love

*You are walking alone on a beach. The stars sparkle above you, and the Moon is waxing to full in the sign of Taurus. The sky is glowing a deep azure, and the horizon is still luminous with the rose gold of the sunset. You hear the gentle rhythmic lapping of waves meeting the shore and walk in the margin where sea meets sand. The water is unexpectedly warm. The gentle breeze picks up and plays with the light dress you are wearing, inviting you to enjoy its gentle caresses over your entire body. You look around and see that you have this magical place to yourself for as far as the eye can see. You pull the gossamer shift over your head, walk over to a rock, and lay down the shift. You take a moment to stretch and lean your head back in ecstasy. A feeling of pure joy and absolute safety flows through you. There is an exhilarating sense of freedom from knowing that no one is watching.*

*You notice a slim opening in the face of the seaside cliff and see pale lunar light illuminating a path through the rock. You decide to see where this path leads. A small white dove flies past you, seeming to beckon you toward a gentle brightening in the distance. You follow the dove, and the path leads you into a secret grotto. The top is open to the sky, and the light of the Moon shines into this hidden world. There is no sign of the dove, but you see a beautiful woman slowly walking toward you. She moves toward you languorously, smiling her welcome. Her long tawny hair falls in voluptuous waves over her generous golden curves. There is an incandescent glow about her, and even though the moonlight dances over the shimmering water and rock walls, you realize the glow is coming from within her. Slowly it dawns on you that this is the goddess Aphrodite before you. Suddenly you realize that you too are undressed. Instinctively you move to cover your own nakedness.*

*She smiles, slightly amused at your modesty, and looks deeply into your eyes. "Why would you cover yourself? You are beautiful. All women are made in the image of the goddess. You do me no honor by hiding yourself and covering the power of your feminine beauty."*

*You allow your arms to drop gently to your sides and take a long, slow, deep breath. Although you are not accustomed to being naked before someone you have just met, you feel a growing sense of newfound freedom as you relax into your body, swaying gently with the rhythm of the ocean with each breath, in and out. In. And out. You feel the layers of protection you have cloaked yourself with over the years dropping from your shoulders, one by one. Feelings of body shame, of not measuring up to a societally constructed ideal, fall gently away. Memories of heartbreak and unrequited love loosen and slip off as easily as a garment that no longer fits. Fears and blockages about connecting with your own sexual desires melt, then release and flow away. You feel a warmth in your sacral chakra that spreads throughout your womb and down into your vulva. This delicious warmth begins to move in a gentle spiral and up throughout each of your energy centers, until you feel the top of your head tingling.*

*You slowly open your eyes and find yourself gazing into the pool before you. Beside you stands Aphrodite, in all her splendor. You see that her luminosity extends and envelops you in its brilliance. She speaks to your reflection in the water: "You see, when you have shed all the projections of the outer world, thou art Goddess. Like me, you must dare to step outside of the expectations of others. Make your own choices. Nourish your body like the temple of love that it is. Indulge your senses and be comfortable in your skin. It is time to reclaim your birthright to pleasure on your own terms and honor yourself as a daughter of Aphrodite. As you do so, you honor me, and the blessings I bestow upon my daughters are rich and abundant. Go back out into the world with my blessing, and know that as you honor me by honoring yourself, I shall always walk beside you."*

*Slowly the reflection fades, and a small white dove flies back out through the pathway through the rock. You look up, and the Moon is shining down on you, bathing you in otherworldly mystery. Just to the right of the waxing Moon, another light has risen, as bright as the Moon. You realize it is Venus, the evening star. Venus and the Moon shimmer side by side, conjunct in the sign of Taurus.*

## Ritual: Dedication to Aphrodite Ceremony

This purification and regeneration ceremony is designed to mark the beginning of a new relationship with your body and your sensual self.

### Aphrodite's Holy Water (Bath Salts)

This aromatic elixir can be used as a salt scrub or, in the following ceremony, added to the bath as Aphrodite's Holy Water. Not only is sea salt a time-honored and ancient protective and cleansing attribute, but it is also sacred to Aphrodite and associated with her birth from the sea.

**You Will Need:**

2 cups sea salt

3 tablespoons baking soda (aura cleanser)

Small handful dried rose petals

Essential oils:

> 10 drops rose absolute
>
> 4 drops ylang-ylang
>
> 2 drops jasmine

Mason jar

Small rose quartz stone

Mix all ingredients in a metal or glass bowl. Visualize Aphrodite and her qualities as you create the mixture. Ask for her blessing to align with your own true beauty, heal a broken heart, or reclaim your relationship to pleasure. Transfer to a mason jar and add the rose quartz. You can put the jar in a window or on a porch with the light of the waxing or Full Moon charging it overnight. The most potent time to align with Aphrodite is when Venus is visible in the sky, either as morning star or evening star. If you can find a time when the Moon and Venus are conjunct (in the same sign and degree—check an astrological day planner), even better. Another powerful time to make and consecrate this elixir is when the Moon is in Taurus or Libra.

### *Dedication to Aphrodite Ceremony*
Smudge (cedar or sage)
Rose quartz or cobaltocalcite (Aphrodite stone)
Seashell
Red rose
Aphrodite's Holy Water
Aphrodite iconography
Wine or grape juice
Pink candle
Drumming music (try some by Layne Redmond)
Old clothes you don't mind parting with or old jewelry it's time to let
     go of
Paper bag
Beautiful soft robe or new clothes that represent your next chapter

First, I highly recommend cleaning your bathroom! Just like any other ritual, preparing sacred space is the first step. Smudge the space and set up a small altar to Aphrodite beside your tub on a little table. Colors for draping could be shades of soft pink and green, colors associated with the goddess of love. On the altar place a single rose in a vase, a piece of rose quartz, a seashell, Aphrodite's Holy Water, the picture, and a chalice of wine.

Turn off the lights and light the candle. Run the tub. Put on the music and allow yourself to get into a light trance state. Dance if you feel called to. Take a moment to recall and clearly name the things, people, and situations that have made you feel "less than"—whatever or whoever has taken a little piece of your sensual confidence. Begin to remove your clothing one piece at a time. With each article of clothing you remove, state aloud,

> *Your words don't define me.*
> *Your actions die on the vine.*
> *This no longer fits me.*
> *My pleasure is mine.*

Feel the sensation of energetically removing what no longer fits you.

> *I hereby reject the burden of another's projections, rejections, and misuse. I hereby refuse any and all cultural messages that minimize me.*

Take the old clothes or jewelry and put them into a paper bag. Fold it up and never look inside it again. Place it outside the bathroom door and close the door behind you.

Re-enter the bathroom. You are now naked. Free. Take Aphrodite's Holy Water bath salts from the altar and pour it into the tub. Swish the water around with your hand until you feel that all the salts have been dissolved. Stand up and pause for a moment, and behold your naked beauty in a mirror. You are made in the image of the goddess and you are beautiful. Turn to the water. State aloud,

> *This is the water that heals.*
> *This is the water that purifies and regenerates.*
> *This water is the fountain of the goddess Aphrodite,*
> *and I am made in her image.*
> *I dedicate my sensuality and sexual confidence to her, here and now.*
> *May I be born anew as the past is washed away.*

The water you are about to enter is sacred. This is Aphrodite's Holy Water, and you are baptized anew starting this moment. You now dedicate your feminine beauty and your sexuality to the goddess. Slip into the tub, close your eyes, and immerse your head beneath the purifying water. Feel the water renewing you—pouring through your hair, moving over every inch of your skin, cleansing your face. Come up for air, open your eyes, and repeat the above affirmation. Take a sip of wine after each affirmation to seal it. When you're done, pour the remaining wine into the tub as an offering to the goddess.

Arise from the water like Aphrodite arising from the sea. You are born anew, ready to begin again from a stronger, clearer, and more confident place. Put on the robe or new clothes you have selected as a symbol of your newly forged connection with your Aphrodite self. When you are ready, take the bag of old clothes or jewelry and drop it off at a charity shop. Resist the urge to look inside the bag. Feel the energy of whatever those old clothes symbolized leaving your life for good. A great way to follow up this ritual is to go through all your clothing and cosmetics, discarding, gifting, and donating anything that is old or torn or no longer fits who you are becoming. Go out and purchase some beautiful new items. You deserve it, and you are worth it.

Aligning with Aphrodite means honoring yourself as a sensual, beautiful, powerful woman. Take time to indulge yourself. Take care of your appearance, and enjoy the feeling of new confidence when you reclaim your right to be beautiful. Although Aphrodite favors fabric that feels good on the skin, such as silk and velvet, she equally loves organic cotton, hemp, bamboo, and other tactile natural fabrics. If your hair is going gray, do your roots or let it all grow out and own your silver with pride. And though Aphrodite adores dressing up and all the feminine accoutrements, such as cosmetics, jewelry, and gorgeous clothing, you don't have to be a girly girl to channel her energy. Wear clothes that you love and that look good on you. Get your hair trimmed regularly in a style that flatters, and moisturize. Everyone can eat nourishing foods and take care of their skin. And we can all benefit from delicious, sensuous treats from time to time—a favorite dessert, a massage, a glass of wine, or new pillows for your couch. If you honor Aphrodite, she will bless you with a sense of well-being and confidence that will enhance every aspect of your life.

# Taurus Correspondences

*Astrological Dates:* April 20 through May 20

*Sabbat:* Beltane

*Taurus Goddess Archetypes:* Aphrodite Pandemos, Aphrodite, Venus, Lakshmi, Gaia, Annapurna, Mara, Zemyna, Dea Nutrix, Ixcacao, Abundia, Mokosh, Xochiquetzal

*House:* Second

*Element:* Earth

*Mode:* Fixed

*Planet:* Venus

*Colors:* Emerald green, pink, earth colors

*Crystals:* Emerald, rose quartz, cobaltocalcite (Aphrodite stone), green calcite, smoky quartz, dioptase, green tourmaline, rhodonite

*Essential Oils:* Rose, sandalwood, vetiver, ylang-ylang, jasmine

*Parts of the Body:* Throat, neck

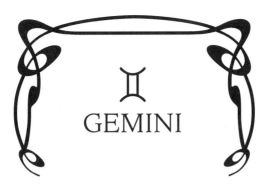

# GEMINI

There is a perceptible quickening that happens when the Sun transitions from Taurus into Gemini. The gentle pace and nurturing cultivation of Taurus has taken root and now seeks to expand and move forward into the world. Inquisitive green tendrils reach up toward the Sun, and bright blossoms begin a spirited communication with bees. Gemini is a mutable air sign, meaning it is a threshold sign, which bridges one season into the next (in this case, spring transitioning into summer), and is associated with the objective, communicative element of air. During Gemini season, all of nature is moving inexorably toward the next seasonal turning point at summer solstice. Echoing this shift as a time of becoming, Gemini is associated with the qualities of curiosity, versatility, and transformation. The motif of a butterfly emerging from a chrysalis is an apt metaphor for Gemini.

Gemini's associated planet is Mercury, the Roman version of the Greek messenger god, Hermes. Hermes was an androgynous deity and a psychopomp associated with transition, guiding newly deceased souls to the afterlife as well as having the magical ability to move back and forth between the world of humans and the divine. Hermes was a mediator, a shape-shifting two-spirited shaman who was said to be the god of travelers and thieves alike. He is tied to the concepts of oratory, poetry, magick, alchemy, and literature, and like Gemini, Hermes is associated with the archetype of the *puer aeternus* (eternal youth). Hermes also embodies the Trickster archetype: he is mischievous, playful, and impish but also sly and sometimes deceptive.

Gemini resonates with the archetypes of the Shape-shifter, the Story-teller, and the Walker between the Worlds, often evading definition by dancing in the liminal spaces between. Gemini tries on different perso-nas and perspectives; plays with ideas, words, and gender roles; and, in doing so, questions entrenched beliefs.

The Gemini archetype is also associated with alchemy and magick, particularly with the magick of words. It wasn't until recently that most people in the Western world could read and write. The written word was almost exclusively the province of the learned ones. For much of history, to be a woman and to be literate almost certainly meant a life dedicated to religious orders. Words are also at the heart of spellcast-ing and ritual, as well as the core of affirmations, chanting, and man-tras. Words are integral parts of our rites of passage throughout our lives and are energetic symbols that can shape and transform our real-ity, both personal and collective. Words frame our perceptions and cre-ate new energetic forms. They can heal, uplift, illuminate, and comfort. They can also deceive, instigate, and distract.

## The Gemini Woman

Like the intoxicating scent of apple blossom on a spring breeze, the Gemini woman is often an evasive creature. She is most certainly so-cial enough, stopping to engage in lively conversation and gathering multifaceted perspectives from as many sources as she can find. She is genuinely curious about everyone. She wants to hear your story and un-derstand your viewpoint. She is also usually lighthearted, nonjudgmen-tal, and flirtatious with everyone, regardless of gender. But try to pin her down, make her choose a side, or make her commit to something that will confine her in any way, and she is as ephemeral as a spring rainbow. The Gemini woman needs the freedom to experiment and ex-plore, to try on different personas and perspectives the way other signs try on clothes. It is in her nature to play with possibilities and imagine new paradigms. She is the *puella aeterna,* the eternal girl, and she often retains this youthful spirit throughout her life. She may indeed get married, have children of her own, and eventually commit to a career path, but she will always keep her inquisitive *joie de vivre*.

As Gemini is attuned with the realm of the mind, she often has a love of words and the ability to use language as an art form. Books, literature, and poetry are often a passion that starts in childhood and continues throughout her life. This is the woman who as a child often daydreamed her way through class, writing poetry in the margins of her notebook, or could be found secreted in a corner of the library, spellbound in the pages of a story. She herself is also usually gifted as a writer. She will often find inspiration and solace through journaling or perhaps have her own blog. Probably several.

However, Gemini can hardly be accused of being sedentary. In between channeling her active mind into reading and writing, she is as animated and changeable as quicksilver. Sometimes her need for constant stimulation and her insatiable curiosity leave her feeling ungrounded. The mutable nature of her sign can pull her in too many directions at once, and she can be something of a dilettante, sampling a little of this and a little of that but never staying long enough on any one thing to really gain any depth. She may find that she knows a little about a lot of things, but only at a surface level. Sometimes, Gemini needs to watch out for posing as a subject matter expert when she in fact has only rudimentary knowledge about a subject.

As Gemini is associated with the nervous system, the constant push and pull of myriad energies can be exhausting if not interspersed with some downtime. There will be occasions when she feels at her wit's end. She might feel overamped, as though she's had too much coffee—jittery and unfocused, uncharacteristically emotional, and even downright bitchy. It is imperative that Gemini schedules in some regular self-care to avoid burnout. Often, what she most needs is respite from the incessant mind chatter that's constantly going through her head. She also needs a break from talk in the everyday world: a break from phone calls, texts, and emails. Gemini would do well to incorporate periodic tech fasts to recharge her psychic batteries. And, although the idea might feel completely foreign to her, a silent meditation retreat could also help her energetically reset. As Gemini is an air sign, any meditations that focus on the breath are often useful. Chanting is also usually a natural fit for Gemini because it is connected to communication with the voice. Yin yoga and tai chi can also help Gemini find her flow and balance her energy.

Another challenge for Gemini that's connected to her vivid imagination and gift for spinning tales is the occasional temptation to be duplicitous. Because of her ability to look at almost anything with a multifaceted range of perception, truth can be subjective. Perhaps she has gotten into mischief of some kind and wants to cover her tracks. Maybe her love of intrigue has led her to talk out of turn—in other words, gossip—and it's landed her in some hot water. Sometimes, when acting from the shadow side of her sign, the Gemini penchant for mind games can run to an aptitude for cunning and double dealing. But, with her impressive verbal skills, Gemini can usually talk herself out of just about any situation. Gemini's tendency to view life through an abstract lens can rationalize hurtful behavior and disconnect her from her sense of empathy. If this happens, it is important that she use her talent for seeing through another's perspective to get her heart and mind working in sync again.

When it comes to love and relationships, Gemini's most erogenous zone is her mind. She is easily intrigued by psychologically complex lovers and will weave a captivating tale about someone she is attracted to that rivals the most descriptive character analysis. It doesn't matter to her if you question whether her fantasies are rooted in truth. With a flirtatious glint in her eye, she'll airily respond to her more pragmatic friends, "But can you imagine if it *were* true?" This is the woman who will spot a handsome yet enigmatic guy pumping gas and, before you know it, will have spun a dazzling yarn about how he is actually an aristocrat down on his luck who came here from a faraway land to find his lost love. She'll then get out of the car and give him her phone number with a beguiling wink and a smile. To Gemini, her flirtatiousness is usually harmless and innocent, a bit of fun to keep things interesting. Gemini, being a bit Fae herself, is also captivated by real-life fairy tales and may actually believe that *The Frog Prince* is based on a true story. Again, who are we to say what is true? Isn't it all relative?

Sometimes her vivacious charm and curiosity coupled with her affinity for seeing what she wants to see can land her in a bit of trouble. She will have fun until someone else catches her interest, and then she'll be on her way. Potential lovers who don't understand her natural vivacity can take her games at face value and feel terribly let down when they realize this is something Gemini does with everyone. She really didn't mean to hurt anyone, and besides, she reasons, it was all in good fun. Gemini is also open to meeting people through online dating. The internet is a Gemini paradise with the opportunity to chat with an unlimited number of fascinating people from all walks of life from all over the world; it satisfies her need for mental stimulation and variety without emotional entanglement.

For all her carefree flirtation, Gemini does fall in love and can be part of a committed relationship. However, it will take someone who can keep her interest—someone who is as multifaceted as she is and who will not try to clip her wings. She does well with a partner who is also a friend, someone she can play with who shares her insatiable curiosity for life. If her partner is willing, some Geminis can thrive in an open relationship. As well, her thirst for experimentation, variety, and novel experience can be an ongoing component within a committed relationship that keeps things from getting stale. Gemini does not tend to get jealous as easily as some other signs and does not have the same propensity for emotional enmeshment as Cancer or Scorpio might. Like the other air signs, Libra and Aquarius, she sometimes has the tendency to abstract or intellectualize love and prefers not to be weighed down emotionally.

Sexually, Gemini tends toward the experimental. She craves variety and can often engage in a sexual experience just for the sheer novelty of it. She may try anything once, just to see what it's about. Gemini has the ability to compartmentalize and rationally file away almost any experience as "interesting," as in, "Been there, done that. Might not choose to do it again, but it was *interesting*." Gemini also often prefers to evade definition of her sexuality in binary terms. Whether she identifies as queer or straight or somewhere else along the spectrum, Gemini does not always appreciate being labeled. Of course, she'll have her preferences, but to label her sexuality is to limit her experience, and experiencing all that life has to offer is what Gemini is here for.

As mentioned above, the mind is Gemini's biggest turn-on. Erotica, a suggestive look, or an intriguing question will get her attention. She may also enjoy role-play or power play as long as it's fun and heady but not too intense. Of course, not all Gemini women are quite as experimental. There are some who tend to a more traditional sexual expression. But make no mistake, fantasy is usually at play in some capacity. Perhaps she is reading a book or watching a series that she finds enticing, and elements will find their way into her mind to make sex that much more fascinating.

The Gemini woman is the original people person and does well in a career where she can engage in a perpetual interchange of ideas, perspectives, and viewpoints. She needs a job where she is mentally stimulated, where change is a constant and keeps her on her toes. Her imaginative genius and thirst for knowledge draw her to explore many paths, and sometimes Gemini can be the proverbial jill-of-all-trades. She can also be a lifelong student, her interests changing with her whims and current fascinations. Gemini finds it difficult to commit to any one career or field of study when there are so many fascinating ones beckoning. She changes her mind frequently and needs a career that incorporates her need for variety and excitement. Some areas where Gemini can excel and satisfy her need for diversity are writing, journalism, acting, promotion, broadcasting, teaching, public speaking, public relations, linguistics, and translation, to name a few. She has a gift for networking and connecting and can shine in a career in marketing and sales. She could also be a brilliant creative director or a savvy spokesperson, as she has a knack for creating a buzz and getting people talking. Her gift for brainstorming and facilitation in the workplace keeps things hopping. She also has a keen eye for trends and intuitively seems to know what the next big thing will be. Gemini would do well to bring her many interests and talents together to create a dynamic career that feeds her need for variety and keeps her from getting bored. Some Geminis will happily work two or more jobs. Repetition and isolation will send her into a tailspin of boredom, so it's best for her to avoid that in a job description or she will just end up leaving.

In the workplace, Gemini is a quick learner, a natural multitasker, clever, and charming. She is usually well liked by colleagues, popular with clients, and known for her spirited sense of fun. However, words are one of Gemini's best assets, and she may wield them for fun and profit, both positively and negatively. For all her charm and sociability, some Geminis do have a bit of a mean-girl streak that can come out at times. She can enjoy being provocative just to keep things interesting, and depending on the Gemini in question, that can sometimes lead to gossip.

Despite her capriciousness, the Gemini woman is a breath of fresh air. She teaches us the magick of living in the moment, and helps us to see the futility of attachment. She reminds us of the beauty of the impermanence of life. Gemini's wisdom lies in her ability to integrate the seemingly disparate dualities of reason and intuition, thought and feeling, action and vision. She is the alchemist who weaves the logical, analytical left side of the brain with the creative, visionary right side to create new magic.

## Guiding Goddess Archetype: Butterfly Maiden

Butterfly Maiden, or *Palhik Mana,* comes to us from the indigenous Hopi tribe from the lands of the American Southwest. She is a *kachina,* or nature spirit, who symbolizes rebirth (and therefore transformation), freedom, balance, and fertility. In Pueblo mythology, kachinas have three aspects: the nature spirit itself, small carved kachina dolls thought to carry the spirit, and dancers embodying kachinas in spiritual ceremony. Butterfly Maiden also symbolizes the fertile energy of spring.[17] Clarissa

---

17. Patricia Monaghan, *The New Book of Goddesses and Heroines* (St. Paul, MN: Llewellyn, 1981; repr., 1997), 175.

Pinkola Estés writes that "Butterfly Maiden is the female fertilizing force. Carrying the pollen from one place to another, she cross-fertilizes, just as the soul fertilizes mind with nightdreams, just as archetypes fertilize the mundane world. She is the center. She brings the opposites together by taking a little from here and putting it there. Transformation is no more complicated than that."[18]

We can equate the transformation process that the butterfly undergoes with the changes that occur in our own life. Both the butterfly and Palhik Mana teach us that change is a part of life and that we must surrender and trust the process. If you are in a place of deep transition, cocooning, or about to cross a threshold, know that this state always precedes transformation and new life. All life is cyclical, but the lives of women are especially so. Perhaps you are even now at one of the thresholds of a new phase in life. Perhaps the change is psychologically, emotionally, or even physically difficult, and you must integrate the new aspects of who you are becoming. Maybe you are about to become a mother for the first time, and your body is changing. Or you could be on the cusp of perimenopause. Maybe you've reached menopause and are wondering what this great shift will mean to you as a woman. Incidentally, the Chinese have a wonderful name for the change that we call menopause: *second spring*. It is considered to be a time of regeneration for women, as well as a time of new self-awareness and an opportunity for personal growth.

The inspiring message from Pahlik Mana is that we always have the capacity to renew ourselves, no matter what phase we find ourselves in. We can reinvent, reawaken, and reimagine ourselves at any age.

## Pathworking: Making Space for Change

If there is one certainty in life, it is that change is inevitable. And yet so often we resist change, as though we might by sheer force of will stop it from happening. Accepting the ebbs and flows of life takes courage,

18. Estés, *Women Who Run with the Wolves*, 211.

faith, and the wisdom to surrender. Two of the great lessons of Gemini are to cultivate curiosity and to realize that we are all works in progress.

*You are walking down a dusty desert road. Red rock formations soar into the brilliant blue sky around you, and the Sun blazes down on the scorched earth. The trail you're walking on glitters with an assortment of pink pebbles, stones, and crystals. You have been walking for a while, and the heat of the Sun has been relentless. It seems that the trail has shifted, for the farther you walk, the more everything begins to look the same. Is that not the same bend in the dry riverbed you passed an hour before?*

*Far off in the distance you hear a rumbling. You pause and glance up. Dark clouds are gathering and heading in your direction. There is an eerie stillness, as if the air has stopped moving and the creatures in this desert landscape have suddenly become silent. The light is ethereal, otherworldly—dream light. You are at a place of transition in your life, and you have come to the desert for insight. You arrived here hoping for a message, some desert medicine to quench your own parched soul. And now it appears you have lost your way. The rumbling gets closer, and the sky darkens ominously.*

*A sudden crack resounds, and a fork of lightning illuminates the scene around you. The sky opens and you find yourself caught in a torrential downpour. You stumble ahead searching for shelter. To your left you make out a path that appears to lead toward a cluster of rocks that you could tuck into and wait out the storm. There is a small opening, and you scramble inside. It is surprisingly much bigger inside than you imagined. In fact, you find yourself in a large cave, the walls luminous and painted with depictions of kachina spirits. Quartz and gemstones sparkle everywhere you look. A small subterranean stream trickles through.*

*You realize you are not alone here. Someone else appears to be seeking shelter from the storm. A young Native American woman wrapped snugly in a blanket of many colors sits folded up before a small fire. She looks up at you, and you see that her eyes are the same dazzling array of shimmering colors as her blanket. "You must be patient," she says. "You cannot force the storm to end before it will, or there will not be enough rain for the new flowers. You must hold lightly and surrender to each rainstorm, each season, having faith that with every turn of the Wheel, each step will take you where you need to go."*

*"Where am I?" you ask. "What is this place?"*

*"This is the dreaming place," she answers, "the place of becoming." She motions to a second blanket folded beside the fire, and you remove your wet clothes and cocoon yourself in its warmth and protection. You slip into a dream within a dream and hear her gentle voice speaking to you from far away. "What is it you fear?"*

*You reflect for a few moments. Why was it you came here? Why did you come to the desert seeking wisdom? You recall your waking life, and it seems very distant. It is so abstract in this place of peace and sanctuary. Reflecting is like trying to grasp fragments of a dream. You dimly remember that you are facing great change in the topside world. Something momentous is shifting in your life, and you are afraid of what that will mean.*

What changes are you facing right now? What are you afraid of? Perhaps you are at a time of metamorphosis in your body's cycles. Your body is changing, and you are afraid of what you will look like or how you will feel when you get to the other side. Perhaps you are at a fork in the road in your career—maybe the company you work for has downsized, or maybe you are about to take a chance and start your own business, but what if it doesn't work out? Perhaps it is your relationship or your marriage that is at a crossroads, and you are unsure of who you will be if that person is no longer in your life. Do not get up from your place of dreaming, but visualize yourself standing and walking to the little stream. Take each one of your fears, place them on one of the dry leaves that are drifting by, and watch them float away one by one, gently, slowly, out of the cave and out of your view.

*Palhik Mana speaks: "Change is inevitable. When you let go of your fear and surrender, you make space for curiosity and open yourself to undreamed-of possibilities. Although uncertainty can be difficult, if you trust the process, you can learn to dance with change."*

*The young woman in the multicolored cloak rises from her folded position and opens her arms out wide. A deep rhythmic drumming from the earth itself seems to be keeping time as she dances herself around the fire, and her outstretched arms become wings. She spins in delight, hopping and gaining air, and transforms before you into a beautiful butterfly. She sweeps out of the cave on her radiant wings, liberated, free. You get up and follow her, blinking in the dazzling sunlight. The storm has passed and droplets of water sparkle like diamonds on new green growth and bright blooms you did not notice before. A monarch butterfly balances in the center of a shimmering orange milkweed blossom and then flutters away. With a growing sense of optimism and lightness, you follow the butterfly, ready to move forward into your next chapter.*

## Ritual: Energy Retrieval

Our energy goes out as words and thoughts on a constant basis. Energy we send out via interactions online, at school, at work, and in our relationships sometimes gets stuck "out there." We end up feeling depleted, emotional, or unfocused, and we're not sure why. Worry is an unproductive energy drain, as is repeatedly replaying a scenario from the past that we cannot change. We may have left our energy with other people in other times when we didn't speak up but feel we should have. Many of us have left energy with old loves or people who betrayed us. Every time our thoughts go to these situations or these people, we lend out a bit of our precious life force, and if we don't call it back, it can stay out there, sapping our reserves.

In our digital age, energy depletion is worse than ever, and it may feel like everyone wants a piece of us—social media, clickbait titles, ads, fake news, real news. The list of things trying to steal our energy via moments of our attention is endless. Add this to our everyday interactions, and it's no wonder we sometimes feel it's hard to concentrate. Although this loss of energy happens to everyone, the mutable signs, especially Gemini, can be most susceptible. If you have a lot of Gemini, Virgo, or Pisces in your chart, you may benefit from doing this energy retrieval ritual from time to time, but especially when you're feeling scattered, devitalized, or distracted.

### Gemini Alchemy Oil

10 drops basil

3 drops grapefruit

3 drops neroli

3 drops vetiver

1 drop peppermint

Aromatherapy is a form of alchemy that truly resonates with Gemini. Not only is Gemini connected to the archetype of the Alchemist, but Gemini is an air sign, and everything you smell is because molecules are floating through the air into your nose, which are then picked up by special receptors that transmit a message to your brain. This alchemical blend invokes the vibrations of Gemini. Use it to focus on gaining clarity of mind, enhancing communication and divination, letting go of the past and embracing the present moment, seeing all sides of a situation, and detaching from heavy emotional energies.

Gemini Alchemy Oil is especially supportive if you are undergoing a time of transition. It can also be used as a sacred offering to Butterfly Maiden or Hermes and is especially helpful for facilitating pathworkings. The most astrologically auspicious time to craft this blend is during Gemini season or when the Moon is in Gemini, to tap into the energies when they are at their peak. It's best to also find a time when the Moon is waxing for optimum potency.

You could also experiment with substituting bergamot for grapefruit. Because peppermint is strong, you will want to start with a very low amount. The total drops of essential oils for this blend is 20. You can also cut the recipe in half accordingly and use 10 total drops to try a smaller amount to start with. Play with the ratios to get it exactly where you want it. Sense of smell is subjective, and everyone will have different preferences.

*Energy Retrieval*

Sage for smudging
Yellow candle
Gemini Alchemy Oil
Feather
Bell

Wear comfortable clothing, and find a place where you will be undisturbed for 20 minutes. If you are inside, unplug all electric and digital devices in the room. Turn off your phone. Clear your space with sage. Anoint the candle with Gemini Alchemy Oil. Light the candle. Anoint yourself with the oil, one drop each for the solar plexus, third eye, and each wrist. Ground and center in whatever way you prefer, and do at least three complete Savitri breaths (see page 54).

When you feel intuitively ready and relaxed, begin to locate your displaced energy. Gain an overview like an eagle, and soar with an elevated view to see where you have left fragments of your power. Some will be easy to see, as you consciously know if you've been obsessing about an old flame or you recently had an argument with your partner. Other places you've dropped energy will be hidden and less easy to access, pushed to your unconscious and forgotten about. It's okay if you don't recall every place. In fact, it may be impossible to do so, as some of our energy is given up even before we have words to name it. Name what you can, and gather what you see.

Focus on your solar plexus. This chakra (*manipura*) is the center of our personal power. It is also connected to confidence, clarity, and the gathering and focusing of energy. Visualize a golden glow beginning in your solar plexus. Breathe slowly in and out, and as you breathe, imagine on the in breath you are drawing the warming, revitalizing energy of the Sun into your solar plexus. Take the feather and fan your energy back into yourself. Feel the golden glow in your center open and spread throughout your body. This warmth is your own energy coming back to you from all corners of the universe—named and unnamed, remembered and forgotten.

Raise your arms and pull your energy into your solar plexus. State aloud three times,

> *I hereby call home to me all my energy that has been left with other people, other places, and other times. I am complete, revitalized, and centered.*

Feel your energy coming home to you. Visualize it restoring and regenerating you on every level. When you are ready and you feel complete and whole, open your eyes, blow out the candle, and take a few moments to stretch and gently come back into yourself. Ring the bell three times to conclude the ritual and clear the air.

## Gemini Correspondences

*Astrological Dates:* May 21 through June 20

*Sabbat:* Threshold sign between Beltane and summer solstice

*Gemini Goddess Archetypes:* Butterfly Maiden / Palhik Mana, Sarasvati, Psyche, Blodeuwedd, Melissa, Seshat, Etain, Niamh, Ismo, Cerridwen, Eris

*House:* Third

*Element:* Air

*Mode:* Mutable

*Planet:* Mercury

*Color:* Yellow

*Crystals:* Apatite, apophyllite, blue lace agate, dumortierite, indicolite (tourmaline), kyanite, tanzanite

*Essential Oils:* Basil, bergamot, grapefruit, vetiver, lavender, neroli, spearmint, peppermint

*Parts of the Body:* Hands, arms, nervous system

# CANCER

Cancer season begins at the liminal moment of the summer solstice. The Sun is at its highest point in the sky, and the natural world is voluptuous, lush, and fecund. Summer solstice is the culmination of the waxing season: the Maiden becomes the Mother. It is a time of ripeness and birth, and the fullness of life force is at its peak. Cancer is a cardinal water sign, meaning that it is a gateway to a seasonal turning point (in this case, summer) and resonates with the intuitive, empathic element of water. Cancer embodies the archetypal feminine and is related to the archetype of the Great Mother, the nurturing, embracing womb from which we all come and to which we will all return. The Great Mother is one of the original archetypes and is so ancient and so vast in scope it would be impossible to convey its breadth in one book, let alone a single chapter.

Much of this is also true for the sign Cancer. Unfathomably deep, connected to ancestral memory and the roots of the subconscious, Cancer is, in a sense, our spiritual home, the home we all subconsciously long to return to. Cancer is also ruled by the Moon, another inestimably ancient archetype. The Moon is inextricably tied to the feminine principle, or the *anima*. Not only does it govern the tides of the ocean, but it also waxes and wanes in sync with the cycles of women's fertility. It is no wonder that the sign of Cancer rules the stomach, the breasts, and the womb.

As an embodiment of the Great Mother, Cancer is cognate with not only the wider family of humankind, but the personal family as well.

Tribe, homeland, ancestral roots, passed-down cultural traditions, and psychological inheritance all come under the embrace of Cancer. So too do the ideas of home, sanctuary, sustenance, and what we belong to— our place in the wider world. Cancer is changeable and, like the tides, moves in and out of waxing and waning cycles from receptivity and emotional fullness to introspective retreat. These shifting internal ebbs and flows sometimes cause Cancer to become entangled in subtle emotional undercurrents, arising in unnameable melancholic longings and inward vision, which has been oft referred to simply as "moodiness." However, as we will see, the archetype and the psyche of Cancer are much deeper than that.

## The Cancer Woman

Ask a Cancer woman why she is feeling pensive, and you are likely to get a vague answer: "I don't know. I just feel weird." She may be ruminating or brooding over an actual concern or event, but it is just as likely that she doesn't know. Part of this is that she's ruled by the fluctuating phases of the Moon, and another reason is that she is subconsciously tuned into the crosscurrents of ancestral memory that have come upon her without warning, dragging her into murky depths and enveloping her in nebulous memories of generations past. Once she becomes conscious of the voices of the ancestors, she can find great healing and wisdom in her lineage, which will also give her useful glimpses into the origins of unfounded fears, patterns, and drives.

Because of her innate emotional and psychic receptivity, Cancer is a natural conduit. It's not only the fragments of ancestral memories that tug at her; she is also keenly attuned to the moods and feelings of those in her most immediate circle. Although her extremely heightened intuitive awareness can make her the most empathic of women, the most gifted healer, and the most attentive mother, the unspoken lesson that accompanies her acute emotional sensitivity is about boundaries.

The Cancer woman cares deeply about her loved ones. She is compassionate, loyal, and often fiercely protective. She has a well of love as deep and boundless as the ocean for those in her inner circle. She is a born nurturer, and whether she is a biological mother or not, she tends to take on this role with her friends, family, and animal companions. While this can be a generally positive and admirable quality, we must remember that there is always a shadow side to every sign. The shadow side, where Cancer is concerned, is the potential of enmeshment. Sometimes Cancer identifies so completely with her perceived role as nurturer or protector that she subconsciously oversteps healthy boundaries with her loved ones, resulting in an emotionally manipulative atmosphere that can foster resentment and guilt. While not all Cancers are biological mothers, it is important to note that siblings, mates, partners, friends, and coworkers can also be affected when the shadow side of this archetype is activated. In Cancer's defense, if this does occur, she is usually not conscious of what she's doing. Cancer is often terribly hurt and bewildered when a loved one asks her to stop meddling. Requests for space or independence can be taken personally, as an affront to her well-meaning efforts. After all, from her perspective, she was only trying to help. She may feel unappreciated and taken for granted and then subsequently withdraw for a time into her shell.

Despite the occasional storms that occur because of being so emotionally tuned in, Cancer is unmatched in the art of comfort. As a natural empath, she can make a powerful healer who knows intuitively what is required to restore someone to wholeness. This skill is valuable whether she is a psychotherapist or an energy worker. It also comes in handy when she finds herself, as she often does, listening compassionately to her loved ones and coworkers, as Cancer is often the go-to person when anyone needs a shoulder to cry on. She has a soothing, calming presence that is often all people need to begin the process of emotional healing. However, lest you begin to get the idea that Cancer is simply a mothering, shy, and retiring soul here to take on the troubles of the world, let's remember that Cancer is by nature cyclical. She has one of the best senses of humor in the entire zodiac, hands down. This woman is seriously funny. She loves to laugh and can have her besties reeling with her impressions, insightful observations, and wacky anecdotes—

all delivered with perfect comedic timing. Her insight and intuition give her the ability (as they say in show biz) to read a room like a pro.

If you are lucky enough to be invited into the inner sanctum that is the Cancer woman's home, you will see why Cancer is aligned with the concept of sanctuary. Cancer is usually selective about who is admitted into her private domain, as this is her safe place of retreat from the harshness of the world. At home, the Cancer woman is in her element. Romantic and mysterious, her hideaway is often decorated with antiques, Oriental rugs, and layers of beautiful fabric. Sentimental objects, keepsakes, and photos are in abundance. Lighting is of great importance in setting her desired ambience: candlelight and Victorian oil lamps provide the atmospheric mood lighting she prefers. In short, the Cancer woman's home is like a bohemian paradise, with more than a nod to the past. Thirties jazz, classical, or seventies folk music is likely part of her music collection, especially if she has fond childhood memories of listening to a particular genre with her grandmother or a beloved aunt.

Food is another Cancerian theme that will be apparent in her haven. Her lush abode is scented with exotic cooking spices and the intoxicating smell of something wonderful pleasantly bubbling on the stove. Many Cancers are serious epicureans. Of course, there are some Cancers who are not cooks, but they still have a deep appreciation for the delicious. Whether she opts for takeout or has friends come over and cook up a storm while she pours the wine, good food will certainly be a central part of the Cancer woman's cozy hearth. To the fortunate few who make it across her threshold, Cancer is an unparalleled hostess who enjoys making her loved ones feel at home.

The protective embrace of her home is also where she conjures her creative magick, as her rich and fertile imagination can soar unimpeded in the privacy of her sanctuary. Cancer is a highly creative sign, and whether she channels it through the written word, with paint and canvas, or with stones and silver, she is compelled to birth something into form with frequent visits from the Muse. She is also usually quite creative with her wardrobe. With her romantic imagination and love of the past, she may have a taste for vintage clothing and antique jewelry. Anything with a story will capture Cancer's heart. She may have a fetish for antique French corsets or shoes from the fifties. Cancer is a born collector, and every piece she covets has a tale to tell. She has a near magical ability for spotting treasures in consignment and thrift shops, and often has a remarkable knack for upcycling some of her finds. She can be quite talented with thread and needle, rescuing a length of antique velvet from a special dress and giving it a new lease on life.

We cannot talk about the importance of Cancer's home without delving into another strong Cancerian theme: security. Security is of near sacred importance to Cancer. And while this encompasses the security of her home itself, it also includes the area of financial security. The Cancer woman has an instinct for protection and does not leave anything to chance. This is not the woman who occasionally forgets to lock the back door, either literally or figuratively. She may have an alarm system installed and is not afraid to defend her home and loved ones if necessary. She is very practical when it comes to home security measures. If she lives in the country, she will want a fence and maybe a dog to warn her both of potential intruders and unwelcome visitors. To Cancer there is nothing more important than the safety of her home and loved ones. However, financial security does take a close second. No matter her income level, the Cancer woman is often financially astute and takes steps to ensure that whatever happens, she will be okay. Like Taurus, she likely has a secret nest egg put away for a rainy day. For her indulgences, Cancer is also very economical and has a natural aptitude for money.

The Cancer woman's need for security also applies to the area of love and relationships. Because of her emotional sensitivity, Cancer can be cautious when it comes to giving her heart away. This is especially true if her heart has been broken in the past. Some Cancerians retreat to the safety of their shells for long periods of time following a relationship gone wrong. They build an impenetrable fortress around themselves and keep potential suitors out with crabby, hard-bitten exteriors that belie the soft, vulnerable creatures they are inside. Some claim they would rather be single forever than allow themselves to be hurt again. Truth be told, in her heart of hearts, the Cancer woman probably wants nothing more than a deeply passionate, committed, emotionally intimate relationship. Even if she is not recuperating from a breakup, it takes Cancer time to develop trust before she gives her heart. When she does, there is no sign more devoted, loyal, and protective of her partner than the Cancer woman. She is also a born romantic. She notices the little things that make her partner happy and never forgets a special occasion. She delights in exchanging love notes, texts, and giving (and getting) sentimental tokens of affection. And many a Cancer woman will keep these emblems of love for the rest of her life. My very good Cancer friend has alphabetized file folders with treasured memorabilia dating back to when she was in her teens and a charming story to go with each one. The Cancer woman often has old-timey values connected to her idea of courtship. No matter how cutting edge or radical she might be in other areas of her life, she has some traditional notions that are nonnegotiable. She appreciates courtesy and respect and loves romantic gestures that show you care: bringing her favorite flowers, opening her car door, walking her to her door in the rain, and calling after a date. She also dearly values the little things that mean you've been paying attention. If she mentioned a favorite something offhandedly six months ago and you surprise her with one out of the blue, you will have scored serious points. Even if she's been married for years, Cancer still treasures every little kindness and never forgets a single one.

Likewise, she also will not forget a slight of any kind. She may forgive, but Cancer's memory is long and her feelings are easily hurt. More spirited signs like Aries or Sagittarius may not even realize they have hurt Cancer. She will expect you to know exactly what you said or did that wounded her and be even more wounded if you don't. If you really loved her, Cancer reasons, you would know. She needs to understand that not everyone is as tuned in as she is, and it doesn't indicate a lack of care. When she's feeling insecure, or her feelings are hurt, Cancer sometimes resorts to passive-aggressive tactics to show you just how deeply your carelessness has affected her.

Even in the early stages of a relationship, there are some Cancer women who are already daydreaming about the names of their future children. Many, but not all, Cancer women yearn to be a mother. This was the little girl who may have spent countless happy hours changing her doll's diapers and couldn't wait until she was old enough to baby-sit. Of course, there are some Cancer women who are not drawn to the path of being a mother or who cannot give birth to children of her own. Her nurturing instinct will then manifest in other ways. Perhaps she mothers her partner. Maybe she has fur babies who mean the world to her. Still others find an outlet for their mothering instinct as dedicated stepparents or aunties or in a career where they can fulfill their need to look after others. The nurturing instinct runs deep in Cancer, and many Cancer women feel as though something is missing in their lives if they do not have someone or something to care for. Family is very important to Cancer. Whether she has a loving bond with her family of origin or can hardly deal with the thought of going home for the holidays, family is never a neutral concept. If her relationship with family is challenged or even damaged, she will focus on creating her own family of choice.

Sexually, Cancer is a sensual, nuanced lover who almost magically knows how to connect with her partner. Most Cancer women take time to build trust, and she will flourish in a committed relationship where she feels safe to explore her passions. For Cancer, at its best, sex is an ecstatic union, a meeting of the sensual and the spiritual, a deep, other-worldly bond that connects her to an ocean of transcendent bliss. Orgasm can be as overwhelming as a tidal wave, and Cancer sometimes finds herself crying after sex, overwhelmed by the vastness and depth of feeling that washes over her. Cancer is drawn to the intensity she experiences through sex, and therefore it is important that she choose her partners wisely. She will usually be disappointed by casual sex, but on the rare occasion that she does experience connection in this way, she will not forget it and will likely want to forge a deeper bond with the person she experienced it with. When she is feeling emotionally secure and confident, Cancer is highly attuned with her sensual nature, and enjoys the gift of being comfortable in her own skin.

The Cancer woman can find fulfillment in a variety of vocations. Her nurturing aspect can make her a gifted therapist, an inspired yoga teacher, a massage therapist, a naturopath, or a physician. She could also be a brilliant family systems therapist or social worker, and her connection with women and children may lead her to work as a doula, midwife, or early childhood educator. Her innate compassion may also lead her to a calling involving working with animals, as a veterinarian or animal protection worker. On the other hand, her affinity with home and food could open a host of possibilities that will feed her soul, such as chef, baker, restaurant owner, or caterer. She would also shine as an architect, interior decorator, or in real estate, helping others to find and feather their perfect nest. Her knack for making people feel at home would also make her an attentive bed-and-breakfast hostess or retreat facilitator. Her penchant for history and love of the past may draw her to a fascinating career path as a museum curator, antiques dealer, vintage shop owner, or history teacher. And of course, the Cancer woman's inspired imagination would make her a gifted natural in any and all of the creative fields. In a completely different direction, Cancer's financial flair can make her an astute investor or business consultant.

## Guiding Goddess Archetype: Demeter

Demeter comes to us from the Greek pantheon. She is the golden-haired goddess associated with the fertility of the earth, as well as being connected to grain and the harvest, signifying her connection to food and sustenance. Her Roman equivalent is Ceres, which is what our word *cereal* derives from. She is also associated with the divine order of nature. However, perhaps most importantly, Demeter resonates deeply with the essential qualities of Cancer, and she is the quintessential mother archetype.[19]

In Demeter's main myth, her beloved maiden daughter is gathering flowers with her friends in a beautiful meadow. Blissfully absorbed in her pursuit, she is drawn by a particularly beautiful narcissus bloom

---

19. Jean Shinoda Bolen, *Goddesses in Older Women* (New York: Harper Collins, 2001), 159.

and bends to pick it. At this precise moment, the ground opens beneath her, and Hades, god of the underworld, comes barreling up out of the depths in his golden chariot and grabs her by her delicate ankle, dragging her back down to his domain to be his unwilling bride. She cries out for help as he carries her away. Moments later, not a trace remains of this violent scene: the fields are once again quiet, except for the sound of birdsong. Morning turns into afternoon, and afternoon becomes twilight.

Demeter begins to wonder where her daughter could be. She is never late. She should be home by now. Demeter begins to worry. With torch in hand to light her way, she sets off into the wilderness to find her daughter. For nine days she searches, neither bathing nor eating. She calls frantically over hill and vale and is greeted by silence. Darkness falls, and Demeter is beside herself. In shock, heart pounding and limbs shaking with fear, she sits—head in hands—thinking of what to do next.

On the tenth day, Hecate—wise crone and goddess of the crossroads—finds her thus, and tells her, yes, she did hear something, but she did not see what befell Persephone. Hecate and Demeter approach Helios, the all-seeing god of the Sun, to see if he witnessed anything that would be of help. Helios takes pity on Demeter and replies that Zeus himself gave her to Hades to be his unwilling bride. Demeter is incredulous. Angry. Horrified. She petitions Zeus for the return of her beloved only child, but he turns her away.

Sinking into despair, Demeter disguises herself as an old woman and covers her bright hair. She roams far and wide, bereft, betrayed, and in deep mourning. In her all-encompassing grief and depression, the crops cease to grow. The once abundant and fertile earth shrivels and dries up. There is no harvest. Humans and animals alike begin to starve. Dressed in a simple dark robe, Demeter eventually wanders into the lands of Celeus, the king of Eleusis, who takes her in and invites her to become nursemaid to his son, Demophon. To repay the king's kindness, Demeter decides to make Demophon immortal. She secretly feeds him ambrosia and places him in the flames of the hearth fire each night as part of the transforming ritual. One night, Demophon's mother, Metanira, discovers Demeter putting the baby in the fire and screams in horror. Although this interruption stops the process of turning Demophon into a god, Demeter now declares her true nature in all her glory. She rises to her full and awesome height, her golden hair tumbles down over her shoulders, and she reveals herself as the goddess she is before the household of Celeus. She commands that a temple be built for her, and here she ensconces herself, enfolded in her deep depression.

Meanwhile, the earth has been barren for a long while. Long enough that the gods on Mount Olympus have not received their sacrifices for many a moon. Zeus is finally persuaded to intervene and agrees to send Hermes, the messenger god, to retrieve Persephone from Hades— provided she has not eaten any food of the underworld. However, upon her departure, Hades covertly offers Persephone the seeds of a pomegranate, and, perhaps to placate him, she eats several.

Persephone returns to the upper world, and Demeter rejoices as she is reunited with her beautiful daughter. In her joy, the fields are transformed once again to a living green, and buds burst open and turn their faces toward the Sun. It is the first spring. Rushing to her daughter in relief, Demeter asks Persephone if she has partaken in any food of the dead. Because Persephone has ingested the pomegranate seeds, she forthwith must spend a third of the year in the underworld with her husband, and two-thirds of the year on earth with her mother, thus explaining the turn of the seasons.[20] When it is time for Persephone to return to Hades, Demeter once again grieves the loss of her daughter, and winter descends: the crops do not grow, and the land becomes barren. However, each spring Persephone is reunited with her mother, and Demeter, in her joy, once again blesses the earth with fertility and renewal.

Demeter also provides humankind with the spiritual sustenance known as the Eleusinian Mysteries, a secret religious order that gave its initiates hope that life continues after passing from the earthly realm.

20. Diane J. Rayor, trans., *The Homeric Hymns* (Berkeley: University of California Press, 2004), 17–34.

# Pathworking: Trusting the Cycles

Cancer wisdom teaches us that all of life is cyclical. The waxing and waning of the Moon, the ebb and flow of the tides, the setting and rising of the Sun, and the turning of the great Wheel of the Year—the change of the seasons that is reflected in the story of Demeter and Persephone. We know with certainty that spring always follows winter. There is great comfort that comes from meditating on the cyclical nature of life. We can rest assured that the adage "it's always darkest before the dawn" is not just a cliché; it is an irrefutable law of nature. The Mysteries teach us that although Demeter and Persephone are mother and daughter, they are also symbolically two halves of a whole. They are inextricably connected. If this instructional tale teaches us anything, it is not only to accept the waxing and waning cycles in our own lives, but also to keep the seed of faith that spring will always come again—and with it, rebirth and wholeness.

*You are walking over a vast plain. It has been a long winter. The fields are bare, and the wind howls forlornly across the bleak landscape. Leafless trees huddle together, as if to try to keep each other warm. The last of the harvest was brought in moons ago, and the earth is in its deep sleep. You shiver beneath your woolen cape. It is easy to believe that this time, this is the winter that will be endless. The flame of inspiration within you seems to have grown dim. It has been difficult to summon your creative spark, and your natural optimism is but a memory. You feel emotionally exhausted and a long way from home.*

*Far off in the distance, you see a large structure, and you are drawn toward it to see what it is. As you get closer, you realize it's a temple. Tall white marble pillars guard the steps to the entrance. You ascend the steps, looking around you to see if anyone is about. All is quiet. There is a desolate air about the place. Perhaps it's abandoned, you muse, and your curiosity brings you to turn the door handle and enter. At the far end of a processional way flanked by bare-branched olive trees, you see what appears to be a woman shrouded in a dark cloak. She sits on a throne decorated with golden sheaves of wheat and dried poppies. Her bowed head is cradled on her arm, and you wonder if she is asleep. She stirs slightly and lifts her head, awoken from her reverie by your presence. She is a beautiful woman in her middle years.*

*She looks at you and smiles gently. "It is not time yet." Her voice is soft, yet warm and embracing. She is Demeter, the all-mother. You have a sudden longing to climb up into the safety and comfort of her arms. As though she reads your thoughts, she reaches out her hand, palm up in an attitude of welcome, and enfolds you in her embrace. You find yourself completely and securely held in the lap of the goddess. You close your eyes and rest your cheek against her chest. How good it is to feel supported. To feel that it is okay and safe just to be. She rocks you gently. You are enveloped in oceanic bliss—a return to Source. You exhale deeply, and your breathing slows and falls into rhythm with hers. You marvel at the surety that is the cycle of breath. In breath. Pause. Out breath. Pause. In breath. Like the certainty of the ocean's tides or the turning of the seasons.*

*Demeter speaks: "Everything has its cycles. Everything has its time. The space between the seasons of life is the same as the space between breaths. A sacred pause in which to trust that spring always follows winter. Emptiness is always followed by fullness. New life invariably comes after death. All you must do is learn to trust. No matter where you find yourself in the cycle, no matter how bleak, remember this is divine law."*

*You rest like this for a long while, healing and gathering strength. After a time, as much as you would love to stay this way forever, you know intuitively it is time to get up. You slide down from the lap of the goddess and turn to thank her. She smiles and looks deeply into your eyes, and then looks off into the distance as though she has heard something. Her eyes dance.*

*"It is time." She rises from her throne and allows her dark robe to drop, her golden hair tumbling over her shoulders. She raises her arms in exultation, palms up, and the olive trees along the processional path burst with delicate green leaves. Her face is radiant—expectant. Mo-*

*ments later, the door bursts open and a lovely young woman rushes in, trailing flowers in her wake. You quietly leave the temple to find that spring has returned to the fields outside. The greening of the land has commenced at last. Renewed and regenerated, you walk into the glorious sunlight ready to begin again.*

## Ritual: Wisdom from Grandmother's Cupboard

Both the archetype of Cancer and the goddess Demeter are deeply intertwined with the motif of nourishment. Food and cooking are more than just a way to feed oneself. They are a connection to the stories and traditions of the past and a direct link to the wisdom of the ancestors, of whispered spells, long forgotten. Cooking invokes all four elements—fire, earth, air, and water—and magickally transforms one thing into another. Cancer is also aligned with the archetype of the Great Mother, as well as ancestral memory, lineage, and roots.

While many traditions and individuals honor both male and female ancestors, the following is a simple way to connect specifically with the wisdom of the Grandmothers. I use the term *the Grandmothers* here interchangeably with *your grandmother* because although you may wish to honor your actual maternal or paternal grandmother, you may also choose to remember the women who came before them in your family line: your great-grandmothers and even those who lived so long ago their names may have been forgotten. You may even wish to delve deeper into your genealogy with one of the DNA-testing kits that are now widely available.

*You Will Need:*

An old recipe from your family (or from the place of origin of your
    grandmothers)
Fresh organic ingredients
Beeswax candle (1-inch-thick pillar candle or votive candle works well)
Photo(s) of your grandmother(s)
Small mementos from your grandmother or from her country or place
    of origin

Implement to inscribe the candle (e.g., inkless ballpoint pen, metal
    skewer with a point, toothpick, etc.)
Paper
Pen

First, find a recipe either passed down in your family or, if that's not
possible, a recipe for a dish from the place of origin of your ancestors.
If, as it does for many of us, your lineage goes back to several places,
choose a recipe from the culture that resonates with you the most. Obtain the ingredients you need in the most direct "farm-to-table" way
possible: buy from a farmers' market, choose local produce, or if you
grow your own vegetables and herbs, this is even better. The exception
is any ingredient you need for the recipe that is grown and harvested in
another part of the world.

Ground and center in your preferred way. Make your kitchen a sacred space: smudge, do the dishes, wipe down the counters, and be sure
to sweep the floor mindfully. Set up an altar to the Grandmothers in
your kitchen. Place the beeswax candle and a picture of your grandmother or grandmothers on the altar. You can also place any small objects that belonged to your grandmothers or are associated with their
places of origin on your altar. If you are lucky enough to have a bowl, a
pan, a knife, or a spoon handed down to you from your family, you may
choose to use it in your cooking ceremony or place it on your kitchen
altar as a symbolic talisman of your roots. As an offering, set a small
portion of the ingredients you will be using on the altar.

Sit in a chair or kneel before your altar and pick up the candle. Take
four grounding breaths. Speak your grandmother's name aloud, to
let her know that it is not forgotten. Carve your grandmother's name
on the candle, light it, and replace it on the altar. Invite her into your
kitchen with a few words of reverence, such as,

*Grandmother, be welcome at my hearth.*

If you wish, you may now ask for specific guidance from the Grandmothers on an issue you are facing, or you may simply wish to connect

with your lineage so you can draw strength and wisdom from those who have gone before. Ask,

*Honored Grandmothers* (or your grandmother's name),
*what do I need to know right now?*

Mindfully begin the preparation of your dish. Allow yourself to slip into a light trance state by reflecting on the ingredients you are using. Visualize where they were grown and harvested. See the sunlight and the rain nurturing the seed of what you are now preparing. See your grandmother using the same ingredients and following a similar recipe. From what you know of your grandmother, take a few moments to actively imagine her life: the smells, sounds, and spirit of place and time she lived in.

Next, turn your attention to the alchemy that is the act of cooking: the heat and the blending of ingredients that transforms and creates magick. As you are cooking, stirring, or kneading, listen for a message. Don't discount what comes to you. Hold an attitude of openness and receptivity. It may be a word, a sudden insight, or an image. Take a moment to write it down and place the paper on the altar so you can return to it later and meditate on the message you have received and what it means to you in your life.

Serve your dish either with family and family of the heart or just to yourself as a moment of personal contemplation. Meditate on the idea that you are the living link in the chain and one day you will be the ancestor. Although you can do this ritual anytime, Cancer season, a New or Full Moon in Cancer, or any time the Moon is in Cancer are especially potent times to connect with the wisdom of the Grandmothers.

## Ritual: Full Moon Scrying

While the Moon is Cancer's ruling planet, the following ritual can be performed on any Full Moon of the year, regardless of what sign it's in. The full phase of the Moon is conducive to all forms of divination, including scrying, as it is a time that is associated with clear vision and revelation. Scrying is the ancient art of gazing into a surface to divine the future or gain insight, and the Full Moon often brings things to light that were previously hidden from our consciousness. The Full Moon occurs when the Sun and Moon are exactly opposite of each other, and the Moon is completely illuminated from our perspective on Earth. The astrological sign of a given Full Moon will therefore always be opposite the sign the Sun is currently in. For example, the full Cancer Moon falls each year in December or January (when the Sun is in Capricorn, Cancer's opposite sign). The Moon is considered full for three days: the day before the Full Moon, the exact day of, and the day after. So if you cannot do this ritual right on the exact Full Moon, not to worry. It is useful to take note of what sign the Full Moon is in, as you can also attune with the themes of that sign and acknowledge the guiding goddesses associated with the sign ruling the Full Moon.

*You Will Need:*
Mugwort smudge stick
Pitcher of water
Large dark bowl
4 white candles
Handful dried flower petals (edible if you plan on ingesting the water)
    or loose herbal tea leaves
Journal
Pen

Find a place where you can see the Moon. It is best to be outdoors for this ritual, but if that's not possible, indoors by a window works well too. Clear your space and ground and center in your preferred way. Smudge your working area with mugwort, a herb long associated with prophecy, divination, and enhanced psychic vision. It is readily available in many natural foods stores.

Pour the water into the bowl. Light the candles. Cast the petals or herbs and the dried mugwort into the water and swish the water clockwise until they are dispersed. Sit comfortably before the bowl and gaze into the water.

Allow your vision to soften and diffuse by half closing your eyes. Slow your breathing and relax into a light trance state. Take note of images and shapes that spontaneously arise in the petals or leaves. Don't try to force the images or control them, just let them shift and morph into whatever they will be. (If you've ever lain on your back in the grass and watched the clouds on a beautiful summer day, just allowing yourself to notice the ever-changing images, it's the same idea). Scry until you feel you're done.

Pick up your journal and record what came up for you. Write down words and thoughts and describe the images you noticed. You may wish to draw them instead. Put out the candles. You may either pour the water and petals from your scrying bowl outside as an offering or leave it to charge in the moonlight for a few hours, remembering to bring it in before sunrise. Moon water keeps in the fridge for up to two weeks. You can use the charged Moon water in a variety of ways, such as in a ritual bath, as a libation, in a recipe, or in other ceremonial work. Be creative.

After Full Moon scrying, you may wish to take a bath; see "A Bath to Ground and Center after a Ritual or Divination" on page 61. If so, bring the candles with you to the bath, and relight them safely around your tub while you bathe.

## Cancer Correspondences

*Astrological Dates:* June 21 through July 22

*Sabbat:* Summer solstice

*Cancer Goddess Archetypes:* Abuk, Anahita, Atage, Ceres, Danu, Demeter, Holdja, Isis, Ixchel, Kupala, Mother Mary, Meskhoni, Parvati, Rhea, Taweret

*House:* Fourth

*Element:* Water

*Mode:* Cardinal

*Planet:* Moon

*Colors:* Blue, aqua, sea green, silver, soft gray

*Crystals:* All moonstones, blue calcite, chalcedony, larimar, morganite, selenite, stilbite, watermelon tourmaline

*Essential Oils:* Clary sage, lavender, chamomile, lemon balm, sandalwood, ylang-ylang

*Parts of the Body:* Womb, breasts, stomach, female reproductive system

# LEO

We have now passed through the gateway of summer solstice and bask in the fullness of the season. The earth is generous, abundant, and life-affirming. Leo is a fixed fire sign, meaning it occurs in the heart of the season (in this case, summer) and is associated with the passionate, visionary element of fire. Picnics at the beach, camping in the mountains, lazy days in the sun—Leo season is a time for gathering with family of the heart, enjoying the incandescent summer twilight. We laugh, dance, play, and celebrate for the sheer joy of being alive. Lughnasadh, or Lammas, the first of the three harvest festivals, occurs during Leo season, and farmers' markets are bursting with ripe cherries, luscious blackberries, and juicy peaches. It is fitting that Lughnasdh is also a traditional time for handfastings and weddings, given the fertility and abundance of the natural world.

Echoing the glorious fecundity of the season, Leo's purpose is to *shine*. It is no coincidence that the Sun is Leo's ruling planet. The Sun in astrology is connected to one's unique sense of self. The Sun symbolizes growth, creativity, illumination, life force, vitality, the divine spark, and the ability to create life. It also corresponds with sovereignty, royalty, nobility, and leadership, all qualities that resonate through the archetype of Leo. Although there are numerous goddesses associated with the Sun, it is also connected with the sacred masculine, or the *animus* in women, our inner king who acts on our behalf and takes action in the outer world. Ultimately, the Sun is symbolic of that mysterious process we call individuation: becoming wholly oneself and standing fully and gracefully in one's power. This is Leo's quest.

Leo embodies the archetype of the Queen (and King) as well as the Divine Child, and tends to view life as an epic drama, with her as the protagonist of her own story. Leo Carl Jung sums it up: "I took it upon myself to get to know my myth, and I regarded it as my task of tasks."[21] Astrologer and author Liz Greene states, "Leo, more than the other two fire signs, loves to make a myth out of himself."[22] Whether or not Leo achieves fame and glory in the pursuit of her personal myth, she does crave recognition for her efforts. Leo likes to be noticed for her own personal brand of creativity and self-expression. Although it is indeed part of Leo's life task to bring her unique creative gifts to the world, when she is feeling insecure, this can sometimes translate to self-aggrandizement and a need for validation. Luckily for Leo, she is usually blessed with her fair share of natural talent combined with vision, heart, and ambition—which often does lead to success. Leo also has genuine warmth and charm in abundance, which makes her quite lovable to those lucky enough to be in her life.

## The Leo Woman

All heads turn when she enters a room. Whether she is a "classic" Leo woman—dramatic, flamboyant, and self-confident—or she is one of the subtler representations of her sign, this woman has an undeniable measure of personal magnetism and has that certain something that might be called "star quality." True, many Leo women have a personal style that garners attention, but this is just all part of the package. Her legendary style is an expression of her innate creativity, her goddess-given right to self-expression. What she chooses to adorn herself with is an integral part of her creative process. Whether she opts for glitter and bling or tattoos and piercings, her style is very much a sacred embodi-

21. C. G. Jung, *Collected Works of C.G. Jung, Volume 5: Symbols of Transformation* (Princeton, NJ: Princeton University Press, 2014), xxv.

22. Liz Greene, *Astrology for Lovers* (York Beach, MA: Weiser, 1989), 120.

ment of who she is—an integral part of exploring her personal myth and a way of getting into character. Even the quieter Leo women have a flair for the dramatic or the romantic, and they thrive on appreciation and recognition. While this may sound vaguely superficial or narcissistic, the validation Leo craves has a deeper purpose. We must remember that part of Leo's soul purpose is self-realization, and through the response of the collective, something of her own essence is reflected back to her, thus deepening her knowledge of her emerging self.

However, as with all signs, there is always a shadow. For all her apparent self-confidence, Leo's shadow is insecurity, not knowing at the end of the day if she really is enough. When self-doubt creeps in, she may try even harder to get the approval or the feedback that she is important. She may also inflate herself and display arrogance or haughtiness to compensate for shaky self-worth. She may grasp at outside validation and display attention-seeking behavior accompanied by dramatic histrionics. She may become competitive. The shadow side of the Queen shows her face, and Leo's natural warmth and affectionate nature become subsumed in the pursuit of recognition.

The lesson for Leo is self-trust. She must learn to develop real self-confidence that comes from a heart-centered place, rather than solely from external sources. Then she can take her rightful place on the throne as the Wise Queen, the Queen who understands that self-sovereignty is the end goal. In coming to this realization, the Leo woman radiates her true regal nature. She is self-possessed, connected to her heart, and true to herself. She steps up to take on the mantle of leadership and wears it comfortably and with grace. She is whole, and she is kind. This is individuation, Leo style.

Although Leo's personal ascent to sovereignty often comes with maturity, there are several life areas she can consciously cultivate to move her purposefully toward this end. The first is to honor her path to individuation through creative expression. She must make space for her creative talents, whatever her chosen medium. Whether she chooses acting, music, writing, cooking, painting, designing, or creating her own business, it is part of Leo's life purpose to be a creator. I cannot count how many times I have seen the potential for significant creativity in a Leo woman's chart and have them answer sadly, "Oh no, I'm not really creative at all. I don't write, and I can't draw anything but stick figures." The problem is not that these clients are not innately creative; it's that their definition of creativity is too narrow, and they may not see themselves as such.

Further, although many Leo women have no trouble embracing their creative abilities and shouting about it from the rooftops, there are other Leo women who find it challenging to accept that creativity is their birthright. Perhaps creative self-expression was not valued when she was growing up. Maybe she had a family that inadvertently stamped out her tiny spark by placing excessive value on conventionally measurable outer-world achievements. For example, she might come from a long line of doctors, and although her heart ached for a creative writing degree, it was expected she take sciences instead of arts in college. Or she may have had an upbringing in a very practical family that thought creative pursuits were fine as a hobby, but to get by in this world she'd need a "real" job. Either way, the message may have been that the creative fields were a waste of time, a waste of money, a waste of effort. Family conditioning can be tricky. But, individuation is about *your* personal myth. This is your journey, and it is never too late to step onto the path you were meant for.

Let's broaden the definition of creativity. Creativity is the imagination embodied. It is an original idea or a new take on something that creates a spark. That spark is new life. Yes, creativity certainly encompasses all the arts from music to dance to painting, but it is so much more. Anytime we are inspired and manifest something tangible out of our inspiration, we are being creative. It can be anything from reupholstering an old chair to decorating the living room. It is thinking up a new solution to an old problem. You can be a creative accountant. You might have a knack for dressing creatively or planning the perfect dinner party. Leo needs to crack the definition of creativity wide open and own it, in whatever guise it shows up for her. Leo must step out of her comfort zone and take risks that create exciting new realities. The secret is that when Leo gets out of her own way, it clears the decks for something life affirming and in line with her true purpose. She will be fulfilled. She will be actualized. She will be on fire.

Another way the Leo woman can move closer to claiming her birthright of sovereignty is by developing her propensity for inspired leadership. With the Sun as her ruling planet, many Leo women are born leaders. And, although this can take the shape of leading others who are fired up by her passion and take-charge attitude, it can just as easily mean that she takes a proactive stance in her own life. Leo both is a mover and a shaker. She gets an idea and, because of the fixed nature of her sign, usually has the follow-through to see it to fruition. Leo also often has the kind of charisma that makes others trust her and want to support her ideas. Perhaps it's her natural self-confidence and abundant enthusiasm that inspires faith in others. A true Leo leader also seems to have a knack for making the people around her feel appreciated and valued. She is generous with her knowledge and her encouragement, bringing out the best in others. When she's coming from a heart-centered place and true to a vision that's a win-win, the Leo woman has an air of grounded self-assurance that echoes the archetype of the Queen.

The third path to self-realization for Leo is to align with her other associated archetype, the Divine Child. For Leo, play, pleasure, entertainment, and fun are all potential paths to self-fulfillment. If she is taking herself too seriously or is feeling insecure and has fallen into the Leo shadow of compensatory self-aggrandizement, connecting with the Divine Child aspect of her sign is the antidote. Tuning in to a sense of childlike wonder and abandoning her carefully cultivated poise rejuvenates Leo. Playing dress-up or allowing herself to be silly regardless of what anyone thinks can be therapeutic. And with Leo's love of the theatrical and her sense of play, it's no wonder you find many Leos at Renaissance fairs and other live-action role playing (LARP) events. Of course, Leo will likely be playing a queen or heroic character in these situations.

Inner child work can also be useful to the Leo woman. Not all Leos had idyllic childhoods in which they were the adored golden child. Some may have experienced childhood trauma. Some may have had their spirits crushed under the weight of family expectation, too much responsibility, or well-meaning parents who for a myriad of reasons never seemed to have the time or energy to make sure their little Leo felt supported to shine. This is often the root of overcompensation as an adult. Beneath every inflated ego is a small child terrified that she isn't special enough to get the love and attention she needs. Leo may have to be the parent she didn't have. She has to be there for herself, have her own back. She may need to dig down deep and find the validation within, not in a self-indulgent, "here's another treat" kind of way but in a real, grounded, "I will always be there for you" way.

Leo carries within her heart an image of idealized love. It is especially exciting to her if there are tests of devotion that noble-hearted lovers must pass if they are to fulfill their quest. Tristan and Iseult, Lancelot and Guinevere, Abelard and Heloise—whether she realizes it consciously or not, these classic love stories are imprinted on her psyche and color her expectations of what it means to fall in love. Indeed, even the phrase *falling in love* describes Leo's idea of what love "should" feel like: an utter loss of control, tumbling headfirst, devil-may-care, us-against-the-world, romantic love. If it feels just like in the movies or the tales of old or as described in the words of long-dead poets, it must be true love. Leo women are born romantics, and in an era of hooking up, they cherish the noble idea of courtship. In Leo's mind, proper courtship sets her love above the tawdry flings and everyday mundane love that everyone else experiences. This is not to say that the Leo woman doesn't exercise her sexual prowess when it suits her—she is a huntress, after all—and has a formidable sexual appetite, but when she is truly interested in someone, she craves all the moments of intrigue and drama, the exquisite torture that is *longing*. Exhilarating highs and lows only prove to her that it's the real thing. The phrase *grand passion* was likely coined by a Leo lover, replete with all the drama, torment, and proof of devotion one would expect. Leo women are often drawn to the concepts of soul mates and the one true love.

For all her love of grandiose gestures and dramatic declarations, the Leo woman is also deeply devoted, warm hearted, and truly affectionate. Once she commits, Leo is amongst the most loyal of all the signs and will often put her love on a pedestal. In turn, she needs respect, admiration, and to feel appreciated. She will not suffer indignity. She is proud and hot-tempered and will not put up with ill treatment in any form. She is a Queen, after all. Even in a long-term relationship, Leo will not settle for the mundane or mind-numbing routine. She delights in romantic surprises and gestures that show her that you still think she is number one. Many Leos desire marriage when they have found "the one." Of course, the wedding will be appropriately lavish, sparing no expense. Alternatively, she may opt for a smaller wedding, perhaps in a gracious countryside setting with imaginative personal touches and the kind of rustic charm that evokes storybook magic.

The Leo woman has a great deal of sexual charisma and a strong sex drive. She is sexually confident and can also be dominant. Knowing she is desirable is like an aphrodisiac to her, and some Leos enjoy putting on a show to show you just how hot they really are. Some Leos enjoy dressing up and role play as an expression of their inherent creative and dramatic flair. Lingerie, wigs, and costumes are all part of the fun. She may be sexually adventurous, but it's not usually to please someone else. It's part of her self-image as a sexy, desirable woman. She can also be highly competitive and will sometimes engage in sexual scenarios where she can be the center of attention. However, Leo's famous claws can come out if she finds she is not the star in the room. Fair warning: Leo's jealousy is formidable, and it's best not to play with fire.

Another face of Leo's erotic nature is connected to her affinity for luxury and extravagance. Rose petals on the bed, champagne in an ice bucket, and a five-star hotel room are true turn-ons for some Leos. They adore being swept off their feet in grand style.

With Leo's formidable repertoire of myriad talents, innate creative ability, and fierce ambition, she can turn her hand to just about any career and succeed to the point where she receives the recognition she craves. Whatever paths they choose to explore, many Leo women become subject matter experts in their field. A few even achieve a degree of fame or celebrity, because when Leo is working in accordance with her heart, she shines. Leo could be a star in the entertainment industry, either as an actor, performer, or musician, but could just as easily sparkle in the role of director, promoter, or publicist. She could also work in the industry as part of the creative team as a makeup artist, hairstylist, set designer, or costume designer. Fashion is another area the Leo woman often shines in, and she may be drawn to a successful career as a designer, illustrator, photographer, or personal stylist. With her affinity for children, play, and fun, she could flourish as a children's author, play therapist, coloring book creator, or game developer. And, of course, her creative abilities would be well matched to a career in any of the creative fields, such as fine arts, writing, poetry, dance, expressive arts therapy, tattoo art, event planning, or interior design. Her natural aptitude for leadership would make Leo a great CEO or brilliant creative director.

## Guiding Goddess Archetype: Rhiannon

Of the many goddesses across the mythological traditions around the world that exemplify Leo's characteristics, Rhiannon from the Welsh *Mabinogion* came to me in meditation as I was writing this chapter. Not only is Rhiannon a sovereignty goddess whose name means "great queen," but she is also closely associated with horses (a solar animal) and inextricably connected to Sun symbolism, which is woven throughout her stories. As we will see, she also demonstrates an array of other Leo correspondences: she is strategic, creative, confident, and lives from her heart.

The great Lord Pwyll of Dyfed rides out one summer morning and comes to the faery mound Gorsedd Arberth, where legend had it that one would either be attacked or witness a marvel. Pwyll, being a great hero and warrior, is unafraid and thinks to himself that he would quite like to witness a marvel. He waters his horse and hounds, sits down in the soft green grass, and waits.

Presently, the most beautiful woman he has ever seen rides slowly by him on a pale horse. She is bathed in golden light and dressed in sumptuous silk the color of the sun, and her long flaxen tresses shimmer with an otherworldly incandescence. Birds fly about her singing the sweetest of songs. Pwyll leaps on his horse and canters after her. Although her horse is walking slowly, no matter how hard Pwyll rides after her, she keeps a maddening few paces ahead, and he cannot reach her. Finally, after three days of pursuing her, Pwyll implores her to stop so that he may speak to her. She turns to him, smiling, and answers that if only he would have asked earlier, she would have gladly stopped, and he might have spared his horse.

She introduces herself to him as Rhiannon, daughter of Heveydd Hen, King of the Otherworld. She informs Pwyll that she has come seeking him, as she has heard of his exploits and has decided that he is the man of her heart. Although she is betrothed to another, she will marry no one else unless Pwyll rejects her, and she has come for his answer. Pwyll can scarcely believe his good fortune and declares that if he had his choice of any maiden in the world, he would choose only her as his queen. Satisfied, Rhiannon states that if this is what he truly feels, he is to meet her at her father's palace in one year's time and they would be wed.

The two part and Rhiannon returns to her otherworldly realm. And to be sure, they long for each other more with each passing day. Finally, the time comes and Pwyll enters the world of Faery to claim his bride. There is great rejoicing. A magnificent feast is prepared, and Pwyll is heartily welcomed. After the feast, a tall young man in royal garb enters the hall. The youth addresses Pwyll, announcing that he has come to ask a favor. Pwyll, feeling giddy with joy on his wedding day, answers that whatever is in his power to grant, he will gladly give. Rhiannon gasps and looks at her husband in disbelief. The young man looks fixedly at Pwyll, his lips curling into a sadistic smile, and tells Pwyll he has come to ask for the hand of Rhiannon. Rhiannon turns to Pwyll and admonishes him for speaking so loosely, explaining that this is the man to whom she had been betrothed. Pwyll is horrified at his foolishness, but Rhiannon takes him aside and whispers that she will find a way to fix the situation. She will agree to marry the youth in one year's time, but she will make sure the marriage does not come to pass. She hands

Pwyll a small bag, instructing him to be at her father's hall again in one year and to bring with him the bag and one hundred of his most trusted knights.

One year later, as Rhiannon is about to be wed, Pwyll shows up at the wedding feast disguised as a beggar, his knights secreted away in the orchard. He takes out the small bag that Rhiannon has entrusted him with and requests that the groom-to-be fill it for him with food from the feasting table. As it is his wedding day, he grants the boon, but no matter how much food is placed in the bag, it does not fill up. Pwyll then tricks him into jumping on top of the bag by telling him it won't be full until a man of noble birth and wealth steps on the bag and claims it full, and the bag magickally swallows him up. Pwyll calls for his knights, and they beat the man in the bag until he cries for mercy and relinquishes his claim on Rhiannon.

Pwyll and Rhiannon are finally wed, and they set forth for his kingdom, where she is welcomed by his people as his queen. She generously gifts his courtiers with jewels and lavish adornments, and she and Pwyll live together happily for two years.

In their third year, Rhiannon finally gives birth to a long-awaited heir. On the night of her son's birth, Rhiannon sleeps beside his cradle with six handmaidens in attendance. In the middle of the night, one of the maids wakes from having fallen asleep on her watch to discover that the baby has disappeared. Terrified, she and the other maids devise a plan to save themselves from punishment for their negligence, whereby they kill a puppy and smear the blood on Rhiannon's cheeks and mouth, thus accusing her of killing her own son. When she awakes in the morning to find her son missing, the serving women tell her they fought her all night and that she ate her own child. Rhiannon, being of generous heart, tells them if they are telling this story out of fear of punishment, she would defend them, but the maids stick with their deceitful tale.

Although his advisors urge Pwyll to be rid of his otherworldly wife, Pwyll loves Rhiannon with all his heart and refuses to divorce her. Instead, he orders that Rhiannon do penance for seven years. Each day she is to sit at a horse block near the castle gate and tell her story to each person who entered. She is also to offer to carry each guest into the hall on her back, as though she herself were a horse. Rhiannon bears her penance with grace and dignity, and all who come to the castle are impressed with her fortitude and can see that she is innocent. Thus, her story is spread far and wide across the kingdom.

Meanwhile, one of Lord Pwyll's subjects finds a beautiful baby with hair of gold tucked in his horse barn. He and his wife raise the child as if he were their own. As the man ponders the sad story of beautiful Rhiannon doing penance for a crime she did not likely commit, he looks closely at the growing boy, and it comes to him that the child he is raising resembles Pwyll in a most extraordinary way. He takes the boy to the palace, and there is great rejoicing in the land. Rhiannon's punishment comes to an end, and she is both exonerated and reunited with her son. The kingdom enjoys prosperity and happiness for many years, and their son grows to be a great hero.[23]

Rhiannon's connections to the Leo archetype are abundant. Not only is she both a queen and goddess of sovereignty, she is also a sun goddess, and Leo's ruling planet is the sun itself. Further echoing the attributes of Leo, she is confident and bold, choosing whom she would marry despite having already been betrothed to another—she has agency. She is also connected to the idea of true love and the quest to be with her beloved against all odds, another Leo motif. Rhiannon is no shrinking violet, and she demonstrates a feisty sensibility when she rebukes Pwyll on two separate occasions: first, when she chides him for not simply asking her to stop and speak to him, and, second, when Pwyll foolishly promises anything to the unwelcome guest at their wedding. She does not just sit there and shiver in woe; she comes up with a plan. She is both proactive and visionary. Rhiannon also corresponds with the inherent generosity of Leo: she gives lavish gifts to the people of Dyfed and then offers to defend her maidservants if they tell the truth. Finally, although she must serve

---

23. Charlotte Guest, trans., *The Mabinogion* (London: J. M. Dent & Sons, 1906; New York: Dover, 1997), 1–15.

penance for a crime she did not commit, she does not play the victim but instead stays true to herself and bears her situation with her head held high and her integrity intact. Echoing the fixed nature of Leo, Rhiannon exhibits perseverance and faith in love and life, even through the bleakest of times. Call on Rhiannon when you need the extra confidence to act on a situation or when you need to recharge your self-esteem and speak your truth.

## Pathworking: Rhiannon's Gift

*The first rose-gold rays of dawn illuminate the sky, and the velvety blackness of night is giving way to soft shades of pearlescent gray and deepest azure, as the Sun is just about to slip over the eastern horizon. You have been sitting vigil through the night on this grassy hillside to catch the sunrise, and from your vantage point you see the rolling green countryside that undulates into the distance in all directions around you. Your vitality and confidence have been flagging lately, and your inner flame seems more like the embers of a dying fire. It seems as if you have been encountering one obstacle after another, and you have come here hoping for perspective.*

*Birds begin their morning courting music, and it's as though time is standing still during this liminal moment between night and day. Something catches your eye to your left, and you sense movement behind the hazelnut trees. A woman on a pale horse rides out from behind the hedgerow, bathed in an otherworldly glow from the rising Sun. For a moment, you are stunned to see someone out riding so early. You call a soft morning greeting to her, and she stops, turns, and then rides slowly toward you. You realize this is no ordinary woman out on a morning errand. She has the bearing of a queen, resplendent in silk, her head held high and her red-gold hair like a dazzling aura around her. The golden light seems to be coming as much from her as it is from the approaching sunrise. She smiles at you and leans down to extend her hand. You take it, and the goddess Rhiannon pulls you up in front of her onto the horse.*

*Together you ride to the other side of the mound, where you come upon a gnarled old hawthorn guarding the entrance to an opening in the hill. The tree is decorated with all manner of offerings: ribbons, shimmering crystals tied on strings, scraps of weathered fabric that must have been left here years before. You feel compelled to leave your own offering here and slide down from the mare to approach the tree. You reach deep into your pockets for something to offer, but your pockets are empty. You turn to Rhiannon, who has dismounted and is now standing beside you. Her eyes are amber in the light of the coming dawn. She unfastens a small golden velvet drawstring pouch from her waist and places it in your hands.*

*"This contains your spark, your sacred inner fire—guard it well. As long as you remember that no matter how dark the night, the Sun always rises, your heart will never be empty. As long as you keep faith and be true to your own heart, I will always be here for you. As long as you speak your truth and take action when it is needed, you will always have sovereignty of self," she says. She leaps up onto her tall white horse and gives you a dazzling parting smile, riding into the blinding brilliance of the newly risen Sun.*

*You reach into the pouch and pull out a piece of citrine. You hold it up to the golden light, and it explodes into a rainbow of colors. You make your way back with your head held high, ready to face the new day with your spark reignited and the knowledge that you have been gifted sovereignty by the Queen of the Land herself.*

## Ritual: Awaken Your Inner Queen

Leo resonates with the archetype of the Queen: she has that inner core of strength and self-worth, personal sovereignty, and the willingness to act on one's own behalf. Look to your chart to see what house the Sun is in; this life area is one in which you have the potential to shine and where you may need to awaken your inner queen in order to step into your power with equal measures of grace and confidence. You may want to cultivate the matters of this life area, as it is the realm where you are likely to achieve special recognition, love, and abundance.

### Leo Sun Queen Incense

1 part each:

   Frankincense

   Cinnamon

   Ginger

   Sweet orange

### Rhiannon's Magick Bag

The magick bag Rhiannon gives to Pwyll is akin to the magick talisman that saves the day in the greatest hour of need. Interestingly, beautiful embellished bags were often given as wedding gifts in early Medieval times from the groom to the bride-to-be. It is rather fitting that Rhiannon gives the bag to Pwyll, rather than the other way around, given her bold and outspoken character. You can either purchase a small bag or find some material you like and sew your own. Fabric colors that resonate with the symbolism of the Sun are especially suitable: gold, yellow, red, and orange. White is also connected to Rhiannon's symbolism. You may also wish to embellish your bag with a symbol, either painted or glued on, that aligns with Leo or Rhiannon: a horse, birds, the Leo symbol, the astrological glyph for the Sun, a heart, or a crown. I have a round copper earring about the size of a silver dollar—embossed with Celtic horses—that I glued onto my Rhiannon bag as a centerpiece. For best results, craft your Rhiannon bag during Leo season or when the Moon is in Leo. Charge it by laying it in the full rays of the Sun for three days if possible. This magickal bag is a reminder that at all times, you carry with you all that you need. Keep it on your altar, or use it in personal ceremony.

### Awaken Your Inner Queen

Cape or other hooded garment

Small tapered gold or yellow candle

Leo Sun Queen Incense

Paper

Pen

Rhiannon's Magick Bag

Symbol of sovereignty: necklace or ring

Remember, Leo loves drama. Leo likes to play and make things special. For this ritual, any extra effort in set decoration is all part of focusing the energies. Go all out. Set your altar up with symbols of the Queen. Drape it in Sun colors: gold, yellow, amber. You can also incorporate purple into your altar colors, as purple has been a symbolic color of royalty since Roman times. Wear something that makes you feel extra queenly, perhaps a cape or other garment with a hood.

Carve a symbol that resonates with Leo into the candle. Light it. Meditate on the flame and visualize what it would look like if you were standing gracefully in your power. Feel the warmth and illumination of the flame transfer to your solar plexus chakra, the seat of your personal power, and then into your heart. Feel these two power centers connected—heart and will. Write down three things you would do if you were acting as Queen of your own life. State these aloud, and pass the paper through the smoke of the incense three times. Fold it carefully seven times and place it in your Rhiannon bag. Remember, this bag is imbued with the magick of the Otherworld and contains all that you need. Take the ring or necklace and pass it through the incense three times to consecrate it, stating aloud,

> *This ring/necklace is an outer symbol of my inner sovereignty. By Rhiannon, by Maeve, by the Morrigan, I align myself with the Queen within and take my goddess-given power to rule my life with grace, dignity, love, and compassion. So be it.*

Put the ring or necklace on, take off your hood, and arise. Close the circle and thank the deities invoked. Although you can wear the necklace or ring all the time if you wish, wear it for at least three days and then keep it in your Rhiannon bag until you need it to boost your self-confidence or need to take action and call your leadership qualities to the fore.

# Leo Correspondences

*Astrological Dates:* July 23 through August 22

*Sabbat:* Lughnasadh / Lammas

*Leo Goddess Archetypes:* Rhiannon, Bastet, Sekhmet, Queen Maeve, Olwen, the Morrigan, Durga, Cybele, Hathor, Qudsu, Amaterasu, Saule

*House:* Fifth

*Element:* Fire

*Mode:* Fixed

*Planet:* Sun

*Colors:* Gold, yellow, red, orange, amber

*Crystals:* Carnelian, citrine, danburite, rhodochrosite, ruby, sunstone, tiger's eye

*Essential Oils:* Benzoin, cinnamon, frankincense, nutmeg, orange, lemon, ginger, tangerine

*Parts of the Body:* Heart, spine, upper back

# VIRGO

The celebratory, sun-drenched days of Leo give way to the second of the threshold seasons. Virgo is summer transitioning into autumn, and this energy is indelibly imprinted into the archetype, which gives way to the mercurial nature in the Virgo personality. There is now an imperceptible shimmer of gold beneath the riotous green that has held sway for the past few months. Virgo is a mutable earth sign, meaning it bridges one season into the next, and resonates with the practical, realistic element of earth. The Virgo archetype is tied to the preparation for harvest. We begin the task of separating the grain from the chaff in our lives. What will we harvest? What will we turn back into the soil to be used as compost for next year's crops? It is a natural time of weighing and evaluating, sifting and sorting. Virgo season has often been equated as the time we clean up after the party that is Leo. It's true that at this time of year, many of us are getting ready to go back to school or work after enjoying the pleasures of summer. There is a simultaneous burst of purposeful activity and organization, as well as a subtle turning within as we prepare for the longer nights ahead.

Virgo relates to the archetype of the Virgin goddess, and no matter how devoted Virgo can be to the people in her life, a certain part of Virgo's psyche will always remain unaffected by the opinions or influence of others. Virgo embodies the aspect of the priestess that is self-purified and dedicated to practical ways of serving the Goddess. To Virgo, the body truly is a temple, and daily ritual and spiritual practice connect her to the innate wisdom of the body as well as allow her to cultivate a deep reverence for the cycles of nature. Virgo aligns with the archetype of the Healer and aspects of the Shaman. She also conjures the motif of the Wise Woman living in a cottage in the woods, crafting healing elixirs and herbal remedies from what grows in her well-tended garden.

Service is a spiritual practice for Virgo. Part of her life purpose lies in improving, purifying, and edifying—not rushing in and rescuing like Aries or being a hero like Leo, but being of use. Virgo resonates with the focused yet humble spiritual archetype of the Zen master. This old Zen adage sums up Virgo's approach to both life and her personal spirituality: "Before enlightenment, chop wood, carry water. After enlightenment, chop wood, carry water." Essentially, the meaning of this proverb is mindfully embracing even the most mundane activities in life as an integral part of spiritual enlightenment; there is no separation between the practicalities of daily life and the spiritual. Virgo brings to mind the quiet contemplation of monastic life and is connected to the tarot card the Hermit. This does not mean that she is destined to spend her life alone but that she is discriminating about what influences and individuals she will allow into her world. Virgo is inextricably tied to the concept of personal boundaries and is not afraid to say no to that which does not make sense to her.

## The Virgo Woman

The Virgo woman is born under one of the most misunderstood signs of the zodiac. Contrary to pop-astrology lore, she is neither boring nor prudish. Truth be told, the Virgo woman often has an earthy sensuality that gives Scorpio a run for her money. She is also highly intelligent and sharply analytical, which are a far cry from the dull Virgo stereotype that is often bandied about on the internet. Part of the reason for her undeserved reputation comes from the misunderstanding of the symbol of her sign, the Virgin. When it's taken out of context from its original mythic meaning of "whole unto herself," the Virgin brings up visions of an inexperienced, uptight, straightlaced, and puritanical woman who is disconnected from her sexual nature. There are many virgin goddesses throughout numerous mythological traditions. Notable virgin goddesses in the Greek pantheon are Artemis, Athena, and Hestia. The main defining characteristic of the virgin goddesses is that they did not marry or have children. In the patriarchal society of ancient Greece, women were considered the property of men and were not a viable part of social life. Women's main role in life was to bear and raise their husband's children. To be a virgin goddess, not beholden to any male authority, was to have a kind of freedom not known to most mortal women. Because they were not preoccupied with the business of procreation and marriage or the distractions of romantic love, these goddesses embody a myriad of other attributes, such as independence, strategy, and self-governance. So in terms of Virgo the Virgin, let us redefine the meaning of the word so it is closer in definition to its original meaning. This is not to say that Virgo women cannot have children or successful marriages, but these things are not the only way she measures success, nor are they necessarily driving forces in her life. She is her own woman: complete, self-sufficient, autonomous.

The Virgo woman is a perfectionist and knows that everything (including herself) has room for improvement. Many Virgo women spend a great deal of time and energy in the quest of self-development, taking classes, workshops, and webinars in the pursuit to better themselves. Virgo has a discerning eye for detail, and if something is out of place in her life or in her environment, it will not escape her attention. The old adage "God(dess) is in the details" is like a Virgo mantra. Her connection to the harvest, especially the aspect of separating grain from chaff, gifts her with an analytical mind that clearly sees what is useful and what is excessive or a waste of time. She is constantly honing her skills, her work, and herself. The alchemical work of streamlining, clarifying, and shaping her psyche is rooted in her connection to her ruling planet, Mercury, whose deity is associated with alchemy and magick amongst other attributes. Because Virgo is an earth sign, she channels Mercury's energy in a practical way, constant perfecting, polishing, and fine-tuning, which is part of Virgo's higher spiritual purpose.

Health is one area of self that Virgo is especially prone to perfecting and is where she can be her most stereotypically obsessive. Whether she is in a healthcare or healing field professionally, Virgo is often an expert on everything from Ayurveda to vitamins. She can be an obsessive label reader and usually knows the exact origins of what she chooses to put into her body. She knows her way around the natural foods store like the back of her hand and is often on a special diet, being in tune with her body and exactly what it needs to run optimally. She is an advocate of whole foods and organic, non-GMO farming practices—she does her research and will tell you everything you could possibly want to know on the subjects. Most Virgos are also highly sensitive and cannot abide harsh chemicals in their skin-care products, housecleaning products, or furniture. She prefers pure and natural and will go the extra mile to make sure she and her loved ones have only the best organic clothing, bedding, and food. Virgo is also a regular at the gym or the yoga studio and often schedules massage and acupuncture treatments to keep her body running like a fine-tuned machine. A Virgo likely coined the phrase "an ounce of prevention is worth a pound of cure."

The Virgo woman is rarely caught without a plan, and you will never hear her say, "We'll just see how it goes" or "Let's just wing it!" She is obsessive about order and abhors devil-may-care improvisation or spontaneity. She is a natural list maker and feels a sense of calm and accomplishment when she puts a neat little checkmark beside items on her to-do list. She has a talent for organization and can magically transform even the most hectic environment into a smoothly running machine. To Virgo, the act of preparation is akin to performing a sacred ritual that will ward off chaos. In fact, Virgo women are intrinsically drawn to practical forms of ritual; it helps them focus and enter a meditative state of mind. Whether she performs a daily morning grooming ritual before leaving the house or lights incense and puts on her favorite music to clean the kitchen, Virgo elevates everyday tasks into an art form.

The Virgo woman is keenly observant and sees the world without romantic illusions clouding her view. To some, her no-nonsense, realistic appraisal may seem cold or judgmental, but to her it is an efficient and logical approach to life. Virgo has a highly developed faculty for critical thinking, and she is often accused of being skeptical. This is not the woman who will buy into anything without having done her research or due diligence, be it a spiritual path or an insurance policy. She is not gullible, and she is rarely naïve. To Virgo, if something sounds too good to be true, it usually is. She is not prone to idle fantasy or escapist delusions, in part because she finds them a waste of time, but also because indulging in psychological opiates would distract her from the real work of improving something to the point where it achieves her high standards.

Virgo is smart as a whip and, due to her Mercury-ruled nature, often has the vocabulary to back it up. She integrates all those self-improvement classes and webinars and classifies all the information into a formidable whole. She is both capable and efficient and often has a repertoire of useful skills that at times make her seem almost superhuman and can have other signs feeling less than "adult" around her. However, she does have a great sense of humor, although she usually is drawn to sarcastic or observational humor. She herself is also quite funny, but beware—her laser-like ability to notice subtle things about others combined with her critical mind can make some people uncomfortable. Remember, one of Mercury's aspects is the Trickster, and he can bestow a way with words that rivals the best stand-up comics.

Of course, every sign has its shadow, and Virgo is no exception. The shadow side of Virgo surfaces when her natural predispositions are taken to the extreme. When she is feeling overwhelmed or unbalanced, her critical thinking may turn inward and become self-doubt. Some Virgos are overly self-critical and may suffer from body image issues. She might zero in on one particular detail of her appearance and obsess about it to the point of seeking cosmetic surgery to "correct" it. In the pursuit of bodily perfection, some Virgos drive themselves mercilessly at the gym to meet a standard that can only be achieved through airbrushing and Photoshop. In her pursuit of perfection in her work, she can burn herself out, with no amount of effort resulting in reaching her impossible standards.

Bouts of self-doubt can also turn her wonderfully analytical mind into a tool for self-deprecation, which can lead to anxiety and obsessive thinking. Although any sign can suffer from obsessive-compulsive disorder, Virgo can be especially predisposed to its tendencies. In an unconscious effort to analyze, organize, and control her environment, Virgo sometimes develops anxiety-relieving rituals, such as repetitive checking, counting, and ordering, when she's feeling overwhelmed. Although Virgo is an earth sign, it is also a mutable sign and has the tendency to become ungrounded, scattered, or anxious when out of balance. Virgo's sensitive nervous system benefits greatly from mindfulness meditation, grounding exercises, and channeling her need for ritual into a conscious daily practice. Meditation, good nutrition, avoidance of stimulants, and flower essences such as Bach's Rescue Remedy can also help. Making lists can get it out of her head and onto the paper, which can go a long way in helping Virgo find moments of relaxation. In addition, Virgo can also tap into the qualities of her opposite sign, Pisces, and consciously work on the art of letting go of that which she cannot control. Virgo must remember that the task of weaving shadow and light equals wholeness.

Virgo's natural discernment is no more evident than in the area of love and relationships. Much like the virgin goddesses, being part of a couple is not usually her main drive. For the most part, she tends to approach love with both eyes open and without romantic projections or illusions. It is very difficult to seduce a Virgo woman or sweep her off her feet. She is rather coolheaded in romance and may initially appear detached. Virgo is generally sensible and levelheaded when it comes to relationships, and her relationships are rarely based solely on romantic attraction. While other signs may pine away for dashing but unobtainable lovers or move from one serious relationship to the next so as not to be alone, many Virgo women are content to live a full life on their own until they meet someone with whom a relationship makes sense. When Virgo does find someone that she considers committing to, she is a devoted and engaged partner and will show her affection through useful and practical gestures that demonstrate she cares. She is not prone to public displays of affection and can be embarrassed by grandiose proof of devotion. Virgo is a supportive mate, sometimes to the extreme. Her well-meaning ideas on how her partner can improve some aspect of their lives can be perceived as controlling or criticism, especially by the more independent signs.

Sexually, Virgo is a technically proficient lover. Contrary to her undeserved reputation as a prude, her attention to detail and desire to master everything she does often make her a brilliant sex partner. What she may lack in creativity or unbridled passion, she makes up for with techniques and positions that may shock even the most amorous signs. Her sexual health is often fastidious, and if it is a new relationship, don't be surprised if she expects you to come back from the doctor with a clean bill of health before sleeping with you. Virgo's alignment with the earth element also means she is attuned with her sensual nature and is no stranger to the physical realm and the things of the body. To Virgo, the body truly is a temple, and she will often pride herself on being healthy and fit, taking scrupulously good care of herself. Some Virgo women make their physicality and sexual attractiveness part of their craft and raise the bar to a whole new level. Notable Virgos that knock over the uptight librarian stereotype include Beyoncé, Raquel Welch, Salma Hayek, Cameron Diaz, Sophia Loren, and Greta Garbo. However, far from being either prudes or sex goddesses, most Virgo women have a very matter-of-fact attitude toward sex and the stuff of the body. Not the luxurious sensuality of Taurus or the seething sex appeal of Scorpio—just pure, natural, and uncomplicated.

On the other hand, there are some Virgo women for whom sex is not a driving factor in life. Parallel to the virgin goddesses, she can be self-contained. She may not be a virgin, but she is autonomous and often concentrated on other areas of life—she quite simply has other priorities. She may choose conscious celibacy for short or long periods of time, as she focuses inward, and finds her own path to fulfillment and awakening. Some Virgo women are drawn to a spiritual path where the body as temple means self-purification and dedication to a way of life that may preclude sex for the sake of sex. They may also choose to eschew alcohol, technology, or dietary substances such as meat and sugar to further facilitate connection with the still point within. The Zen monastery, certain yogic paths, the Christian convent, or other forms of cloistered spiritual study may be the call she answers.

The concepts of right livelihood and meaningful work are an integral part of Virgo's life purpose. She also has an inborn need to serve in a way that contributes to the greater good. Although as an employee she is reliable and humble and has impeccable standards, service is a concept that is easily misunderstood. Virgo's desire to serve does not mean that she wants to literally be a servant, although old-school astrology and many pop astrology columns certainly seem to think that this is her role in the zodiac. I think it's time to update this, just as it's time to update the outdated notion that it's hard to be an Aries woman because she has natural leadership skills. The sign Virgo's archetypal connection to service stems from the Vestal Virgins of ancient Rome. For over a thousand years, these priestesses were chosen between the ages of six and ten to serve the goddess Vesta by tending the sacred flame that would ensure the continuation of the empire. As Vesta was the goddess of the hearth, the Vestal Virgins were essentially the sacred hearth keepers for all of Rome. Amongst their other duties were preparation of ritual food, maintenance of sacred objects in the sanctuary, and, perhaps most importantly, keeping their vow of chastity. Although the terms of their contract stated that they were to remain celibate in service of the goddess for thirty years, they enjoyed privileges that were not the norm for women at the time. For one thing, as they were considered married to Rome, they were not under the control of a father or husband. They could own property, and their persons were protected under law. However, if it was suspected or proven that a Vestal Virgin lost her virginal status, she would be severely punished and in some cases buried alive for her transgression, as it was considered taboo to spill the blood of a priestess of Vesta.

In terms of vocation, the Virgo woman's on-target sensibility and sharp eye would make her an exceptional editor, proofreader, researcher, statistician, systems analyst, or auditor. That same meticulous attention to detail would also make her a brilliant surgeon. With her exceptional organizational ability, she is often a sought-after executive assistant, or she might channel this superpower into a successful career helping others clear and organize their clutter. On the other hand, her connection to the body opens up careers in the healing arts, such as teaching yoga, herbalism, making natural products, and hands-on healing work like massage or acupuncture. Further, she may find a fulfilling career in health and medicine as a naturopath, nutritionist, fitness instructor, physician, or veterinarian. She can also make a down-to-earth sex educator. Virgo's reverence for nature may draw her to holistic living and turning her talents to homesteading, organic farming, landscaping, animal care, beekeeping, and horticulture. Virgos also make exceptional craftswomen. Whatever medium calls her, she has the attention to detail as well as the patience and drive for perfection that produces sought-after, high-quality artisan work. Whatever Virgo does, she does well and often elevates it to a whole new level of perfection. Once she has found her calling, she aligns herself so completely with her work that it becomes synonymous with her identity.

Virgo tends to work well on her own, with minimal supervision. Even if she is part of a team, she needs solitude to focus. For this reason, Virgo excels in a work situation where she can preserve and control the quality and environment of her work. Many Virgo women appreciate quiet working environments where they can concentrate on the task at hand. A calm work space also helps her keep her anxiety at bay. The Virgo woman can also happily work behind the scenes or in a support role. She does not need to be the center of attention or receive personal glory for her work, but she does appreciate respect.

## Guiding Goddess Archetype: Hestia

Hestia is one of the three virgin goddesses from the Greek pantheon and is the first daughter of Kronos and Rhea. Both Poseidon and Apollo desire her, but with Zeus's blessing Hestia rejects both suitors and instead chooses eternal virginity, thus preventing rivalry between the two gods. In gratitude for her keeping the peace, Zeus honors Hestia by making her one of the most important deities in ancient Greece: every home and temple has a shrine to her, and she is honored with the first offerings of any sacrifice. Hestia embodies the hearth fire itself, and as such she is the very center of family life. Although the hearth is a gathering place and provides heat and the means to cook food, it is also an altar: it holds the sacred fire that represents the soul of the home and the innermost circle of the sanctuary. In later times, the Roman equivalent of Hestia, Vesta, is also the goddess of the hearth. Her perpetual fire is tended by the Vestal Virgins and is considered the collective heart and hearth of the entire city.

There were numerous rituals connected with Hestia. Moving to a new home, marriages, and consecrating the birth of a child were all accompanied by rituals that invoked Hestia's blessings. When a new colony was built, fire was taken from the central hearth fire of the host city to light and bless the new village. When a woman married, her family would light a torch from their own hearth fire and light the very first fire in the new couple's home. Underlining the magickal or ritual use of the hearth fire, in *The Greek Myths* Robert Graves speaks of the connection between the Great Goddess of the Mediterranean and the charcoal mound, or hearth. He describes how a prophetess would induce trance through inhaling the smoke of barley grains, hemp, and laurel, which were warmed over the fire to produce visions.[24]

Although Virgo is an earth sign and Hestia is associated with fire, there are many parallels between Virgo and Hestia. The most obvious is that both are identified with the Virgin archetype. Both are self-contained and autonomous, without the need or desire for personal glorification. In *Goddesses in Everywoman,* author Dr. Jean Shinoda Bolen refers to Hestia as "Hestia, Goddess of the Hearth and Temple, Wise Woman and Maiden Aunt," all apt epithets for the Virgo archetype.[25] Virgo's propensity to work behind the scenes suggests a self-effacing or humble quality that she shares with Hestia. Hestia's synthesis of the everyday and the sacred, which are embodied by the hearth fire, echo Virgo's pro-

24. Robert Graves, *The Greek Myths*, rev. ed. (Harmondsworth, UK: Penguin, 1960), PDF e-book, chap. 20.

25. Jean Shinoda Bolen, *Goddesses in Everywoman* (New York: Harper & Row, 1984), 111.

pensity to find spiritual sustenance in the mundane—both Hestia and Virgo are connected to the rituals of daily life. And finally, Hestia and Virgo share an ability to create and maintain personal boundaries. Virgo is known for her ability to say no, to draw the line in any situation that does not work for her. Similarly, Hestia said no to the attentions of both Poseidon and Apollo and chose eternal virginity as her path.

## Pathworking: Hestia's Hearth

The first time I met Hestia, I was in the integration phase of my Saturn return. I had recently extricated myself from an abusive marriage and was rebuilding my life from the ground up. This was the era of Lilith Fair, back in the late nineties, and I felt a quiet, nurturing support with all the women's music and poetry that embodied that time. More than that, I felt that I had crossed a threshold into a place of peace and solitude: the incredible sense of being alone, or *all one*. There was no one to placate. No one's mess to clean up, and no need to walk on eggshells. I was completely self-sufficient, and my time was filled with the calming everyday tasks of getting my house in order on my own terms. When I reflect on that time now, it glows with quiet magic and a centered feeling of serenity.

*You are walking through a noisy, bustling cityscape, trying in vain to shut out the cacophony of the street vendors, the clatter of wheeled carts, and the jostling of passersby. The discord and harshness match your jangled nerves, and you yearn for a moment of respite from the tumult, both inner and outer. Ahead of you, you see what appears to be a temple. Although you are not sure if you are permitted to enter, you take a chance and quietly open the door and step across the threshold, closing the door behind you.*

*Immediately the chaos of the outside world disappears, and you find yourself in a quiet, softly lit sanctuary. The silence is soothing, and you feel yourself exhale as a sensation of calm envelops you. The subtle scent of natural incense perfumes the air. You breathe slowly for a few* moments, every breath releasing the distractions of the outside world and taking you deeper into your center. You look around you and notice that there is an order to this place of hushed serenity: the stone floors are neatly swept, and the space is uncluttered except for a wooden chair with a white cushion sitting near the fire and a simple altar before the hearth. Atop the altar is a clay vessel holding several small unlit torches.

The round hearth is in the center of the sanctum, a small fire glowing amongst the coals. Slowly, reverently, you make your way to the hearth fire and kneel before it. The fire is welcoming. Not a crackling blaze, but a steady, comforting fire that seems to have a presence of its own. As a gesture of respect, you feel moved to cover your head with the hood of the garment you are wearing and take a few moments to gaze into the dancing flames.

As you allow yourself to enter a light trance state, a voice comes to you that seems to be coming from the fire itself. It is the voice of a wise old woman that comes to you: "The three tasks before you now are simple in nature but of great importance. Your first task is to learn to find the calm within so that you can weather any storm. Your inner hearth fire is always there. You need only to seek it. Your second task is to remember that you are whole and complete, just as you are. And your third task is to honor your own boundaries, to be true to yourself without the need for the approval of others. You can always enter the temple and shut the door behind you, finding sanctuary and sustenance within. My fire belongs to all who seek it. You may take an ember with you to light your way, and if you remember my words, you will not allow it to burn out."

You bow and give thanks to Hestia, goddess of the hearth. You take a torch, light it from the hearth fire, and quietly make your way back into the world with a newfound sense of calm focus.

## Ritual: Sorting the Seeds

Virgo teaches us the value of sorting, selecting, sifting, and evaluating the things in our lives so that we may purify, prioritize, and grow as self-actualized beings. Sorting seeds is a common archetypal motif in mythology and fairy tales. The Russian tale "Vasilisa the Wise," also known as "Vasilisa the Beautiful" and "Vasilisa the Brave," tells the story of a maiden daughter sent into the forest to face the fierce Baba Yaga and bring back light for the fire. One of her tasks is sorting poppy seeds from dirt. In Greek mythology, Aphrodite also gives Psyche the impossible task of sifting and sorting a variety of seeds. And in the Grimm Brothers' version of "Cinderella," the wicked stepmother casts a bowl of lentils into the fire and assigns her the job of sorting them from the ashes to prevent her from going to the ball.

On an archetypal level, sorting the seeds is the first step toward forward motion and psychic growth. Seeds symbolize potential and possibility, and when we take the time to sort them, we decide what is important, what is essential in our lives, and what is dross. In *Women Who Run with the Wolves: Myths and Stories of the Wild Woman Archetype*, Dr. Clarissa Pinkola Estés beautifully sums up the archetypal dimension of sorting the seeds: "Like Vasalisa, we have to sort out our psychic healing agents, to sort and sort and sort to understand that food for the psyche is also medicine for the psyche, and to wring the truth, the essence, out of these elements for our own nourishment." [26]

### Hestia's Purifying Oil

1 part each:
    Rosemary
    Camphor
    Eucalyptus
    Laurel leaf

### Sorting the Seeds

Hestia's Purifying Oil
Small pure beeswax candle
An assortment of seeds: rice, beans, lentils, corn, etc. (choose two or
    more types depending on what you are sorting in your life)
Paper

---

26. Estés, *Women Who Run with the Wolves*, 100.

Pen

Digging implement

First, clear your space by burning Hestia's Purifying Oil. Ground and center. Anoint the candle with Hestia's oil and light it: this is her hearth fire. Meditate on the flame and find your center. Spread the seeds on the floor before you or on an altar or table. When you are ready, take the paper and pen and make two or more category headings. Each type of seed symbolizes one category. You can write "Harvest" and "Release," or you may want to be more specific depending on what it is you are sorting. Write down your specifics in each category. When you are ready, call on Hestia and say,

> *Hestia, lady of purity, integrity, and personal boundaries,*
> *Help me to sort the seeds in my life.*
> *What to harvest, what to release and give back*
> *to the earth that it may be recycled.*
> *May my life be designed by divine order.*

Mindfully sort the seeds into piles. Each seed represents a potential, a possibility, or an actuality in your life. Give thanks for what you are harvesting and for that which you choose to continue to nurture. Reflect on that which you now see needs to be sacrificed back to the earth or integrated back into the psyche. Dreams, plans, and hopes that you know need to be recycled so something new can be born. Take the seeds to be recycled and go outside and bury them for the goddess to transform them into something new. Remember, nothing is ever wasted, only transformed. Take the seeds of harvest and possibility and place them on your altar as a reminder of what is truly important in your life now. Do not extinguish the candle but let it burn out safely. Give thanks to Hestia for her wisdom.

This ritual is best done during Virgo season, when the Moon is in Virgo, or when the Moon is in its waning phase.

# Virgo Correspondences

*Astrological Dates:* August 23 through September 22

*Sabbat:* Threshold sign between Lammas and autumn equinox

*Virgo Goddess Archetypes:* Hestia, Vesta, Astraea, Hou Ji, Inari, Austeja, Airmid, Frigg, Iden-Kuva, Pszeniczna-Matka, Baculbotet

*House:* Sixth

*Element:* Earth

*Mode:* Mutable

*Planet:* Mercury

*Colors:* Pure white, green, brown, earth colors, gray, gold (the color of fields during Virgo season)

*Crystals:* Amazonite, axinite, chiastolite, jasper, peridot, petrified wood, vesuvianite

*Essential Oils:* Frankincense, peppermint, camphor, eucalyptus, cypress, rosemary, juniper

*Parts of the Body:* Digestive system, nervous system, spleen

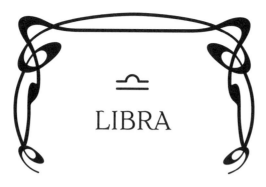

# LIBRA

Black crows dot cornflower-blue skies, and leaves edged in gold provide dazzling contrast. The mornings are noticeably cooler now, and at night we snuggle back into our favorite sweaters and kindle the first fires in our hearths. The transitional time of Virgo gives way to the next seasonal shift, and in a moment perfectly balanced between light and dark, autumn equinox heralds Libra season. Libra is a cardinal air sign, meaning that it is the gateway to a seasonal turning point (in this case, autumn) and relates to the impartial, objective element of air.

Autumn equinox is the Second Harvest. The earth is at its most abundant, and we gather baskets of apples, harvest the grapes, and celebrate this time of plenty with cozy candlelit suppers. At its core, the Libra archetype is about balance. However, on the journey to attaining that balance, Libra learns the fine art of reconciling contradiction—the ability to hold space and see all facets of a given situation. Libra is a natural bridge builder, a connector, a peacemaker. We often hear of Libra being indecisive or vacillating, unable to pick a side. This is because Libra's task is to bring things into alignment, to be objective and find the common ground.

For Libra, seeking symmetry extends to every area of life. The Libra archetype resonates with the golden ratio—the perfect relationship between two proportions. From interpersonal relationship to the relationship between line and color or form and function, Libra is an artist, and her medium is life. Many Librans are drawn to the arts in some way, and their eye for proportion, balance, and beauty shows up in the visual artist, designer, architect, and curator. And of course, Libra's ruling planet is Venus, the goddess of love and beauty, which further underlines the connection to beauty, art, and relationships. Libra is connected to Venus in her aspect as Aphrodite Urania, or "Heavenly Aphrodite," associated with the "higher" principles of love: lofty, spiritual, intellectual love as differentiated from the earthy physical love of Aphrodite Pandemos. If you think that the Libra archetype sounds rather abstract, you would be right. Libra is the only sign that is not symbolized by either an animal or human. Libra is symbolized by the scales of justice, and at its core, is aligned with the democratic concepts of equality and fairness. Although Libra is a social sign and is innately tied to the idea of relationship, there is a rational, logical impartiality about it. At its core, Libra is an idealist.

## The Libra Woman

The Libra woman can be a contradiction. On one hand, she is the epitome of what we have come to think of as stereotypically feminine: charming, gracious, and often stylish. On the other, she can also be one of the most success-driven and strategic signs in the zodiac. And, although she is a born romantic, she can also be a dyed-in-the-wool commitment-phobe. She is constantly trying to balance and align all the factors in her world so she can find the elusive state of harmony. Not too much or too little of this or that. The Libra woman is a bit like Goldilocks, looking for the porridge that is just right. Creating peace and harmony is at the heart of Libra, but sometimes in the pursuit of this ideal, her carefully balanced scales will tip one way or the other and knock over the apple cart.

Libra is a social sign. It is the evolutionary point where the soul has reached a place where it looks outside its own development and recognizes that where there is an "I," there is also an "other." Where first sign Aries is all about the birth and nurturance of the self, Libra is about "we"—the drive to form partnerships and find mutually beneficial ways to approach life. Libra is about the fine art of balancing the needs between "you and me" and finding a common purpose. In other words,

Libra is innately concerned with building relationships of all kinds, and in her pursuit of harmony, Libra has earned a well-deserved reputation for being amicable, cooperative, easygoing, and fair. She really does mean well. However, when she is acting from her shadow side, we will see that in her quest for keeping the peace, all is not always as it seems with Libra's carefully cultivated equilibrium. Keeping the peace can be hard work. Because we all have different agendas, different opinions, different ways we think life should be, there's bound to be friction in any relationship; it's simply a part of life. However, as Libra is an idealist, she doesn't agree that this necessarily needs to be the case. She reasons that if she has anything to do with it, there won't be any need for friction. She will smooth, placate, and charm. She will put on her sweetest smile and keep her opinions and feelings to herself so as not to rock the boat.

Of course, this might be called codependence. In her drive for peace and harmony at all costs, Libra can be a people pleaser. In a sense, it's a survival tactic. Somewhere along the line she learned that telling people what they want to hear can keep things running smoothly. Always smiling and being agreeable can keep everyone happy, and no one gets angry. But there is a price, and ironically the price is disharmony and internal conflict. Where do all those stuffed feelings go? They get relegated to the shadow of the psyche, where they can transform into resentment. And in turn, resentment can turn into passive-aggression and anger that erupts at a terrible time at an undeserving person. Libra needs approval, perhaps more than any other sign, and sometimes has one face that she shows the world—the calm, perennially cheerful woman who never gets ruffled—and quite another face to those she knows best. Perhaps she feels it's safe for her to vent on the people closest to her, and she finally releases all those pent-up feelings she so carefully conceals behind her public persona. However, Libra has also been known to smile agreeably in the face of discord in her personal relationships too, sometimes resorting to covert, passive-aggressive behavior in a misguided attempt to keep the peace. When she is really feeling unbalanced, instead of confronting an issue head-on, some Libras can even resort to manipulative tactics to maintain their façade of reason and poise, while making the other person look like the bad guy.

Libra must remember that her quest to attain harmony starts with herself. Instead of sublimating her own opinions, needs, and desires, she needs to take a page out of Aries's (her opposite sign) playbook. Aries is about drawing clear boundaries and speaking one's truth no matter how many feathers get ruffled in the process. In any event, Libra can learn to clearly express her own needs and opinions, which ironically will go a long way in helping her to find the peace and interpersonal harmony she craves.

For all Libra's considerable charm, she can be one of the most ambitious women in the zodiac. She has a head for strategy and a persuasive way with words. She truly is a people person and has a wonderful knack of dealing gracefully with even the most difficult situations. As an action-oriented cardinal sign, the Libra woman will usually have a game plan. Many Libras reach their desired level of financial success at a relatively early age (Venus is connected to resources and wealth), and I have worked with many Libra women who are CEOs, bosses, and managers. Libra's people skills are superlative, and it has been said more than once that Libra can be the iron fist in the velvet glove. She gets things accomplished with friendly diplomacy, and people are usually happy to do what she asks. She also has an inborn sense of fairness that can place her head and shoulders above other leaders. She abhors injustice and will work hard to make sure that her employees and colleagues are treated with respect.

Being Venus ruled, Libra women have an affinity for beauty in all its forms. She herself is usually impeccably groomed and thinks nothing of spending an afternoon at the spa. To her, it's time well spent. Libra knows that if she looks good, she feels good, and she never balks at spending money on clothing or cosmetics. To her, they are necessities, not luxuries, as pampering herself raises her self-esteem. She rarely leaves the house without having her game face on. Remember that Venus is connected to the concepts of worth and value—Libra invests in herself because it ups her sense of self-worth. She also firmly believes that if you make an effort, people will treat you better. She reasons that if you put your best foot forward, you will look successful and therefore attract better opportunities. Libra also often has good manners: she is usually courteous and well-spoken. Many Libras cannot abide anything or anyone gauche or vulgar—they have a refined sensibility and enjoy the pleasantries of polite, congenial company. Libra women often have what would be termed a "cool beauty" rather than the earthy sensuality of Taurus, the other Venus-ruled sign. Think of the elegant and sophisticated poise of Grace Kelly, who had Venus in Libra, or Dita Von Teese, the burlesque star who has graced many a best-dressed list, bringing a polished and refined aesthetic to her classic vintage style. Even the Libra women who are not into cosmetics and self-adornment (there are a few) have a certain effortless style about them that always looks on point.

The Libra woman's appreciation for beauty extends to every element of her life. Even if she's young and still on her way up, there will be a certain style evident in her environment. Even if everything she owns is from the thrift store or is recycled, she has an artistic eye and ability to source out aesthetically pleasing pieces. Whether her style is bohemian, vintage, or contemporary, she has a way of putting her space together so it looks like it's been styled for a magazine shoot. Libra is also drawn to the romantic and often has a genuine love and appreciation for the arts, including literature, music, and poetry. She may have a collection of her favorite prints on the wall or originals created either by herself or her artist friends. She herself is usually artistically gifted in some way, and whether her medium is words, clay, or canvas, Libra is the sign of the Artist.

We need to remember that Libra is here to learn about relationships; it is a major part of her life purpose. You would think that she would be all about commitment and happily ever after. She is a born romantic, after all, and needs companionship probably more than any other sign. However, Libra can also be a notorious fence-sitter when it comes to commitment. As an air sign, Libra loves the *idea* of love. She likes thinking about it, planning for it, reading articles on it, and the concept of two people living the dream, together. She adores being courted and appreciates all the little rituals that go along with it—the flowers, nice restaurants, tokens of affection. She believes in notions like true love, the one and only, and twin flames. Because she is so charming and attractive, she usually has no shortage of available suitors. Perhaps herein lies the issue: she's spoiled for choice! How does she pick one? What if someone better comes along as soon as she's made her pledge of love everlasting? Commitment usually does win out in the end. Libra is, after all, the sign of "we." She needs a partner who looks good, who smells good, and who she can be proud of. Good manners and an appreciation of culture are a definite plus. On the other hand, she also needs a partner who is intelligent, romantic, fair-minded, and balanced in their own life.

As much as Libra loves to be properly pursued and adored, she may be turned off if someone pursues her too ardently. In some cases, Libra women can get caught up in the dance of the push-pull relationship, which could also be called hide-and-seek or the chase. A push-pull relationship is counterproductive and emotionally exhausting, and it's one of the reasons it sometimes takes Libra so long to commit. Of course, underneath this dance is the fear of intimacy: as much as Libra loves love and desires companionship, she sometimes subconsciously sabotages her relationships when things start to feel too intense. When Libra finally does find the one, she commits 100 percent and usually desires marriage. Libra is, after all, *the* sign of marriage and partnership. Once she is in a committed relationship, she is a loyal, engaged, and congenial partner who knows how to keep the romance alive.

As with the other two air signs, Gemini and Aquarius, sex is more a mental turn-on. The Libra woman is playful, has a vivid imagination, and often enjoys the use of fantasy in sex. For Libra, sexual fantasy is often preferred to actually acting out the scenarios she entertains. Some enjoy mental stimulation from erotic stories, poetry, and visuals, but they must be tasteful and not in any way crass or vulgar. She loves all the trappings of proper seduction and needs beautiful surroundings, candlelight, soft music, and pillow talk to get her in the mood. She has a taste for expensive lingerie, which will always be elegant, beautiful, or vintage—never tacky. Some Libra women, given their creativity, can turn lovemaking into an art.

With her exceptional people skills, artistic flair and ambition, there are a variety of careers the Libra woman would excel in. Although she is independent and not afraid to take initiative, Libra needs to work with others to bring out her best. Libra shines in one-on-one relationships, and her aptitude for working with people would make her a first-rate therapist, especially a couples counselor. Her interest in relationships and penchant for romance could lead to a career as a wedding planner, officiant, or professional celebrant. She also makes a valuable team player, and her convivial personality as well as her grace under pressure are assets in any office setting or other environment that requires teamwork to get the job done. Libra dazzles in any role that utilizes her natural charm and charisma: she would be a natural in promotion or as the spokesperson and face of a company. She'd also excel in a sales role, perhaps in a high-end luxury industry, where her poise would be an asset.

Alternatively, Libra's leadership skills coupled with her charismatic personality could draw her to a career in politics. Because she has a thirst for justice along with a rational mind and a gift for clear communication, Libra also makes a brilliant lawyer, negotiator, arbitrator, diplomat, or judge. She would also be a top-notch advocate or social justice activist given her proclivity for fair play and equality. Libra's connection to beauty and the arts opens another host of possibilities. She can channel her natural artistic talent into a variety of media, depending on her interests. Some possibilities include design, the fine arts, merchandising, photography, architecture, or interior decorating. Libra's connection to beauty and self-adornment would make her a natural in any related field, such as hair and makeup artistry, esthetics, cosmetics representation, fashion design, or merchandising.

## Guiding Goddess Archetype: Lakshmi

Although Libra is associated with the planet Venus, specifically in her aspect as Aphrodite Urania, there are of course numerous goddesses that correspond with each sign from different cultures and pantheons.

While I was writing this chapter, the Indian goddess Lakshmi kept arising both in my meditation and in little synchronicities throughout the time I was immersed in Libra. For instance, after having gone through profound transition over the last three years, including two moves that necessitated many of my treasured belongings being placed in storage, I was delighted to finally unpack my remaining boxes and find a tiny statue of Lakshmi gifted to me long ago by a dear friend. Also amongst my recovered treasures was a painting I did of Lakshmi for a goddess-inspired art show back in 2008 that I hadn't been able to find for years!

Lakshmi does indeed resonate with many of Libra's attributes. She is the Indian goddess of beauty and abundance and is also connected with love and marriage, all of which are defining characteristics of Libra. Lakshmi is the consort and wife of the god Vishnu the Preserver. When Vishnu came to earth in his incarnation as Rama and then later as Krishna, Lakshmi also descended and joined him as Rama's wife, Sita, and then Krishna's wife, Rukmini.[27] This suggests that she is not only a goddess of wealth and prosperity, but also of love, devotion, and marriage, all of which can arguably be described as forms of abundance. In "Lakshmi: Hindu Goddess of Abundance," Constantina Rhodes states that Lakshmi and Vishnu "constitute the quintessential divine couple." Further, she adds, "It is the unified image of Lakshmi and Vishnu that also sets the paradigm for the bride and groom in the Hindu wedding ceremony."[28] The Libra archetype with its connection to relationships and marriage as a central motif reflects this essential aspect of Lakshmi.

Lakshmi is one of the most popular deities in the Hindu pantheon. Nearly every home and business has a statue or image honoring her.[29] She is worshipped year-round, but she is especially honored during the festivals of Navaratri and Diwali, the Festival of Lights. Diwali is a time of joy and plenty, for gathering together and celebrating. Before the fes-

27. Steve Rosen, *Essential Hinduism* (Santa Barbara, CA: Praeger, 2006), 72, 136, 163.

28. Constantina Rhodes, "Lakshmi: Hindu Goddess of Abundance," in *Goddesses in World Culture*, vol. 1, ed. Patricia Monaghan (Santa Barbara, CA: Praeger, 2011), 5.

29. Constantina Rhodes, *Invoking Lakshmi* (Albany: SUNY Press, 2010), 26.

tival, people thoroughly clean their homes and prepare their space to welcome Lakshmi. Lights and lamps are lit in her honor to celebrate her arrival and to dispel the darkness. Diwali takes place during the New Moon, usually in October, which is Libra season.

In her iconography, Lakshmi is depicted as a beautiful woman with a serene expression, usually dressed in an exquisite red and gold or magenta sari. Most of her images show her gracefully seated or standing in a pink lotus, adorned with jewels and surrounded by symbols of prosperity and abundance, such as gold coins and bowls of ripe fruit. Some of her depictions show her being gently showered with water by a pair of joyous elephants, indicating her embodiment as a fertility goddess, as well as her role as a provider of wealth and abundance.[30] The lotus has many layers of symbolism in Eastern mythology. The roots reach down deep into muddy water while the flower opens clean, pure, and majestic in the upper world, suggesting the balance between the fertile unconscious channeling into manifestation and beauty in the conscious world. The flower of consciousness is literally fed by the rich hidden depths just beneath the surface.

Hindu mythology is very complex. The Churning Sea of Milk is a common motif that arises in many stories involving different deities and has a long and complicated backstory. Legend has it that Lakshmi is angered by the god Indra's arrogance and leaves the earth. She, along with several other wonderful treasures, is discovered long after, when the sea is churned. It is said that upon her reemergence, she chooses Vishnu as her divine consort and is devoted to him ever after. Constantina Rhodes writes of the "four wealths" or the "four meanings" of life that are connected with Lakshmi. Rhodes states, "Let us consider the four categories to be addressed in living a balanced life: (1) *kåma*, or pleasure and enjoyment; *artha*, or material prosperity: (3) *dharma*, or virtuous conduct and harmonious relationships; and (4) *moksa*, or spiritual liberation."[31] This suggests that to live a life of abundance and wealth on all levels one

---

30. Rhodes, *Invoking Lakshmi*, 26.

31. Rhodes, *Invoking Lakshmi*, 30–31.

must be mindful of balance, which of course is also a Libra motif. Lakshmi is a divine manifestation of *Shakti* energy, the sacred feminine, and it is said that all women are an embodiment of Lakshmi.[32]

Although Lakshmi is a distinct goddess from a separate pantheon, there are some interesting correspondences between her and Aphrodite. It is said that Lakshmi arises from the Churning Milky Sea on a pink lotus. Similarly, Aphrodite is also born from the foam of the sea and floats to shore in a scallop shell. When Lakshmi arises from the Sea of Milk, she chooses Lord Vishnu as her divine consort, which reminds us of Aphrodite and her agency in choosing her own lovers. Another correlation between the two goddesses is their offspring. Lakshmi in her incarnation as Krishna's wife, Rukmini, gives birth to Pradyumna, who, according to some versions of the myth, is the reincarnation of the god of love and desire, Lord Kama, while Aphrodite is the mother of Eros, another god of love and sexual attraction.[33]

## Pathworking: Meeting the Goddess of Abundance

*You sense a change in the air. A single bird begins his morning song, and soft pink and violet tint the deep blue of the lightening sky. Stardust shimmers across the horizon, and you catch your breath to see one bright star twinkling in the east. You realize this is Venus in her guise as the morning star, bigger, brighter, and more beautiful than all the stars in the sky.*

*You begin to walk toward the low hills that she appears to be rising from. You follow a mossy path through the flowering trees, and in the distance you hear the soft sound of running water. You make your way toward the sound. The Sun is rising, and all around you everything is touched with gold. A gentle, warm breeze is coaxing an intoxicating scent from the blossoms, and each bloom is more exotic, more beautiful than the next. You bend to pick the most remarkable flower you have ever seen and tuck it into your hair, inhaling a fragrance that is sweeter*

---

32. Rhodes, *Invoking Lakshmi*, 26.

33. Rhodes, *Invoking Lakshmi*, 32.

*and more layered than any perfume. The scent envelops you, and you feel yourself carried into a deeper state of trance, yet a heightened sense of awareness.*

The path opens and you find yourself standing on the edge of a natural pool. Its softly rippling surface reflects the blush of the tie-dyed sky. There is a small waterfall feeding it, joyously bubbling, cascading over stones, like the sound of silvery laughter or the strains of shimmering sitar music. In the center of the pool, you see a large rose-colored lotus, and nestled gracefully between its voluptuous petals is a beautiful woman seated in lotus pose, her eyes half lowered and a serene smile playing around her lips. She is resplendent in a magenta silk sari, her skin glowing gold in the morning Sun that is just kissing the edge of the distant hills. Jewels sparkle at her throat, wrists, and ankles. You kneel in reverence, knowing this is Lakshmi, the goddess of abundance, beauty, and love, before you.

She slowly raises her eyes and smiles dreamily at you in benevolence. "You have found your way here to me at last. What is it you seek?"

You think for a moment. What is it you need right now? What would enhance your life, bring you more joy? Are you currently searching for the right person to share your life with? Could you use more harmony and balance in an existing relationship? Would more prosperity and opportunity in a certain area of your life bring you true happiness? You gaze into the pool before you, and the rose-tinted water begins to churn, bringing you a kaleidoscope of images of your most heartfelt desires. You breathe in slowly to the count of seven and hold it for the count of seven as you reflect. Then you exhale slowly to the count of seven.

A sense of calm descends upon you as you realize the essence of what would bring you the most joy right now in your life. You take the scented flower from your hair and place it in the water as an offering to Lakshmi. It floats languorously toward her, and she reaches out one of her bejeweled arms to receive it. You bow your head and speak your desire to the goddess. All is silent but the sound of the water and the birds singing in the trees.

*She speaks: "Love, beauty, and abundance are your birthright. You need only to balance the gifts you receive with integrity, being ever mindful of the natural law of harmony in all things."*

*Lakshmi smiles at you and raises her palm in blessing. You feel a sense of deep joy suffusing your entire being, knowing that your boon has been granted. You bow deeply to her, your forehead touching the earth in gratitude. When you are ready, you rise and make your way back along the path that you came by, the entire forest now alive with the sounds of the dawn chorus greeting the new day.*

## Ritual: Love Magick

Love magick must be one of the most common, yet one of the most misunderstood, reasons for working with energy. It's been said before, but I'll say it again: it is *not* a good idea to use magick to draw a specific person to you. For one thing, it isn't ethical. It goes utterly against the principle of free will to even consider using magick to make someone fall in love with you. Like any other covert tactic, it's manipulative and usually doesn't end up working at all, or it goes awry in a way you cannot possibly imagine from where you're currently standing. Usually those who are drawn to attempting magickal means to persuade someone to fall in love with them are projecting on the other person. In a nutshell, projection is seeing someone for something they're not. What you're "falling in love with" is an outwardly projected manifestation of your own animus. Often the Other will have a few qualities that match or subconsciously resonate with your inner idea of your ideal partner. You project this outward onto them as if they're a movie screen, and you see them as you want to see them, the perfect embodiment of all you've ever dreamed of. Here is a truth: if someone is "meant" to fall in love with you, and you are "meant" to be in a relationship with that person, it will happen. You will not need to use magick to draw them to you, because you will naturally click. If someone does use manipulative means to get the guy or girl of their dreams to fall in love with them, and it happens to work temporarily, it will eventually backfire. The projection will eventually crumble, usually as soon as the real relationship starts, and you will wonder what on earth you ever saw in them in the first place. Yes, there are always obstacles in life, but real love does not include excuses. Someone who cares about you and who is worth your time will call you back and answer your texts. They will be emotionally available for you and not perennially "just about to leave their wife or girlfriend." They will be courteous and considerate of your feelings. And, as Libra teaches us about balance, *they should be just as into you as you are into them.* Real love is based on mutual respect and kindness. Yes, there are ups and downs in any relationship, but if it's the real deal, these are the bottom-line requirements. Full stop.

Do not despair—you can still use magick to draw love into your life, or to enhance an existing relationship. However, there is a caveat. If you are wanting to draw the perfect love into your life, *you do not name a specific person*, for the reasons outlined already: because it's manipulative and likely based on projection—but also because if you focus on a specific person, you might be missing out on the one who actually could be your one true love. I can hear all of you who are hung up on the most amazing person in the world (who is currently not returning your texts) groaning right now. I get it, I've been there too, and there are few things more painful than unrequited love. But, here's the good news: if you do a love spell and you send out to the Goddess for the perfect person for *you*, if he or she is the perfect person for you, it will happen. The following ritual can be used to attract the perfect partner for you, or to enhance an existing committed relationship. Adapt it to your own specifics.

*Lakshmi's Love Incense*
1 part sandalwood powder (start with 1 or 2 teaspoons for a small
  batch)
Couple of drops rose oil
1 drop lotus oil
A few lightly crushed dried rose petals

1 drop honey
Sprinkle of cinnamon or traditional chai spices

*Love Magick*
Lakshmi's Love Incense
Iconography of Lakshmi
Iconography of Vishnu (you can also use a Rama or Krishna image, as
they are both incarnations of Vishnu)
11 pink and/or white candles

You can offer Lakshmi's Love Incense and/or any of the following: ripe fruit, honey, sweets, figs, dates, milk, rose petals, flowers (especially roses, lotuses, or water lilies), gold jewelry, and coins. There are many mantras dedicated to Lakshmi that are readily available online either to learn or listen to. If you wish, you may play or chant one of these before you begin the ritual to align yourself closer with her energy. Alternatively, you can play traditional Indian music as an additional offering to her.

Clean your space thoroughly to welcome Lakshmi. Clear your space and ground and center in your preferred way. Set up your altar to Lakshmi; incorporate her sacred colors, which include red, gold, magenta, white, and pink. Make sure to add flowers or flower petals and something sweet. Place the pictures or statues on the altar, turned slightly toward each other. Reflect for a few moments on the divine relationship between Lakshmi and her consort. Light Lakshmi's incense and say the following. After each line, light a candle.

*Lakshmi, beautiful goddess of abundance, beauty, and wealth,*
*I hereby call on you in your aspect as Divine Consort, Lover, and Devoted Wife.*
*You, who emerged from the Sea of Milk and chose your beloved for all time.*
*You, whose love is deep and boundless as the sea,*
*as wide and limitless as the universe.*
*You, who in your devotion chose life again and again*
*to walk by the side of your beloved.*

*Bring to me a love as perfect for me as your own is for you.*
*Bring to me a love that honors the divine love of Lakshmi and Vishnu.*
*Bring to me a love that is a mutually beneficial exchange of heart energy.*
*Bring to me a love that is kind, respectful, deep, and true.*
*My heart is now open, and I am ready to receive your blessings.*
*In deepest gratitude, so be it.*

Visualize breathing the light from the candles into your heart chakra, lighting it up with the light of the goddess and filling you with love. Feel the light in your heart center magnetizing the right person for you, wherever he or she may be. If you are already in a committed relationship and you want to enhance and deepen your union, visualize a rose-pink light surrounding you both and a golden thread connecting you at your heart chakras. See you both smiling into each other's eyes, coming from your highest self. All obstacles and petty, ego-based arguments are now melting away. Thank Lakshmi for her blessing, and trust that it is so. Let the candles burn out safely, or extinguish them and burn them for a little while each night until they are done. This ritual is best done on a New or Full Moon, when the Moon is in Libra, or on a Friday, a day sacred to Lakshmi.

# Libra Correspondences

*Astrological Dates:* September 23 through October 22

*Sabbat:* Autumn equinox

*Libra Goddess Archetypes:* Aphrodite Urania, Aphrodite, Venus, Pallas, Lakshmi, Radha, Ma'at, Nana, the Graces, Dike, Eirene, Hera, Nemesis, Juno

*House:* Seventh

*Element:* Air

*Mode:* Cardinal

*Planet:* Venus

*Colors:* Sky blue, indigo, pink

*Crystals:* Fluorite, hemimorphite, hiddenite, lepidolite, prehnite, seraphinite, scolecite

*Essential Oils:* Clary sage, geranium, rose, frankincense, bergamot, basil

*Parts of the Body:* Kidneys, lumbar region

# SCORPIO

As with all the signs, the best clues to the formation of Scorpio's archetype are found in the season it presides over. As the Sun moves into Scorpio, there is a collective turning inward as ancestral memories tug at our consciousness and let us know the agricultural year is ending in the Northern Hemisphere.

There is no denying that Scorpio season is a time between the worlds, a liminal place both physically and metaphorically, as we turn toward the Final Harvest of Samhain. Scorpio is a fixed water sign, meaning that it is a sign that takes place in the heart of a season (in this case, autumn) and resonates with the intuitive, flowing undercurrents of the water element. The archetype of Scorpio is associated with the deepest mysteries of life: birth, sex, death, rebirth, and transformation. Scorpio is connected to the idea of the mythical phoenix rising time and again from its own ashes. Scorpio season invites all of us to shed old skins, dig deep, and release whatever patterns are keeping us from growing. We then have the opportunity for rebirth, to come up on the other side, regenerated and reborn. Look to your chart to see where Scorpio is for you. This will show you the life area where you will likely experience your most profound transformation, healing, and regeneration in this lifetime.

The Scorpio archetype asks us to embrace the shadow, to move into it, not only shining a light on our deepest wounds and fears, but also recovering our forgotten talents, desires, and soul treasure. Scorpio is aligned with the goddesses that are associated with the sacred dark, such as Persephone, the Morrigan, Cerridwen, Kali, and Inanna. Each of these deities has wisdom to share with us that can only come from digging in the dirt with our own hands and surrendering to the sometimes messy, cathartic process of release and rebirth. Like the goddess Inanna, Scorpio keeps one ear open always to the Great Below and is attuned to that which is relegated to the shadows, hidden, or shrouded in mystery. Scorpio is drawn to depth psychology, shamanism, magick, medicine, and healing. It should come as no surprise that the midwife, the sacred prostitute, and the death doula are each symbolically associated with Scorpio.

Scorpio is intrinsically connected to the idea of *compost,* alchemizing what some might consider waste materials into the rich, fertile creative potential of the psyche. If we reflect on the time of year that this sign embodies, this is just what is happening in the natural world as well. Scorpio is also associated with death and grieving, whether that be the death of a part of ourselves, a relationship that we know it is time to release, or remembering a loved one that is no longer on this plane. Scorpio wisdom asks us to open and surrender, because it's futile to fight when it's time for something to die—it is simply another part of the cycle. Scorpio knows that no new life can come unless we willingly enter the sacred dark and allow ourselves to be transformed.

As Scorpio is associated with the planet Pluto and traditionally with the planet Mars, its archetype also resonates with the deeper nuances of sexuality and power. Scorpio is also deeply passionate and highly sexual, but, again, this is not always obvious. Although her journey to self-knowledge is often through exploration of the sexual, it is often connected more to a personal process of transformation than promiscuity. Taboos of all kinds, but particularly those of a sexual nature, attract Scorpio, as they are a means to understand the layers beneath the façades of personality and society, as well as her own responses to the shadow side of human nature. Scorpio understands intuitively that where something is taboo, the question of power is at hand—who has it and who wants it—and she is driven to untangle and understand the various psychological games at play. To Scorpio, knowledge truly *is* power.

## The Scorpio Woman

Scorpio is a psychologically complex woman whose desire above all else is to pierce the veil of illusion and get to the truth at the heart of any matter. Intriguing, usually self-confident, and emotionally intense, the Scorpio woman often gives off a subtle air of mystery. And when her passions are stirred, she is focused, strong willed, driven, and not afraid to show her teeth. Although some are daunted by her intensity, once you have her trust, Scorpio will have your back if she considers you worthy of her respect.

When a Scorpio woman commits, she cares deeply. She is emotionally courageous and demands complete honesty and loyalty from her loved ones. She is also keenly perceptive and knows intuitively that all humans are capable of a great range of behaviors. Because she understands the nuances of human psychology, she will usually be able to summon compassion for you if you come clean about your own underside. However, if you do manage to fool her and she finds out later that you have skeletons in your closet, forgiveness for this kind of transgression comes hard to this woman, if ever. In her mind, this constitutes one of the very worst kinds of betrayal, and even if she does eventually find it in her heart to forgive you, she will always keep one eye open for any hint of future deceit on your part. Contrary to popular belief, Scorpio women are not simply suspicious. In her mind, she is not being suspicious; she is being savvy. She is being strategic. It all comes down to self-protection.

We cannot talk about the Scorpio woman without talking about sex. Much has been written of Scorpio's sexual prowess: the very embodiment of seething sexuality wearing the cloak of the seductive femme fatale. The popular conception that Scorpio is a raving nymphomaniac who will jump into bed with just anyone is usually far from reality. Although this sign is associated with sex, it does not follow that Scorpio women are indiscriminate. To Scorpio, sex is one of the great mysteries of life and a means for self-exploration. Sex can be an integral part of her spiritual path and a channel for connecting with the sacred. Tantric practices often resonate deeply with the Scorpio woman. *Tantra* is a Sanskrit word that can be translated roughly as "woven together" and suggests a weaving of the spiritual and the mundane, of bodies and souls. The focus of deepening intimacy and increasing potent sexual energy is highly attractive to Scorpio. Another sexual area of inquiry that some Scorpio women are drawn to is BDSM and other forms of kink. The complexity of power dynamics that can be present in BDSM can be enticing to the Scorpio woman, as she is drawn to delving into the deeper layers of the psychology of sexual exploration. She is also sometimes drawn to what some would consider the shadow aspects of sex.

For some Scorpio women, early life experiences have acquainted her with the darker side of human sexuality, which can produce a variety of effects. Some Scorpio women harden themselves, setting up a barricade between themselves and the outside world. But for all its brooding intensity and whip-cracking bravado, Scorpio is a water sign, and like the other water signs, Scorpios are emotional creatures at heart who yearn for connection at the soul level. The hardest Scorpio women are usually those who have been hurt the deepest early on in their life's journey. Some respond to the deep wounds inflicted on them by trying to control their own desires and manipulate the desires of others. For them, sex becomes a battleground of wills.

The evolved Scorpio woman learns what she wants and, perhaps more importantly, what she doesn't want. She has developed healthy boundaries that enhance her life rather than restrict it. She has come to know that her wounds can be healed and that she can also heal *through* her connection to her sexuality.

Sometimes it takes many years for the Scorpio woman to come to a place of healing. She realizes that the price of forsaking the balm of true intimacy comes at too high a cost and that the split between her body and her spirit has left her fragmented. But the rewards of wholeness are so great that, little by little, she will emerge from the ashes of her old life and do what Scorpio does best: regenerate.

Many healing modalities seem to be tailor-made for Scorpio issues. It's not always easy being queen of the underworld. Among the many options, acceptance and commitment therapy is a healing therapy that addresses many Scorpio challenges, which can include trust issues, forgiveness, the need to control, anxiety, and letting go. Scorpio can also benefit from a regular practice of mindfulness meditation and yoga. Journaling and seeking ways to reframe her stories in an archetypal light can also be useful. Additionally, Scorpio can find the peace she craves and the balance she seeks by drawing on the qualities of her opposite sign, Taurus—consciously finding ways to get out of her head and into her body more often. Ecstatic dance, drumming, massage, creating art, and other earthy, body-centered practices can be very helpful in bringing Scorpio back to center.

In relationships, Scorpio wants nothing less than to plumb the depths of her own and her partner's soul—to find the meaning of life, death, and transformation. Consequently, the thought of sex as a mere distraction will often usually leave her as cold and remote as a mountain lake in November. At its best, Scorpio sexuality is intense, ardent, and transformative at a soul level. It is a path to the numinous realm of sex magick, a sacred threshold to individuation.

Because she has the propensity to view sexuality as a profound exchange of energy, the Scorpio woman will sometimes choose periods of celibacy. This will usually happen when she is in a descent phase: she may be experiencing a time of emotional upheaval, undergoing an important transition, or in a state of deep personal transformation. She intuitively understands the potential power of sex and the intense psychic energies it can unleash. Much like when a snake sheds its skin, the Scorpio woman has a deep need for privacy and knows when the time has come to seek solitude, sexually and otherwise.

You will find many Scorpio women working in careers assisting others in navigating the real-life underworlds of addiction, depression, and mental illness. Like the goddesses who made the descent to the underworld, she herself has often experienced times when she made a descent and found her way back up to the topside world to share the wisdom she has accrued. Remember that one of this sign's symbols is the phoenix, the mythological bird that dies and rises again from its own ashes, and death and regeneration are at the heart of the Scorpio archetype. Scorpio does not tend to be squeamish about death, and some find fulfilling careers in the death and dying industry as a coroner, mortician, funeral director, natural burial advocate, death midwife, or hospice worker. Scorpio's connection to human sexuality would make her a brilliant sex therapist, sexologist, or sex educator. Her penchant for delving into the psychology of others could lead her to a career in psychology, psychiatry, or hypnotherapy. Alternately, her natural enthusiasm for digging deep could be channeled into working in the field of geology and mining or as an archaeologist, forensics specialist, investigative journalist, researcher, or private investigator. Scorpio's cool demeanor under pressure and her propensity to be drawn to crisis would make her a great first responder or an indispensable member of an emergency medical team. Her sharp attention to detail and her willingness to work tirelessly until she uncovers the truth would make her a brilliant litigator. Scorpio would also be in her element as a shrewd market analyst, stock broker, or investment banker.

## Guiding Goddess Archetype: Inanna

Inanna is a Sumerian goddess whose stories come to us from the ancient land of Mesopotamia and who embodies many of the qualities of the Scorpio archetype. She was an immensely powerful goddess known as the Queen of Heaven and Earth, and she presided over love, sexuality, and war. In one of her two main myths, *The Courtship of Inanna and Dumuzi*, we see a fiercely sensual goddess who owns the power of her sexuality in one of the steamiest pieces of ancient erotica ever written. In Sumerian myth, Inanna is connected to the planet Venus. Her journey to the underworld and back is reflected by the transits of Venus in the sky, where it sets in the west as the evening star and then rises again in the east as the morning star, completely disappearing and then reappearing in the heavens. When the planet is invisible, it is said Inanna is in the underworld. Inanna's main myth is *The Descent of the Goddess*, which describes her perilous journey to the underworld and back. The tale is deftly woven with Scorpio imagery. The mysterious opening lines immediately capture the reader's attention:

> *From the Great Above she opened her ear to the Great Below*
> *From the Great Above the goddess opened her ear to the Great Below*
> *From the Great Above Inanna opened her ear to the Great Below* [34]

Translators and scholars Diane Wolkstein and Samuel Noah Kramer explain that "in Sumerian, the words for *ear* and *wisdom* are the same."[35] Inanna, the great Queen of Heaven and Earth, becomes receptive to the call of something outside her experience, and is called to seek the wisdom of the "Great Below," or the underworld. The story of Inanna's descent to the underworld is at least five thousand years old, and it carries much symbolic insight not only for the Scorpio woman, but for any woman who finds herself in a time of descent. Inanna resolves that she must make a pilgrimage to the land of the dead, but before she embarks on her quest, she prepares herself by dressing for the journey, donning seven protective talismans that symbolize her status as queen of her own realms:

> *On her head she wears the shugurra, the crown of the steppe.*
> *Across her forehead her dark locks of hair are carefully arranged.*
> *Around her neck she wears the small lapis beads.*
> *Her body is wrapped with the royal robe.*
> *Her eyes are daubed with the ointment called,*
> *"Let him come, let him come!"*
> *Around her chest she wears the breastplate called "Come, man, come!"*
> *On her wrist she wears the gold ring.*
> *In her hand she carries the lapis measuring rod and line.*[36]

---

34. Diane Wolkstein and Samuel Noah Kramer, *Inanna: Queen of Heaven and Earth* (New York: Harper Collins, 1983), 52.

35. Wolkstein and Kramer, *Inanna,* 156.

36. Wolkstein and Kramer, *Inanna,* 56.

Inanna sets out on the road with her faithful servant, Ninshubur, at her side, instructing her to appeal to the gods for help should she not return in due time. As she approaches the first of seven gates that guard the entrance to the underworld, the guardian, Neti, stops her in her tracks and demands that she relinquish her crown before she can enter. At each successive gate, she is stripped of an article of power—and of the protection it confers—until she kneels, "naked and bowed low,"[37] before her dark sister, Ereshkigal, Queen of the Underworld.

Ereshkigal is not happy that her sister has entered her realm uninvited; she "fastened on Inanna the eye of death" and hangs her on a peg.[38] For three days and three nights Inanna hangs on the hook like rotting meat. Her faithful friend Ninshubur sounds the alarm when her mistress doesn't return, beating the drum and tearing at her face and clothes in mourning. She approaches the gods for assistance as she was instructed, but one by one they turn her away, exclaiming that Inanna got what she deserved. Finally, the god Enki shows concern for Inanna and, from the tip of his fingernail, conjures two creatures to help bring Inanna back from the land of the dead. These beings descend unnoticed into the underworld and find Ereshkigal in the throes of labor. They sympathize with her pain, and, in gratitude for their compassion, she grants them whatever they wish. They reject her offerings of a field filled with grain and a full river and ask instead for the corpse rotting on the peg. Ereshkigal acquiesces, and the creatures sprinkle Inanna with the food and water of life, thus reviving her.

On her way back to the land of the living, Inanna is accompanied by demons of the underworld who must bring back a substitute, for no one escapes the underworld without providing a sacrifice in return. The first person they encounter is loyal Ninshubur, but Inanna refuses to sacrifice her. It is obvious that Ninshubur is truly in mourning. Each person they find is deeply distressed over the death of Inanna, and she forbids their being taken in her stead. Finally, they come to the palace, where her consort

37. Wolkstein and Kramer, *Inanna*, 60.

38. Wolkstein and Kramer, *Inanna*, 60.

Dumuzi sits proudly on her throne, bedecked in jewels, enjoying his lofty position and clearly not mourning the loss of his wife.

"Him!" she cries. "He is the one who shall go down in my place!" The demons pounce on arrogant Dumuzi and drag him away as sacrifice to Ereshkigal.

The descent and the return are at the heart of the story of Inanna. Symbolically, it signifies a woman's journey into the shadow aspects of herself in order to come face to face with the powerful wisdom that has been disowned or otherwise banished to the unconscious. Journeying into the underworld and coming back up regenerated and whole can involve the shedding of outworn personas, relationships, or self-images that are no longer viable in our lives. Going into the sacred dark can sometimes unearth powerful sadness and anger that we thought was long buried. When Ereshkigal is writhing with birth pangs and the creatures sympathize with her pain, she is finally heard and her feelings are validated. In other words, the shadow has been recognized and integrated.

However, before rebirth can occur, a sacrifice must be made. The sacrifice is something that does not support us—whatever (or whomever) doesn't have our back. In the myth, it is Inanna's consort Dumuzi who must be released as sacrifice. He may have once served an important role in her life, but now she can see clearly that he no longer has her best interests at heart. When Inanna resurfaces, she has become tempered. She has gone through the darkest night of the soul without the comfort and protection of the seven talismans. And so it often is when we ourselves go through a dark night of the soul. The things that identify us in our everyday lives—careers, education, youth, beauty—lose their significance. The only way to enter the underworld is "naked and bowed low." It is only then that we can be receptive to the hidden wisdom and the transformation that may follow.

There are virtually countless similar interpretations of *The Descent of the Goddess*, as this myth has become a popular motif both in Jungian and Pagan circles. If you are interested in learning more about the descent of Inanna, I recommend the book *Descent to the Goddess: A Way of Initiation for Women* by Sylvia Brinton Perera.

# Pathworking: The Descent and the Return

*Tonight is the long-awaited night of your initiation into the myster-*
*ies of the goddess Inanna. The excitement rises like a tide within, but*
*you also fight to contain the anxiety that threatens to overtake you. If*
*it hadn't been for one of her priestesses coming across you in the mar-*
*ket, bruised and broken, running from the brothel your family threw*
*you into when they discovered your "impurity," you would never have*
*found your way here. But the instant Anahita laid her eyes on you, she*
*recognized you as belonging to the great goddess Inanna and brought*
*you back with her to the temple, where kind hands bathed you and gen-*
*tly dressed your wounds, mending not only your body but, in time, your*
*spirit.*

*That was many moons ago, and what a joy it was to finally find*
*a family that accepted you, a family of women who embraced you as*
*one of their own! Inside the sanctity of the temple, you were sheltered,*
*protected, and welcomed. The outside world and its betrayals seemed*
*very distant inside the perfumed courtyards of Inanna's sanctuary. Of*
*course, there was hard work too. You learned the duties of the novice*
*under the ever-watchful eyes of the elder priestesses: tending her sa-*
*cred flame and learning to quiet your thoughts in order to go within*
*and hear the voice of the goddess. You also learned one of the most*
*important parts of being a priestess of Inanna: to honor your sensu-*
*ality as a divine gift. They showed you how to move your hips in sinu-*
*ous circles, feeling the ancient power of the feminine awakening deep*
*in your sacral chakra, building in intensity and then pulsing through*
*your body in waves of ecstasy as you felt yourself opening to your sen-*
*suality and connecting to the infinite wellspring of your own creative*
*power as a woman. Although at times you struggled with the discipline*
*it took to learn the rites, your favorite duty was assisting the priestesses*
*with their preparations to honor Inanna as the Queen of Heaven and*
*Earth. Among your tasks was grinding kohl for the smoldering eyeliner*
*that would transform the women you worked alongside each day into*
*the living image of the goddess herself. How exotic they were! Their*

*beauty and embodied sensuality hypnotized you. Like glorious, other-worldly creatures, they swayed and undulated to the throbbing beat of the drums, eyelids lowering as they slipped into the trance that aligned them with the goddess.*

*Although you don't feel quite ready, the time has finally come for your own initiation. In the last rays of the setting Sun, a new acolyte comes to you, her head lowered respectfully in silence as she leads you to the baths. There you are bathed and anointed in oils of frankincense, cedar, and myrrh. You are then carefully dressed in the ritual finery you yourself have helped the senior priestesses with so many times, and a necklace of brilliant blue lapis lazuli is placed at your throat, the center of speaking your truth. You are then led down a darkened passageway, flickering candles in wall sconces casting dancing shadows along the way. The ominous, far-off sound of drums beating a slow and insistent rhythm makes the hair on your arms stand up. You become aware that the passageway is beginning to descend. You catch a glimpse of yourself in a mirror and gasp. The woman before you is the image of Inanna, resplendent in diaphanous saffron and shimmering white silk.*

*You come to a doorway blocked by a fearsome guardian who will not allow you to pass until you remove your gossamer veil. You bow your head and offer the veil, and the guardian takes it and steps aside. The passage becomes steeper, spiraling down as you descend ever deeper into the secret heart of the temple. You make out a shadowy outline ahead of you, and soon you are approaching another threshold. A second guardian blocks your way and demands that you surrender the lapis necklace you are wearing. At each threshold, one after another, you are stopped and required to give up a piece of the finery that identifies you as a novice priestess. You find yourself in utter darkness, naked and shivering.*

*Suddenly, you realize a shadowy female figure is materializing before you. You recognize the entity as Ereshkigal, Inanna's underworld sister. As her features begin to take shape, a strange realization dawns on you: it is like looking in a mirror, and indeed, Ereshkigal is the mirror image of the Queen of Heaven. She fixes you with an unwavering*

*gaze and says, "Symbols of status, power, and wealth have no value
here in the underworld. What do you offer me as sacrifice?"*

*For a long moment you are silent.*

Take a slow, deep breath and allow yourself to reflect. Name three
things you have learned during a time of personal darkness, things you
could not have learned any other way. Perhaps you learned how much
inner strength you have. Maybe you learned to define your personal
boundaries and stand up for yourself, or you came to a place where acceptance of a painful situation was the first step to freedom. Everyone
has their own unique initiation in the underworld. Take a deep breath
and make your offering to Ereshkigal.

*Ereshkigal holds you in her gaze for a moment that seems to last an
eternity. Then her face transforms into an expression of wise compassion. "Go with my blessing. You have been harrowed, deepened, and
reborn. You have descended into the heart of darkness and survived.
May you emerge tempered, to share the wisdom you have found in the
darkest nights of your soul," she says. She places something in your
hand; it might be a symbol, a message, an object, or an image. Her vis-
age fades slowly away.*

*From far off, you sense rather than see a brightening in the dark.
You turn toward it and make your way in its direction. With each step
you feel a growing sense of strength and confidence and a deep inner
calm. You passed the test. You are Priestess. The other priestesses joyfully welcome you as you step into the light of the rising Sun to the
triumphant sounds of drumming, sistrums, and singing. You open your
hand in the brilliant light and see what you have been given as a symbol
of your initiation, which you will take with you as a talisman into
your new chapter.*

# Ritual: Release and Renewal

At its core, Scorpio is about death and rebirth. It is about shedding our old skins and letting go of what no longer serves us. Scorpio wisdom knows exactly what is required and does not fear the dark, for it knows innately that there lies our greatest healing. Do this ritual when you feel you must release something that is keeping you stuck. The best time to do this ritual is during the waning or dark of the Moon, when the Moon is in Scorpio, or at Samhain.

*You Will Need:*
Small black candle
Heatproof dish or shell
Paper
Pen
Sage for smudging
Small green candle
Indoor or outdoor plant

Smudge and clear your space, and ground and center in your preferred way. Light the black candle. Take a minute to acknowledge the sacred that is woven into the descents you have undergone—the betrayals and deep losses, the disappointments and heartaches you have experienced. Perhaps you may even now be in a descent.

Write these initiations on a piece of paper in as much or as little detail as you wish. Consider all the ways you have been tempered through the dark times in your life.

When you are ready to release the pain, resentment, anger, or grief you have been carrying, touch the paper to the candle's flame and burn it safely in the heatproof dish. Watch as the fire consumes that which it is time to let go of. Feel yourself becoming lighter, stronger, and wiser as the cleansing flames transform. Reflect on the gifts that have come to you through the difficult steps on your journey.

Ground and center yourself again. Smudge your working area.

Remember, one of Scorpio's symbols is the phoenix rising from its ashes. Take the ashes and either bury them somewhere away from your yard or, better, take them to a river or to the ocean when the tide is going out, to be carried away by the current.

On the following New Moon, take the green candle—the color of new growth—light it, and place it in the plant. On a piece of paper, write all the new intentions you would like to put forward. When you are done, mulch the paper carrying your intentions into the earth of your plant. Visualize your intentions becoming part of the new growth of the plant, being carried out to manifestation in your new chapter.

Allow the candle to burn out safely while you meditate on the intentions of growth that you have set into motion.

# Ritual: Dancing in the Temple of the Queen of Heaven
*Inanna's Incense*
3 parts frankincense
2 parts myrrh
7 drops cedar essential oil
A few dried rose petals
1 tiny pinch cinnamon
Several drops of wine
¼ tsp. honey

*Dancing in the Temple of the Queen of Heaven*
Kohl
Inanna's Incense or spikenard oil
Candles
Music (try slow belly dancing percussion)

Inanna is intimately connected with the sensual expression of the sacred feminine and with owning and celebrating our sexuality. We are bombarded on a regular basis with cultural messages that say we need to look and behave in societally prescribed ways to be validated as sensual or sexual beings. Inanna stands for being proud of our bodies and our own brand of sensuality in whatever package we come in. In my more than two decades as a professional dancer in my early life, I did a variation of the following meditation before every show. I called it "getting into the zone." This meditation is designed for you to connect deeply with your sensual body or as preparation for lovemaking.

Wear something comfortable that you can move in freely, such as yoga clothes. Consecrate your space by burning some spikenard oil or Inanna's Incense. Set up your altar to Inanna, Queen of Heaven and Earth. (Refer to the correspondences at the end of the chapter for altar ideas.) Light a candle and dedicate the flame to her.

Ground and center yourself, and take some time to connect with and tune in to Inanna. Play some slow drumming music, belly dance music, or 5Rhythms. Allow yourself to begin to shift consciousness and get into a light trance state.

Prepare yourself. Outline your eyes with kohl. Do this mindfully and with utmost reverence. If you wish to apply more adornments or makeup, you can do this now. Self-adornment is an activity sacred to Inanna.

Look into the mirror and affirm that you are Goddess. You might feel strange doing this at first; it can be unnerving to speak to your own reflection. Stay with it—it gets easier with practice.

Begin doing some slow, gentle, succulent stretches with the music. Feel the power and glory of your female body, the body of the goddess. Affirm that you are beautiful. Run your hands over your body and give yourself permission to be bold in your self-appreciation. This is the time to banish any negative self-talk. You are an expression of the goddess, and it is her that you are praising. Be extravagant!

Slowly stand up and allow your body to sway to the cadence of the drums. Visualize yourself a priestess of the goddess Inanna. You are offering your womanly beauty and sensuality to her. Arise and feel the rhythm in your hips; practice rocking back and forth into your hips, and then try a figure eight. Let the music take you ever deeper into a trance state, until your movement becomes one with the beat of the drums. Slowly raise your arms in honor of Inanna, welcoming her to your dance. Do not edit your movement. There is no wrong or right way to dance for the Queen of Heaven. Your unique way is exactly what she requires. Allow her to guide your movement. You are raising energy. Try not to stop until you reach that ecstatic moment when you feel yourself become the dance. Feel your beauty and power as a woman, a being made to create, love, and celebrate the dance that is life.

Give thanks to Inanna for being able to freely delight in the joy of your body and feminine gifts. Focus and ground the energy through self-pleasure or lovemaking.

# Scorpio Correspondences

*Astrological Dates:* October 23 through November 21

*Sabbat:* Samhain

*Scorpio Goddess Archetypes:* Inanna, Ereshkigal, Kali, the Morrigan, Ishtar, Persephone, Hecate, Cerridwen, Amokye, Ammut, Selkhet, Mary Magdalene, Green Tara

*House:* Eighth

*Element:* Water

*Mode:* Fixed

*Planet:* Mars (traditional), Pluto (modern)

*Colors:* Black, deep red

*Crystals:* Charoite, iolite, labradorite, lapis lazuli, moldavite, pietersite, obsidian

*Essential Oils:* Patchouli, spikenard, frankincense, myrrh, cedar

*Parts of the Body:* Sexual/reproductive organs

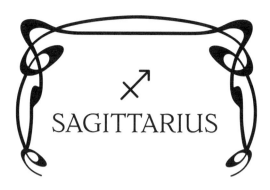

# SAGITTARIUS

In many places in the Northern Hemisphere, the first snows of the approaching winter have already dusted the distant mountaintops. We feel a collective lightening as we turn to the task of understanding that which was unearthed while the Sun transited Scorpio. Sagittarius is a mutable fire sign. It is the third of the threshold signs, taking us from autumn into winter, and is aligned with the enthusiastic element of fire. Sagittarius is also the last of the fire signs, which started with the spark of new life that is Aries, passed through the ardent flame of self-actualization that is Leo, and now culminate with the visionary fire of Sagittarius.

Sagittarius is the Truth Teller, the seeker of life's mysteries. Sagittarius is aligned with the impetus to develop knowledge and wisdom and resonates with Joseph Campbell's hero's journey, the archetypal Quest. Throughout that journey, Sagittarius pushes the boundaries and aligns with several core archetypes along the way, the Explorer, the Hedonist, the Philosopher, and the Sage among them. Sagittarius is searching not only for the endpoint of individuation but also ultimate meaning, and on her mission she can cover a lot of ground. No stone is left unturned in the search for knowledge. Sagittarius has the heart of the seeker, the mind of the philosopher, and an unquenchable thirst for the next horizon. Hers is the unfolding royal road of the journey, and she will happily travel the unfolding inner and outer paths to see what's around the next bend. She is drawn by the mysteries of faraway lands, the scent of exotic spices, and the intoxication of different perspectives. She is the sign that will throw a few belongings into a backpack and hitchhike across Europe, staying on the couches of friendly strangers and collecting stories along the way.

Sagittarius is ruled by expansive, magnanimous Jupiter, and as such is connected to the idea of *faith*—faith in self, faith in life, and the ability to see the big picture. Sagittarius asks, "What is my place in the universe?" She requires a great measure of personal freedom to fulfill her quest and cannot abide being tied down for long. On her journey, especially in her younger years, Sagittarius occasionally aligns with the Hedonist archetype: jumping in over her head and throwing caution to the wind. However, her unshakable faith in herself and genuine friendliness usually gets her out of many a scrape, giving Sagittarius the reputation for being lucky. At any rate, she gathers many allies on life's adventure and has an incredible time doing it.

## The Sagittarius Woman

Confident, courageous, and optimistic, the Sagittarian woman is equal parts bon vivant and wise woman. She has a thirst for adventure, a buoyant sense of humor, and a generous spirit. She is always up for a new experience, whether it be strapping on her hiking boots and heading for Patagonia or exploring the subcultures in her own city. She will happily strike up conversations with people from all walks of life—in fact, the further from her field of experience the better. Sagittarius embraces diversity and welcomes cross-cultural connections that open her to new perspectives. She has a jovial sensibility and a shoot-from-the-hip straightforwardness that is refreshing. She may lack subtlety and is known for being honest to a fault at times, but at least you always know where you stand with a Sagittarius woman. Unlike Scorpio, she doesn't hold grudges, and she has no hidden subtexts or agendas. What you see is what you get. She shines with authenticity and has a wonderful habit of always looking at the bright side of any situation. Although she can sometimes get herself in trouble with her bluntness, her affable nature usually makes up for it. Because she's so up front, people usually tend to accept whatever she says without making any bones about it.

On the other hand, she does exemplify the Wise Woman archetype, or at least the Wise Woman in training during her younger years. She often has a whole shelf full of books on world mythology and comparative religion, from Yakut shamanism to witchcraft to yoga philosophy. Stacked beside these are travel guides and maps of all the places in the world she's been or plans to go. Sagittarius rarely travels just to lie on the beach and get a tan. She wants to be changed by her adventures. All her wanderlust is part of an ongoing vision quest that serves as inspiration on her life's journey. Her quest is nothing less than to find the meaning of life, as well as her place in the cosmos, and she will climb every mountain and peer over every ridge to find it. As a fire sign, her goal is to move outward and reach outside herself to find that meaning. Seeking Truth with a capital *T* is an important part of Sagittarius's life task, and she usually comes to realize that truth can be found in many different places. Sagittarius corresponds with both the Student and Teacher archetypes, and although she is usually a lifelong learner, she will also gravitate toward being a teacher or mentor in some way as she integrates the wisdom she accrues. She often attains higher education, and many Sagittarians in their pursuit of knowledge have advanced academic degrees.

On the other hand, she can be unconventional in the way she gathers her wisdom, preferring self-study through her own personal curriculum of nomadic wandering and studying what inspires her passion. Many Sagittarius women find themselves studying or living abroad during periods of their life. Pilgrimage travel often leads her on a quest to the great spiritual power centers of the world, such as Glastonbury, Machu Picchu, the El Camino trail, and the great temples of Southeast Asia, such as Angkor Wat. Sagittarius needs freedom, and sometimes that means freedom from what she perceives as the claustrophobic structure of academia. She does not like being told what to do and hates having to commit to being in one place for too long. Many Sagittarians are drawn to alternative paths of acquiring knowledge and immerse themselves in spiritual or metaphysical study. They are also often interested in the study of archetypal psychology as well as cross-cultural mythology and folklore, as these help her further her personal understanding of life's mysteries.

Nature and the outdoors also call to the Sagittarian woman and her thirst for adventure. She often loves camping and hiking and can have quite a formidable repertoire of outdoors skills and wilderness survival tips in her backpack. Some Sagittarius women are more comfortable starting a campfire and identifying animal tracks than they are sitting at home with a glass of wine watching Netflix. Many Sagittarian women are also athletic, and they like testing themselves and setting personal challenges. Sagittarius has an affinity for animals and may acquire a dog or a horse just so she has an excuse to get out more often. At any rate, she has a genuine love of nature and for the most part will prefer being outside to being indoors. Of course, if being temporarily indoors means sampling the newest Nepalese restaurant or a hidden wonton spot in Chinatown that only the locals know about, she'll make an exception.

Because her mind is so often on higher learning or philosophical study and her body is usually on an adventure of some kind, fashion is not typically a Sagittarian preoccupation. Unless she's shopping for new hiking boots or merino wool base layers, she rarely gets too excited about it. One exception is bohemian style. Sagittarius women love to collect meaningful or exotic pieces of jewelry and clothing on their travels and incorporate them into their wardrobe. If she does happen to be shopping for wardrobe items at home, she might gravitate toward natural fibers and fair-trade garments made in developing countries. Depending on the Sag in question, there are some that make the bohemian-luxe look quite a statement, and she'll delight in the likes of vintage tribal beads and ethnic embroidered pieces from places she's been or has studied and plans to visit one day.

Sagittarius champions the idea of personal freedom, and she will fight for her right to autonomy. She is a born feminist and actively resists patriarchal notions and oppression in its many guises. Most Sagittarius women have a thirst for social justice, and she can become a fierce activist for causes that stir her sense of righteousness. She may be especially interested in gender equality and supporting access to education for girls, as well as promoting awareness of sexual harassment, domestic violence, and sexual assault. Sagittarius naturally takes on the role of "big sister" and can find satisfaction in mentoring and empowering girls and young women. Some Sagittarians are passionate about women's and gender studies and major in it in college. I've also met several older Sagittarius women who go back to school and get a degree in these subjects later in life, enabling them to better challenge essentialist views on gender, question male sexual entitlement, and support women's reproductive rights.

Much like the other astrological archetypes, the shadow of Sagittarius lies in the extreme expression of its positive traits. Her absolute faith in herself and in life can run to self-righteousness if not balanced. She can lose sight of the fact that there are as many truths on the planet as there are humans and dogmatically stick to her opinions and beliefs in a way that may verge on fanaticism. On another note, if she allows the hedonistic part of herself to go unchecked, it can put her in some precarious positions: with her inclination to learn about everyone, she sometimes lacks discretion in whom she connects with, which can have unpleasant, or in some cases dire, consequences. Taking everyone at face value means she can be lured down roads better left untrodden. Sagittarius needs to learn that having healthy boundaries does not mean she is being judgmental.

In a perfect storm, her desire to experience everything life has to offer can draw her to substance misuse. What starts as boisterous camaraderie and a few drinks can sometimes turn into an issue. Sagittarius's openhandedness can also lead to extravagance, not knowing when to draw the line, or neglecting to take care of essentials. Blowing all her savings on an impromptu trip or eating out every night and forgetting about the dull necessities of life, like rent, can sometimes land Sagittarius in hot water. Sagittarius can be magnanimous and generous to a fault and will often give her last dollar to help someone in need. As a mutable sign, when Sagittarius is feeling scattered or ungrounded, she can be irresponsible and reckless. However, with time, she usually learns valuable wisdom through experience and eventually finds her way to embodying the archetype of the Wise Woman. But she rarely ever loses her lust for life or sense of humor in the process.

Relationships can be a tricky area for Sagittarius women. They want someone they can adventure with, travel with, and engage with in philosophical discussions around a campfire. But they also need someone who will respect their need for personal freedom, even within the parameters of a committed relationship. Many Sagittarius women are content to be single for long stretches of time. She values her independence and usually has lots of friends—she doesn't feel a lack of companionship or like she's missing anything if she's not part of a couple. On a certain level, Sagittarius fears commitment. She is a free spirit at heart, and although she can be happy in a committed relationship, she should never feel like she is tied down. She needs her space, sometimes to a disconcerting degree for more sensitive signs. She is usually not possessive or jealous and expects the same openmindedness from her partners. Although she would probably enjoy traveling with her significant other, she has no problem with taking separate vacations. In fact, she may insist on it. She may be restless if she feels stifled in her relationship and may begin to look for new horizons. For Sagittarius, companionship and camaraderie are the cornerstones to a successful union. She cannot abide clinginess, suspicion, or anyone trying to control her. If she finds that person who understands that life is a mythic quest, who gives her the freedom she requires, and who shares her passion for learning, spirit, and lifelong adventure, it just could be a match ordained by the gods.

The Sagittarian woman has a lusty, physical appetite for sex. She is fiery and dominant and not afraid to take the initiative. She is spontaneous, and doesn't always need romance or love to go with her sexual endeavors. She looks at sex the way she looks at the rest of life: as a grand adventure to be enjoyed for all it's worth. She may be experimental with different partners and different scenarios. Until she commits to someone, she is more than happy to play the field and experience all the nuances and flavors that pique her interest. Sagittarius may lack subtlety, and she certainly doesn't engage in coy flirtation to gain the attention of someone she's interested in. Like every other part of her life, she is direct, is up front, and doesn't feel the need to play games. Sagittarius is sexy in a natural, fire-sign kind of way: passionate, bold, and exciting.

Because of her broad range of interests and passions, the Sagittarius woman has a wide range of career paths open to her. She needs freedom and variety in whatever she does, so it's good if she chooses a career she loves. In fact, there are certain careers that are especially suited to Sagittarius, as not only does she tend to get bored if stuck in one place for too long, she also does not like to be told what to do. Sagittarius cannot abide the dreaded micromanager! Therefore, consulting or contract work can be a good choice. Owning her own business also appeals to Sagittarius: not only is there no boss monitoring her every move, but she also doesn't mind taking risks and has plenty of energy and drive to successfully implement her big ideas. Sagittarius women need a target to aim for and accept challenges with enthusiasm. Repetitive, dull work will drive her crazy. Although she has what it takes to be a first-rate entrepreneur, she shines as a team player too. She is flexible, versatile, and a natural multitasker, as well as being all-around good natured and fun to work with, provided she's getting enough mental stimulation. She's also never short on good ideas, which can keep things on a forward track.

Sagittarius's spiritual and metaphysical interests can lead her to a successful career as an officiant, minister, working priestess, or spiritual writer. Her love of travel could lead to a career path in tourism, teaching English abroad, or pilgrimage guiding. She could also turn her affinity for travel and other cultures into a successful importing business. Some Sagittarius women have very fulfilling careers as flight attendants or pilots, for which they get paid to travel. If she is a nature-loving Sagittarius, she could be a wilderness guide, run her own outdoor company, or work with animals. Education is yet another area that Sag excels in as a mentor, teacher, facilitator, writer, publisher, archetypal psychologist, folklorist, or university professor. If she explored her way into the hedonistic shadow of her sign in her early years, Sagittarius can be a brilliant experiential drug and alcohol counselor, someone who has been down that road and has gained hard-won wisdom firsthand. Young people struggling with addiction often trust her and appreciate her tell-it-like-it-is candor. Finally, her passion for social justice can lead her to meaningful work as an advocate, sex educator, youth worker, human rights lawyer, or social worker.

## Guiding Goddess Archetype: Artemis

There are many parallels between the Olympian goddess Artemis and the Sagittarius woman. As we will see, Artemis, like Sagittarius, is the epitome of the free-spirited woman who makes her own choices and lives as she decrees. Virgin goddess of the hunt and the Moon, Artemis roams the high mountains and woodlands with her pack of hunting dogs and her band of nymphs. She wears a short tunic so she can run and hunt in the forest unimpeded and carries a bow and arrows. Oak groves, quail, deer, and bears are sacred to her. She is known as the protector of wild spaces and young girls. Artemis is the "illegitimate" daughter of Zeus and Leto and the firstborn, twin sister of Apollo. Legend has it that after giving birth to Artemis, Leto lay in anguished labor for nine days. By the ninth day, Artemis helped midwife her brother into the world and saved her mother's life. From that moment, Artemis became known as the goddess of women in childbirth, and women would appeal to her for an easy labor.

There are many myths and stories connected with Artemis that illustrate her independence and how she values her freedom above all else. One of her earliest stories takes place when she is just three years old, sitting on her father's knee. Amongst her requests, Artemis, straightforward and outspoken, asks for a bow and arrows, a pack of hunting dogs, a band of nymphs for company, a short tunic she can hunt in, and mountains and woodlands as her domain. Zeus magnanimously grants her everything she asks. It is of note that the Roman equivalent of Zeus is Jupiter, which is Sagittarius's ruling planet.

In another story, the hunter Actaeon comes across Artemis bathing in the woods. He hides himself behind a tree and spies on her in her nakedness. In one version of the myth, she transforms him into a stag, and his own dogs, not recognizing their master, tear him to pieces. In another version of the tale, it is her own hounds she unleashes on him.

The myths and stories connected with Artemis suggest that she values her autonomy, which she will defend at any cost, a trait shared by Sagittarius. She is also fiercely protective of her freedom and chooses the wild over a domesticated existence. Artemis also prefers the company of her female friends over a romantic relationship, which would only tie her down. She has no specific place she calls home but roams the untamed wilderness with her nymphs, beholden to no man and unburdened by offspring.

A fascinating cult connected to Artemis is depicted in artwork on the remnants of ancient pottery and vases. A myth tells the story of a young girl who teases a bear sacred to Artemis and is then killed by the bear. Her brothers in turn kill the bear, which enrages the goddess, and she sends a plague in revenge. Artemis will stop the plague only if the people of Athens surrender their virgin daughters every five years to propitiate her.[39] At the sanctuary of Artemis in Brauron, on the eastern coast of Attica, a select group of prepubescent girls engaged in a rite of passage known as *arkteia*, or "acting the She-Bear."[40] They would wear bear masks and assume the guise of she-bears, dancing in a wild ritual before they crossed the threshold to womanhood. We must remember that life for women in ancient Greece was in many ways little more than a half life. The only role open to most women was as wife and mother, with no place in society outside the constricted realm of the home. After marriage, she would be the property of her husband and completely under his dominion. Given the cloistered life that the women of ancient Greece endured, their time of unbridled and carefree wildness was probably cherished. Acting the bear honored the Virgin goddess Artemis by ritually embracing the untamed fundamental feminine before

39. J. Donald Hughes, "Artemis: Goddess of Conservation," *Forest and Conservation History* 34, no. 4 (Oct 1990): 191–97, doi:10.2307/3983705.

40. Sue Blundell and Margaret Williamson, eds., *The Sacred and the Feminine in Ancient Greece* (New York: Routledge, 1998), 33.

girls had to surrender their intactness to a patriarchal society that essentially stole their natural connection to their own wild female nature.

As goddess of the waxing crescent Moon, Artemis is further archetypally aligned with Sagittarius. While they both share an independent spirit, they each also embody a philosophical, mystical aspect. In many magickal traditions, the Moon has been traditionally seen as the Triple Goddess in her guises as Maiden, Mother, and Crone, which correspond to the Moon in her waxing, full, and waning phases, respectively. As the waxing Moon is connected to the goddess in her Maiden aspect, it symbolizes growth and outward directed energy, the ability to set one's eye on a target and move courageously toward one's goals.

## Pathworking: Reclaiming Your Wild Self

*You are walking up a winding mountain path. Deep green shadows of spruce and pine stand like sentinels, and the oaks and beeches are nearly bare. A light snow has begun to drift lazily down, dusting the crunching, leaf-carpeted ground underfoot. It is twilight, and a waxing crescent Moon appears overhead, glowing slim and bright in the late autumn sky. You have needed this, needed to get away from the constraints of civilized life—the constant harangue of school, work, and other people's expectations. You have felt caged and listless, and you wonder where your vitality has gone. You take a deep breath, inhaling the sharp green scent of the forest, and feel its living essence fill every part of you, instantly awakening and enlivening both your body and spirit. With each breath, you begin to feel a tingling sensation spreading throughout your body.*

*A feeling of freedom overtakes you, and you burst into a run for the sheer joy of being outside. You feel your lungs expand and grow larger. Your arms and legs become heavier, more powerful, and you realize as you're running that you feel the cool mountain air rippling through your coat. The strength and power within you is intoxicating, and you easily jump over a large mossy log, leaving the path and plunging joyfully headlong through the woods. Nothing is an obstacle. You pause and stand up on two legs, raising your great shaggy head and sniffing* the air. Your sense of smell is heightened, and images flash through your mind's eye, showing you a panoramic view of the terrain. In one direction, not far off, a mother deer and her fawn lie secreted in the foliage. In another area further afield, you pick up the scent of the charred remains of a campfire that was vacated the day before. From several miles away, a sweet, moist scent comes to you: a spring. You lumber off in that direction and hear the trickling before you see it.

You arrive at the edge of the spring and bend your head to the water to slake your thirst, your sides heaving and flecked with sweat. You have never felt so satisfied or alive. Gradually, you realize that you are returning to your human form, and having had your fill of mountain water, you settle cross-legged with your back against a great old oak. Night has fallen. Your breathing slows and deepens, and you take in the sounds of the forest.

From somewhere far off, but getting closer, you hear the sound of dogs barking and of women singing and laughing. They come out of the woods just downstream from where you're sitting and make the motions of preparing to set up camp. As if she is alerted by your presence, the tallest of the women turns her head and fixes her sharp eyes on you. She is wearing a short deerskin tunic and carries a bow in her right hand, with a quiver of arrows slung over her shoulder. She strides confidently in your direction on silent feet. One of the dogs trots after her and sits at her side as she stops before you, hand on hip. She raises one eyebrow and beams a hearty welcome.

"What have we here? Have you come to join our merry band of wanderers?" Her voice is rich and throaty, and she shines with healthy, youthful radiance, good humor, and absolute self-assurance. You realize that you are sitting before Artemis, goddess of the hunt and the Moon. She holds out a sturdy hand and lifts you to your feet. "Come, join our celebration. We've just returned from a successful hunt."

She slings her arm around you and walks you over to where the other women are laughing boisterously and slapping each other on the back. A woman wearing antlers begins beating a drum, and another joins in on an aulos, or double flute. Drawn to the rhythm of the music, *the women begin to dance, throwing their heads back, whooping and howling joyfully at the swelling Moon. Some mimic the movement of bears in time with the cadence of the drum, shaking themselves out, grunting and turning their heads this way and that like a bear scenting the wind. Others leap high into the air like does.*

*You feel the throbbing pulse of the drum and join the ecstatic dance around the campfire. Although you have resumed your usual form, the experience of taking the shape of the She-Bear resounds within you, and you move with wild abandon, embodying her ursine power. You are one with your body, moving alongside the blur of the other women who dance around you. In the dance, you lose all sense of time.*

*You awake beside the glowing coals of the campfire, wrapped against the morning chill in a deerskin blanket. A pale Sun is rising. Artemis and her band of nymphs have already moved on to their next adventure. You rise and stretch, feeling recharged and empowered, ready to take your place at the helm of your waking life.*

## Ritual: Hone Your Vision

Sagittarius is about having the courage to push past limitations and step into authenticity. Where do we feel restricted? How do we let go of self-consciousness and audaciously claim our connection to our wild heart? Both Sagittarius and Artemis encourage us to shake off other people's expectations and to show up as we are with confidence and loyalty to our instinctual selves. If possible, this ritual is best done outdoors, at twilight or after dark, and preferably during a waxing Moon or when the Moon or Sun is in Sagittarius. Set up your altar to Artemis; this can be as simple or elaborate as you wish. Try to incorporate some items that are sacred to her: oak leaves, sustainably harvested deer antlers, arrowheads or arrows, a fallen branch, iconography of Artemis or She-Bear, a crescent Moon, and deer. A white or silver altar cloth corresponds with her aspect as goddess of the Moon. Alternatively, you can use midnight blue, as this color is associated with Sagittarius. If you are doing this ritual in a wild space, a flat top of a large stone or fallen log would work well as an altar. If you are indoors, bring something of the wild into

your ritual to honor Artemis. When I did this ritual last Sagittarius season, the weather was so bad I had to move it indoors—the wind and rain
kept putting the candle out! So, I collected some oak leaves, respectfully
harvested some Douglas fir sap from one of the trees on our property,
and set up my altar in my studio while the storm raged outside.

## Clear Vision Oil

1 part each:
> Basil
> Clary sage
> Camphor
> Rosemary
> Juniper

## Hone Your Vision

Small white, silver, or dark blue candle
Clear Vision Oil
Paper
Pen
Quartz crystal point or wand with quartz crystal tip
Heatproof dish

Clear your space and ground and center in your preferred way. Anoint
the candle with the oil and light it. This is the flame of your vision. Next,
anoint your heart space. Finally, anoint your feet, which symbolically (or
literally) will carry you on your quest. Focus your gaze on the candle's
flame for a few minutes and ask Artemis to lend you the heart and courage you need to begin a new adventure. Recall how a three-year-old Artemis sat on Zeus's knee and confidently asked for exactly what she wanted.
She was clear and direct and knew exactly what her core values were. You
can also ask for what you want, but you need to clarify your vision before
you can hit your mark. Take your paper and write down the following
questions. (You can also write the questions beforehand, in which case
have your paper ready on the altar so you can write your answers during

the ritual.) Remember, Sagittarius is about the Quest, which entails getting focused and setting goals. The following questions are designed to psychically clear space so you can release your arrows of intent directly at your target. Take some time to really reflect on your answers; you are honing your vision.

- What lights your fire?
- How would you like to show up in the world? Envision yourself free to be who you're becoming. What would that look like?
- What is holding you back from taking your first step?
- What can you realistically do to push past these limitations? Be creative.
- Who are your allies?
- What is your first step on your quest? Are you willing to commit to it? When?

Take the tip of your crystal or wand tip and touch it gently to the candle flame. Say aloud,

*This is the flame of my vision.*

Bring the tip toward your heart and say,

*Connected to the clear fire that burns in my heart.*

Raise the wand up and outward, visualize your goal as clearly as you can on the horizon, and say,

*I now release my arrow of intent and take the first step*
*of my journey to begin my quest.*

Fold up your paper with your answers on it and place it on your altar to allow it to charge. You may allow the candle to burn down as you reflect on your intent, or you may extinguish it with a candlesnuffer. As Sagittarius is a fire sign, you don't want to use air to extinguish it, in respect for the fire element. If it is a waxing Moon, you may wish to light the candle for a few minutes each night until the Full Moon. When you are ready, thank Artemis for her energy and presence. Open your circle. When you have attained your goal, burn the paper in a heatproof dish, and take the ashes to the woods as an offering to Artemis.

## Sagittarius Correspondences

*Astrological Dates:* November 22 through December 21

*Sabbat:* Threshold sign between Samhain and winter solstice

*Sagittarius Goddess Archetypes:* Artemis, Atalanta, Diana, Fatna, Sanene, Bixia Yuanjun, Kang-kys, Flidais, Luot-Hozjit, Mielikki, Callisto, the Vila

*House:* Ninth

*Element:* Fire

*Mode:* Mutable

*Planet:* Jupiter

*Colors:* Purple, violet, sapphire blue

*Crystals:* Ametrine, azurite, chrysocolla, rutilated quartz, sapphire, sodalite, topaz, turquoise

*Essential Oils:* Tea tree, rosemary, eucalyptus, bergamot, basil, juniper, marjoram

*Parts of the Body:* Hips, thighs, liver, sciatic nerve

# CAPRICORN

In the Northern Hemisphere, the darkness of winter has descended, and the trees are leafless and bare. Life contracts in order to survive, and many living things make important energy choices to see themselves through the season of scarcity. The light has dwindled to its lowest point, and around December 21 we turn within to face the longest night of the year, the winter solstice, which marks the beginning of Capricorn season. Capricorn is a cardinal earth sign, meaning we are once again at the gateway of a new season (in this case winter) and connected to the strong foundational energy of the earth element. Echoing the season it's rooted in, Capricorn is about defining life purpose by pruning away the excess of the sign that precedes it (Sagittarius) and committing to the long view.

The process of *defining* entails the recognition of boundaries and limitations, which crystalizes an objective. Capricorn is ruled by Saturn, the planetary archetype that is traditionally associated with boundaries. Before telescopes, Saturn was the farthest planet visible to the naked eye and therefore came to be identified with boundaries, limitations, and endings. Consequently, Saturn is also related to the limits and structure of our physical reality: skin, hair, and bones. Starting most noticeably with the Saturn return around the age of twenty-nine, the major Saturn cycles in our lives coincide with rites of passage that lead to new levels of maturity. Therefore, Saturn is aligned with aging, milestones, and taking on the mantle of responsibility. Saturn is also associated with the concept of time. His older Greek equivalent was the god Kronos, who was the personification of time itself.

In Jungian parlance, Capricorn is connected to the archetype of the *senex,* the Wise Old Man, or the Elder, which also exemplifies the archetype of the Crone. The *Cailleach,* the "old woman of winter" from the Gaelic lands, as well as Hecate, crone goddess of the crossroads, especially relate to Capricorn. Deeply resonating with the wisdom of the Grandmothers, passed-down traditions, and time-honored ways of knowing, Capricorn represents our psychic ancestral bones. Although the Capricorn archetype is aligned with the Father, and the animus, it is actually a yin sign and is therefore conjointly an expression of the sacred feminine. With Capricorn, I am reminded of the symbolism of the *hieros gamos,* or sacred marriage, between the polarities of masculine and feminine.

## The Capricorn Woman

When I reflect on Capricorn, I cannot help but think of my beloved grandmother, a Capricorn who, in my mind, embodied the archetypal qualities of this sign in a very literal way. If not for her perseverance in the face of the most austere and unimaginable conditions, I would not be here today. My grandmother lived in the beautiful, lush countryside in what was once a part of Hungary. Her people were called the *Donauschwaben,* a Germanic community that made its home in this idyllic land for over two hundred years. After the Second World War, the victors seized the homes and land of the people who remained, and as reparation systematically murdered most of the men, tore children from mothers' arms, and sent the women to labor camps in Russia. The children were rounded up and placed in orphanages, and most were never to be reunited with their families again. My own mother was just two years old when my grandmother was taken, and she was one of only nine children left alive in the entire village. My grandmother, who was twenty-three at the time, spent the next years in a Siberian labor camp not knowing if her family was alive or dead. She told us stories of women lying on the railway tracks to end their misery, but the thought that her children might be alive somewhere kept her from joining their numbers. The conditions in the camp were the stuff of nightmares; starvation, rape, and beatings were commonplace. With a shudder, my grandmother would tell us tales of women digging with hands and sticks in the frozen earth to bury fallen friends and sisters. Then she would look off and say, "But that is not something we should speak about now."

My grandmother found her way from Russia to East Germany and hid in the forest with a small band of other women desperate to find their scattered families until they made their daring escape over the Berlin Wall. Once in the west, and finally free, she made her way from camp to camp for displaced persons, asking everyone she met if they knew what had happened to the children of her village. Eventually, her perseverance paid off, and with the help of the Red Cross, she was reunited with her daughters on Easter Sunday 1951. My mother was eleven years old.

Although my grandmother's story of survival and determination is the stuff of screenplays, many Capricorn women have their own tales to tell of surviving hardship of one kind or another, of putting one foot in front of the other until they have left an abusive situation, beat the odds of poverty, or otherwise endured, overcame, and attained hard-won peace and security. Of course, not all Capricorn women have undergone these same extremes, but most know a thing or two about real-world responsibilities and the value of perseverance.

Capricorn seems to have an inner acceptance that anything worth having is worth working for. She is not afraid of hard work or putting in the time to attain her goals. She is often suspicious of things that come too easy, like get-rich-quick schemes of any kind or online courses that promise mastery of a subject in five easy payments. She knows that to become a person of authority in any area means putting in one's time, making the effort, and being patient. She knows real accomplishment and wisdom are a process, and in our "instant"-everything world she would rather take the long way and have something stable, solid, and genuine that will stand the test of time. Integrity and self-respect are driving principles that motivate her to strive for accountability.

The desire for material security is a Capricorn theme that arises time and again. Capricorn is pragmatic. This is not the woman who throws caution or money to the wind and assumes that the universe will magically provide. Not only does she work hard, but she also saves judiciously and invests wisely. Speculative financial gambles put cold fear into her heart. A Capricorn likely coined the old adage "better safe than sorry." Not that she really thinks anything is ever completely safe, but she will carefully consider the safest route before diving into anything. She usually has a contingency plan and is prepared for any eventuality. Capricorn is nothing if not prepared.

For all her integrity and practicality, Capricorn's shadow is the underbelly of Saturn's realism. The desire for material security can easily become materialism, the idea that the only thing worth anything is money and status in the outer world. Bottom-line thinking without heart can produce a calculating, cold, and opportunistic mindset. Blind ambition just for the sake of prestige or power reflects the dark side of the masculine that is connected to the Capricorn archetype: the patriarchy. Some Capricorn women are not exempt from siding with patriarchal ideology when they are expressing from the shadow side of the sign. They can be just as ruthless and identified with hierarchical power structures as any patriarchal male. On the other hand, there are some Capricorn women who collude with the patriarchy by espousing a traditionally male-dominant society, taking on the guise of the good wife—for example, in a secondary support role to her husband. And, unfortunately, there are those who are content to live a half life as a kept woman. To them, being taken care of is a form of security. These are the few who align themselves with a financially powerful man to get by in the world. Examples of this lifestyle are currently paraded in reality TV shows ad nauseam.

Behind all three of these Capricorn shadow situations lurks a survival tactic in a still-sexist society. They are each a response to living in a male-dominated culture and are rooted in fear. We must remember Capricorn is at heart a survivor, and though that's usually a positive trait, fear and self-preservation can shape her reaction to situations and to life itself. She may also collaborate with the status quo in other ways. Fear of being disenfranchised can prevent her from being her true self and taking risks that will broaden her horizons. Some Capricorns side with the dominant power and become overly conservative in their worldview, trading authenticity for a life of unquestioned *shoulds* and *musts*. Fear of self-expression or being kicked out of the club can turn Capricorn into a straitjacketed, reserved woman afraid to do or say the wrong thing. She may also be drawn to a life of empty social climbing, as Capricorn in her shadow can be very preoccupied with keeping up with the Joneses.

Finally, there are the Capricorn women who have been down some very hard roads, made some unimaginable sacrifices, and know what it's like to be between a rock and a hard place. Instead of alchemizing her experience into hard-won wisdom, she has allowed fear and disappointment to carve a deep furrow into her psyche, and she may be pessimistic, cynical, and hardened as a result. If this has happened, she must find a way back to her heart. The way back may be difficult, and she may be slow to trust that something can grow again in that fallow earth. However, with her natural propensity for commitment, she would do well to remember that one of her main tasks in life is to be a wise guide for the next generation. To take on this role, she will have to commit first to herself, to the work of healing and nourishing the places in her psyche that have become constricted in self-protection.

Like most other life areas, Capricorn women take love and relationships very seriously. Once she has made a commitment, she is amongst the most loyal of signs and will stick by her partner through thick and thin. She wants a stable relationship built on a firm foundation. She is trustworthy and is not prone to cheating, as security is her top priority and she wouldn't do anything that would potentially destabilize the stability of the relationship. If things do go south, she is apt to keep a rational head, a stiff upper lip, and do her best to push forward against all odds. She can occasionally play the martyr and will stay in a passionless relationship even if it is unhealthy to do so, especially if leaving means jeopardizing her security. Capricorn usually wants marriage and children, either her own or adopted, to create what in her mind is a real family. She makes an exceptionally dedicated and devoted mother and will be sure to teach her children impeccable manners, how to be resourceful, and how to be respectful of their elders.

However, as much as she is commitment oriented, she is usually cautious when it comes to love. Contrary to her sometimes cool and detached demeanor, Capricorn loves deeply and fears rejection. First and foremost, she needs to know she can depend on someone. She also needs to know whether they share the same values. She has very high standards and expects accountability. Capricorn women often also expect a potential mate to prove their worth and suitability in some way. It's not simply proof of devotion she requires—it's proof that her beloved will share responsibility for ensuring a secure future. Even if she works tirelessly to this end at three jobs or is on her way up to CEO, her partner will have to contribute to building their future nest egg.

Sometimes Capricorn can come across as cool or reserved, even when she is in fact interested. She does tend to suppress her emotion at times and suffers from a fear of vulnerability. Capricorn women exercise a great deal of self-control because they are afraid of losing that control. Beneath her serious, self-possessed façade often beats the heart of a secret romantic who is afraid of losing herself and becoming subsumed by the unruly, chaotic feelings that love can unleash. However, her practical nature often overrides her emotions, and with steely determination (and often great sadness) she can turn her back on someone she has feelings for. Perhaps the object of her affection is moving to another continent for the next two years or she's beginning med school and knows a serious relationship could derail her from her career path. Either way, she is a realist and will sacrifice what she must if it doesn't make rational sense.

Although most Capricorn women work very hard and are deeply loyal mates, there are those who operate from the shadow side of the sign who are materialistic and even somewhat mercenary when it comes to relationships. Yes, some Capricorns can be consummate gold-diggers. It's interesting to observe this type, for in true Capricorn form they are committed to this lifestyle as if it were a career. They treat a relationship as a business, and in some cases it is quite literally their livelihood. They are savvy, strategic, and do not lose sight of their end goal (security) by allowing themselves to fall in love with worthy partners with modest bank accounts. I remember the chilling, matter-of-fact words of a Capricorn friend who had adopted this stance: "They're going to use you anyway. You might as well beat them to it." This is really the saddest direction for the Capricorn woman. In her fear of rejection or past situations of disappointment, she has closed her connection to her heart, which will only serve to diminish her sense of self-respect and cut her off from her many wonderful qualities as well as the possibility of having real love in her life.

Sexually, Capricorn is an earth sign and is far more physical and sensual than might be expected from her usual no-nonsense demeanor. If she drops her inhibitions and feels safe with her partner, she can discover a lusty appetite that helps her to let go and enjoy this side of life. In fact, some Capricorns find that the only place they can abandon control is between the sheets. It's as if by the very nature of the physicality of sex, she can finally drop her guard. She has a strong sex drive, but her practical nature usually prefers straightforward sex rather than variety or elaborate sexual fantasy. She is not known for being particularly experimental, although there are exceptions to the rule. Some Capricorn women can only really let go in bed, and when they finally have an opportunity to unleash their wild side, they let it rip. For Capricorn, there is a time and place for everything.

When it comes to career, finances, and work, the Capricorn woman is most in her element. She will always aspire to the top of whatever mountain she's climbing, but she will plan her ascent with measured steps. Although she is ambitious and competitive, she has the patience and humility to start at the bottom and learn the ropes from the ground up. She is self-sufficient and has the discipline to stay her chosen course. While she craves honor, milestones, and outer-world accomplishment, she has immense endurance and usually outpaces her competitors in the long run. Capricorn values the ubiquitous "piece of paper" and often only feels qualified to do something if she has the stamp of approval from the authorities that be. Whether it's an MBA or a certificate in aromatherapy from the continuing education department at the local high school, she requires proof of her qualifications. She has a natural respect for authority, and while she is a born leader, instead of resenting her superiors, she strives to learn from them while quietly strategizing her own rise to the top. Capricorn can be a workaholic, and although this can be tied to her need for security and personal accomplishment, there is a side of her that craves respect and status. Some aspire to power and prestige, rubbing shoulders and making strategic alliances with people in high places that can give them a leg up the ladder.

Although it's been said all too often, Capricorn can be a good company woman. Some do tend to thrive in a corporate atmosphere and deftly run board meetings in pumps and a pencil skirt, but I find this stereotype limiting. It doesn't take into account that most Capricorn women the world over do not happen to live in New York City, devouring business magazines instead of a sandwich on their lunch hour. I have met Capricorn women who work as contractors, firefighters, small-business owners, farmers, architects, exotic dancers, occupational therapists, and just about every other job title in between. Because, with Capricorn, it's not so much what they do; it's the way that they do it. And although Capricorn can be a banker or a CEO, these are just two examples of careers that resonate with the earth element. Yes, earth is connected to resources like money, but money is just one form of resource. Capricorn is a deeply practical sign, and you will more often find her working in a career that is still earthy but has nothing to do with trading commodities or pulling off the big corporate takeover.

As an employee, Capricorn is efficient, dependable, and trustworthy. She shines in any position where she is given a measure of responsibility. She is hardworking and organized and will often go above and beyond to get the job done. Her talent for leadership makes her a natural boss or mentor. As a business owner, she has both the financial acumen and determination to be successful. Any business she operates will likely be built on a solid reputation and will often outlast competitors in similar fields. Some career areas that are connected to her ruling planet Saturn include government, orthopedics, osteopathy, dentistry, and working with elders. Her respect for the past and love of provenance could lead her to become a museum curator, antiques dealer, or appraiser. With her flair for finances she could excel as a financial advisor or stockbroker. Her talent for building means she could succeed as an architect, engineer, contractor, natural materials builder, or real estate developer. Some Capricorns have built an empire fixing up old houses and flipping them for a profit. With her need to produce something tangible, any kind of production would be a good fit, whether it be film production, fiber arts, or food production. She may also choose a practical career working outdoors, such as land surveying, house painting, or working in forestry or as a park ranger.

## Guiding Goddess Archetype: Frau Holle

Frau Holle, alternatively known as Holda, Hulda, Holla, and Pertrecht, is the ancient Teutonic goddess of winter and is especially connected with the renewal that coincides with the winter solstice. In one of her best-known stories, we see a grandmotherly figure who is aligned with the concept of just reward for integrity and hard work, attributes that correspond with Capricorn. She is also related to the tasks of spinning and weaving, which suggests a deeper symbolic meaning, as the repetitive, cyclical nature of these activities has long been associated with ritual and spell work. Although her story is widely known through the Grimm Brothers' rendition, her origins appear to be much older. In *The Language of the Goddess,* professor Marija Gimbutas underlines Frau Holle's connection with the regenerative motif of the winter solstice, which is at once a time of darkness and also the return of the light: "German Holle regenerates the sun, and she herself is the sun, addressed as 'The Mother of all Life' and 'The Great Healer.'"[41] Gimbutas further refers to Holle as "the Killer-Regeneratrix, the overseer of cyclic energy, the personification of winter."[42] Although she is a goddess of winter and a weather deity, Holle is also a goddess of rebirth and renewal. Gimbutas explains how she appears as a dove once a year and also as a frog bringing a red apple from the well, after it had fallen in during the previous harvest.[43] Both are symbols of regeneration and fertility. However, she was also referred to as "Mother of the dead."[44] The elder tree was sacred to Holle, and it is said that the dead lived beneath it, as it had healing and regenerative powers.[45] It is clear from her many layers of symbolism that Holle is a powerful goddess who encompasses all the cycles of life and death. She is a foundational goddess whose "realm is the inner depths of mountains and caves."[46] This implies that she is the personification of the great power of the turning wheel that is beneath all things.

If we read carefully between the lines, we see that the goddess Holle story as retold by the Brothers Grimm is rife with ancient motifs and symbolic underpinnings. The following version of the tale is one my grandmother would tell us when we would come to visit, tucked beneath homemade feather blankets, with the smell of fresh-baked *kipfel* scenting the air. There are obvious similarities to the Grimm Brothers' rendition, which makes me think my grandmother was told the same story when she was a child. However, there are a few differences, which illustrates how stories evolve and change with the teller but still retain the same roots.

The tale begins with a widow, her daughter, and a stepdaughter. The mother cherishes her own daughter, although she is lazy and ill-tempered. The stepdaughter is fair, sweet-natured, and made to do the hardest work in the house. Each day the stepdaughter spins the flax from

41. Marija Gimbutas, *The Language of the Goddess* (New York: Harper Collins, 1989), 211.

42. Gimbutas, *The Language of the Goddess*, 319.

43. Gimbutas, *The Language of the Goddess*, 319–20.

44. Gimbutas, *The Language of the Goddess*, 320.

45. Gimbutas, *The Language of the Goddess*, 320.

46. Gimbutas, *The Language of the Goddess*, 320.

morning until nightfall without complaint. One day she is spinning at the side of a well when her hands become bloody from all her work and the spindle slips from her fingers and falls to the bottom of the well. Horrified, she runs home and in great shame tells her stepmother of her negligence. Her cruel stepmother orders her to go back to the well and fetch it back at once. The girl returns to the well, and in her fear and sadness throws herself headlong into the well so that she may find the spindle. Everything goes dark.

Sometime later she opens her eyes and finds herself in a beautiful spring meadow. Flowers are bursting into bloom. She straightens her *dirndl* and begins to walk in the warm, golden afternoon Sun. Soon the delicious smell of baking bread reaches her, and a voice calls out to her to take the bread out of an oven before it burns. She takes a big baker's shovel and rescues the bread from burning just in time. Not long after, she comes upon an apple tree, heavy with ripe red fruit. The apples call out to her beseechingly to please pick them before they drop on the ground. She goes to the tree, and picks every apple and sets them in a basket. She walks on and comes at last to a little thatched roof cottage. A very old woman with wrinkled skin like a walnut and hair as white as newly fallen snow comes to the door, wiping her hands on her apron. She smiles a warm welcome, and her teeth are so big the girl almost runs away in fear. But it is evident that the old woman is kindly, and she invites the girl over her threshold and into her warm, comfortable home.

In exchange for helping with the household chores, the girl is invited to stay with the old woman. Amongst the chores, the most important task is shaking out the down comforter each day until the feathers fly like snow. "For I am Frau Holle," the woman tells her. The girl stays happily with Frau Holle for a long time, listening to her stories and eating delicious suppers in front of the fire each night.

One day, the girl realizes she must return to the upper world. Although she is content, she is homesick and, more, has begun to wonder if it is in her future to marry one day and have children of her own. Frau Holle is delighted that she has this in her mind and agrees to take her back to the upper world. They leave the cottage, and a door appears, which Frau Holle encourages her to walk through. The girl steps over the threshold, and gold coins rain from the sky, filling her pockets to bursting.

She walks through the door and finds herself back at her old home, where she tells the stepmother and stepsister her story. Seeing the prosperity bestowed on her stepdaughter, the mother insists that her daughter also go down the well so she can get her share. The stepsister complains but sticks her hand in a prickle bush to make it bleed and goes to the well, where she throws the spindle in and jumps in after it.

She arrives in the same golden field and soon smells the bread, but shrugs and walks on, ignoring its pleas to take it out. When she comes to the apple tree, she tosses her head and pays it no attention. Finally, she arrives at the door of Frau Holle and presents her services. The first day she does as she's asked. But by the second and third day, she has reverted to her lazy ways. Frau Holle tells her her time is up and walks her to the door that leads to the upper world. But when the stepsister crosses the threshold expecting a shower of gold, a bucket of tree sap is dumped over her head, and she is covered in it for the rest of her days.

This story is rife with the symbolism of initiation of a maiden into womanhood. The motif of the blood on the spindle suggests first menstrual blood. Falling down the magickal well is a theme used in many stories to transport the protagonist from one world to the next, or from one form of existence to another. Once the girl has found her way to the Otherworld, which is symbolic of liminal space or the unconscious, she meets the old woman, who is archetypally the Guide, the wise elder who teaches her the wisdom of the cycles of life. The tasks of taking the bread out, picking the apples, and helping Frau Holle with the household chores suggest that the girl has integrity and acts on what she knows is right, not skipping any steps that are part of her initiation.

Interestingly, both the apples and the bread are at the point when they are ripe and done, which is symbolic of the girl herself having reached the brink of womanhood. Finally, when the girl has completed all her tasks, including shaking out the feather bed, a seasonal reference that signifies the cyclic motif that underlines the entire story, she tells Frau Holle that she is ready to return to the upper world and take her place in the next phase of her life. Note that Frau Holle is delighted that the girl feels thus—she has completed all the steps and is ready. The girl then goes through the door, crosses the threshold, and is rewarded for her integrity and willingness to work. Conversely, her stepsister essentially fakes the entire initiation process, including faking the blood, and ignoring all the tasks required to gain her reward. This tells us that there is no rushing initiation. There is no skipping steps and no faking it to get the prize at the end. Like Capricorn, one must commit oneself to the task at hand. One must do the work.

## Pathworking: Weaving the Tapestry

*It is the eve of winter solstice: the longest night of the year. A fierce wind picks up, cutting through your clothes and making you aware of every bone in your body. You huddle deeper into your woolen cape and breathe out puffs of steam. Snow has begun to fall, at first as soft as feathery down, but now falling out of the darkening sky in large white pieces. You hurry along the wooded path in search of somewhere to shelter. You come upon a small opening flanked by two snow-covered elder trees. It looks like the entrance to an animal's den. You hesitate, but you need to get out of the approaching blizzard. You flatten yourself on your belly and squeeze through the small space.*

*Inside, the small space opens into a tunnel, high enough that you can get to your feet. You find that it is quite warm inside, and you walk toward a faint light glowing in the distance. As you walk, you realize that the tunnel appears to be formed from the gnarled and curving roots of trees. Small offerings are tucked here and there amongst the roots: a length of scarlet flax thread, a perfectly ripe apple, and an earthenware cup. The light becomes brighter, and you continue toward it. The tunnel opens, and you walk out into the dazzling sunshine of a spring afternoon. The air is scented with the perfume of flowers, freshly baked bread, and apples.*

*You walk on until you come to a small cottage with a neat fence. As you move toward it, an elderly woman appears on the porch. She smiles broadly at you, and you feel an instant sense of homecoming. You approach her, and she introduces herself: "I am Mother Holle, and you are most welcome here." You realize the delicious smell of baked bread is coming from her kitchen as she beckons you over her threshold.*

*Inside, the only sound is the comforting tick of an old clock. Her furnishings are spare but comfortable, and she motions for you to sit at her kitchen table. In the corner, you notice a shuttle and a simple frame loom, as though Mother Holle had just put aside her handiwork when she heard you coming up her path. The piece is in progress; the warp threads are sturdy, and the weft is an intricate pattern of red and white. You look closely at the shuttle and see that it is made from old, yellowed bone, with curious carvings of elderflowers intertwining with images of young women and old crones in various postures of weaving.*

*Frau Holle sets a cup of elderberry wine before you and sees you admiring her work. "There are no shortcuts. Although one can weave any pattern and colors one wishes into the weft, a strong warp supports the integrity of the entire piece, and the threads must always be tied securely. You can be creative when weaving, but you cannot miss any steps," she says. Her blue eyes twinkle, and she reaches into her apron pocket and offers you a skein of scarlet flax thread tied securely with an elder twig. "Plan your steps carefully and do your work willingly, and you will be rewarded with the finest cloth, both beautiful and enduring."*

*The old clock chimes, and you realize it is time to go. You thank Frau Holle for her gift, ready to pick up the loom and begin the work of weaving practical magick into your weft. You go back through the tunnel the way you came, and when you emerge, the storm has passed and a blanket of newly fallen snow sparkles in the solstice sunrise.*

## Ritual: Frau Holle's Protection Charm

Weaving magick is one of the oldest forms of spellwork and is featured cross-culturally in mythology and folklore. Although weaving is an art unto itself, the following ritual is a simple braiding charm that evokes the same meditative light-trance state as weaving. If you know how to weave or feel called to learn this ancient craft, feel free to substitute.

*You Will Need:*

3 lengths of ribbon, yarn, or string

Black tourmaline beads with holes big enough for string or ribbon to pass through

Ground and center in your preferred way. Visualize your intent for a few moments. Tie the three pieces together, and leave a loop at the top. Begin to braid, and intersperse the tourmaline pieces when you are intuitively called to do so. Envision yourself protected and perfectly safe. A simple chant that doesn't distract you from the work at hand works well, such as,

> *Frau Holle protects me, I am perfectly safe.*
> *Frau Holle protects me, I am perfectly safe.*

Depending on the length of string or ribbon you use, you can use this charm as an ornament that you can braid into your hair, make into a bracelet or necklace, hang from your rearview mirror to protect you while in your vehicle, or hang in your window or over a doorway in your home.

## Ritual: Frau Holle's Protection Powder

The elder tree (*Sambucus nigra*) has long been associated with protection magick and with the realm of the Fae. Folklore had it that having an elder tree outside one's home protected the inhabitants therein. It is especially sacred to Frau Holle and connected with the mysteries of the cycles of life, particularly regeneration and rebirth. Elder also has many practical medicinal uses for the respiratory system, asthma, and colds, amongst other ailments. In addition, the flowers and berries make a wonderful cordial, a soothing tea, and a delicious wine. Unless you're an herbalist and know what to look for, it's best to obtain elderflowers or berries from your local natural foods store. Elderflowers and elderberries are also readily available as packaged tea and bottled cordial or wine in a variety of places, including online. The following magickal recipe is best made when the Moon is in Capricorn, during Capricorn season (especially winter solstice), or when the Moon is waning.

*You Will Need:*
1 part each:
    Dried organic elderflowers
    Dried organic elderberries
    Dried organic apple bits
    Dried organic white sage
Mortar and pestle

Grind all ingredients with mortar and pestle until reaching a slightly coarse blend. Scatter around your doorway to repel negative energy and unwanted guests, or around your property to widen your sphere of protection. Alternatively, you can place it in a small offering bowl on your altar in honor of Frau Holle, with the intention of manifesting right livelihood or new work that you love. You can tuck a small amount in a pouch and wear or carry it for extra protection. It can also be burned as an incense. Although folklore tells us that it is ill luck to burn the wood of an elder tree, the flowers and berries, if harvested ethically, are appropriate to use as a ritual incense.

# Capricorn Correspondences

*Astrological Dates:* December 22 through January 19

*Sabbat:* Winter solstice (Yule)

*Capricorn Goddess Archetypes:* Frau Holle, Mother Hulda, Hecate, the Cailleach, Baba Yaga, Illinti Kota, Budi Ma, Etugen, Emegelji Eji, Colleda, Sudice, Agischanak

*House:* Tenth

*Element:* Earth

*Mode:* Cardinal

*Planet:* Saturn

*Colors:* Black, winter white, icy gray, silver, earth tones

*Crystals:* Aragonite, aventurine, black tourmaline, hematite, jade, malachite, pyrite, smoky quartz

*Essential Oils:* Douglas fir, pine, vetiver, ginger, cypress, oakmoss

*Parts of the Body:* Knees, joints, skeletal system

# AQUARIUS

Although it is the heart of winter, after the Sun's rebirth on winter solstice, we now begin to notice the return of the light. While only a few short weeks ago it was velvety black at five in the evening, there is now a golden glow on the western horizon that infuses hope into the most winter-weary soul. The cross-quarter festival that occurs during Aquarius season is Imbolc, also known as Candlemas or the feast of the waxing light. Sacred to the Celtic goddess Brigit, Imbolc is a time of inspiration and hope, a time to look to the future and contemplate what seeds one will plant. Aquarius is a fixed air sign, which means that it occurs in the heart of the season and resonates with the intellectual and objective element of air. Reflecting the natural world's promise of awakening and the anticipation of the rebirth that will come with spring, the Aquarius archetype is forward looking and visionary. After the survival-oriented, conservative worldview of Capricorn, Aquarius is a wild card: a nonconformist rule breaker who speaks without filter and unabashedly celebrates its differences. The modern ruler of Aquarius is Uranus, known in astrology as the Great Awakener, and those with Aquarius prominent in their charts do tend to challenge the status quo and question assumptions, which often leads to a paradigm shift, aligning Aquarius with the archetypes of the Revolutionary and the Rebel.

Aquarius is connected to the collective, and although the sign is highly creative, her visions and revelatory flashes of insight are usually about the bigger picture in some way. And while she is innately concerned with community, Tribe, and group consciousness, Aquarius can be somewhat detached on a personal level. Her eye is on the wider, more holistic view of any given situation. This identification with the collective gives Aquarius a finger-on-the-pulse awareness, as she is gifted with the intuitive ability to read patterns and know which way the tides are turning. This gives way to Aquarius's reputation for being progressive and futuristic: always on the forefront or cutting edge of a new social movement or direction. Because they are often amongst the first to pick up on subtle shifts in the collective unconscious, it is sometimes not until much later that they are recognized as the visionaries they are. Aquarius is often ahead of her time, and her radical ideas and brilliant originality sometimes lead to a reputation of being quirky or eccentric.

Aquarius marches to the beat of her own drum, a true individual who often finds herself at odds with the dominant culture. She is often more comfortable in subcultures that resonate with her ideals, many of which become absorbed into the overculture as society catches up in the years and decades that follow. The ideals of the hippie generation of the 1960s are prime examples of Aquarian ideals, and their time has now come. Ideologies and practices that were once considered far out and fringe have made their way into the mainstream—vegetarianism, yoga, religious freedom, preservation of the environment, animal rights, and human rights, to name just a few. Of course, there's still a long way to go, and the far right might still not be entirely enthusiastic about all these Aquarian ideals, but progress has been made and can be built on. Certain laws have been changed. And, perhaps most importantly, there is arguably more shared conscious awareness in the collective than ever before.

## The Aquarius Woman

Fiercely independent with a brilliant mind and always radically authentic, the Aquarian woman is the quintessential free spirit. She can be provocative and enjoys shocking people out of complacency with her controversial views on a wide range of subjects. She has a penchant to wake up and shake up the tried and true and get people thinking. She is a born instigator and a change maker, a Truth Teller who is as true to herself as she is idealistic. Inspired and inspiring, she has the gift of intuition and is blessed with illuminating flashes of uncommon insight. She is often seized with moments of inspiration, the "fire in the head" alluded to in the ancient Celtic poem, the "Song of Amergin."[47] When she channels these brilliant insights into creative inspiration, her ideas bring hope and optimism that serves the greater good.

However, she is also known to be highly unpredictable, and while some find that unpredictability exciting, others can be put off by what they consider erratic. She does tend to have some inherent contradictions. On one hand, she seems to be friends with everyone, and cannot walk down the street without bumping into an acquaintance. On the other hand, only a very few ever get close enough to be allowed into her inner circle. She is always friendly and usually kind, yet there can be a slightly reserved, cool, and somewhat detached quality about the Aquarius woman. Although Aquarius is the sign of the Humanitarian, and she's often found championing equality and upholding the rights of her fellow citizens, it does not follow that she is emotionally demonstrative. She can be distinctly uncomfortable around what she considers irrational displays of emotion. She prizes logic and rationality over maudlin sentimentality any day. Whether she is aware of her apparent contradictions doesn't matter; she's of the mind that what other people think of her is none of her business, and she is always unapologetically and wholly herself.

Aquarius accepts that in following her dreams, and her unique vision of the future, she is bound to encounter some resistance. Although she may ruffle some feathers as she pushes forward on her path, she has the conviction to walk alone if it means being true to her ideals. She senses that if she stays on a path with integrity and personal meaning, she'll eventually find her true Tribe and be surrounded by like-minded individuals who share similar hopes, goals, and dreams. As an air sign, Aquarius is considered social, but unlike Gemini and Libra, she does not

47. Augusta Gregory, *Gods and Fighting Men* (1905; repr., Floating Press, 2012), PDF e-book, 96–97.

need constant stimulation or companionship—she enjoys her moments of solitude. At heart she is a bit of an intellectual and has a thirst to learn about everything from art history to archetypal psychology to astrology to Nietzsche. Aquarius is a diverse thinker, and what some might think of as offbeat or bizarre notions are often the seeds of ideas whose time has yet to come. While many Aquarians spend an inordinate amount of time in their head, they are rarely bored or lonely. However, most will jump at the chance to discuss their views on politics, science, or philosophy with equally intelligent and open-minded peers.

Aquarius women treat everyone with equal respect and actively resist racist, classist, and sexist ideologies. Many are activists in some way and work tirelessly to bring awareness to those causes that resonate with their strong sense of equality and fairness. She can be contemptuous of the status quo and defiant of structures that she sees are plainly antiquated and irrelevant in the new world she envisions. When she channels her vision constructively and works toward change in a balanced way, she can be an excellent social reformer, advocate, or environmentalist. A few Aquarian women have what some might consider unconventional, utopian ideas about community, and they embrace the concept of ecovillages, land trusts, spiritual or artists' communities, and other types of cooperative, sustainable-living arrangements.

Although she is altruistic at heart, when the Aquarius woman is unbalanced and coming from her shadow, her idealism can turn into zealotry. Aquarius is a fixed sign, and she can fixate and obsess on her ideals to the point where, in her all-encompassing fervor, she stops hearing others' perspectives. It is interesting to note that for all her Uranian libertarian ideals, the traditional ruler of Aquarius is Saturn. It may not be evident at first glance, but if you look closely, you'll see some surprising examples of compartmentalized either-or thinking or a strong adherence to the "way things *should* be." She is absolutely dedicated to her concepts of right and wrong and may succumb to the-end-justifies-the-means thinking to implement her vision. Ironically, she may not see that in her zeal to improve one area of society, she may begin to objectify anyone who is not part of her plan and doesn't care if she crosses their boundaries or erodes their rights. And there are those Aquarius women who rebel just for the sake of stirring things up, the quintessential rebel without a cause. She may be blatantly defiant about rules, even when there's no good reason to flout them—she does it just because she can. Although she values logic and rationality, when she is acting from her shadow, the fixed nature of Aquarius tends toward brooding resentment, which on occasion can erupt into explosive rage. She can also turn her brilliant originality into empty, bizarre, and eccentric theatrics for mere shock value. Her behavior and ideas may be erratic, or she may detach herself from society to the point where she becomes the archetypal Outcast. On a subconscious level, she may identify with what she perceives as the glamour of outsider status and do all she can to not belong, wearing it as a badge of defiance. If she has gone to this extreme, it is likely that she gets secondary gains from this identification. For example, she may use it as proof that no one understands her after all.

Of course, there are many Aquarius artists and performers who use their outsider status as part of their art or persona, which is a very different thing. Artists and performers are usually using the platform of their work to wake people up, make them think, or highlight the hypocrisy of social convention and privilege. Aquarius women are born creatives and, no matter their medium, do their best work when they utilize their ability to tune in to the collective and give voice to their insights and observations to make a statement that illuminates, informs, and creates change. Whether she is a painter, writer, or a spoken-word or hip-hop artist, Aquarius can be a creative genius and has the gift to tap into the group mind and inspire an expansion of consciousness in others. It is then that she is fulfilling her life's task, and her need to instigate, push boundaries, and break paradigms not only has an impact on the collective but also feeds her at a soul level.

As might be expected, when it comes to love and relationships, the Aquarius woman needs a great deal of space and freedom. She is ultrasensitive to any hint of someone trying to control her in any way and will walk away with scarcely a backward glance. She may be slow to commit, but when she does, her partner needs to be a unique combination of open-minded, intelligent, and hopefully a bit quirky and should not curb her creativity or idealism. For the Aquarius woman, compatibility is usually based more on mental connection than physical attraction. She is intrigued by intelligence and attracted to the unconventional: the fascinating, eccentric suitor will beat out any competition for her attention, hands down. Some Aquarians choose partners with different cultural, spiritual, and socioeconomic backgrounds, especially if she grew up in a family that did not recognize that she herself was cut from a different cloth. Remember that Aquarius likes to challenge tradition and will often rebel against parental expectations, especially if those expectations are rooted in unquestioned assumptions. Although she is not usually romantic in a traditional sense, she needs someone who can be her best friend and share her political, intellectual, and creative visions. But once she does make a commitment, she is intensely loyal, a good listener, and a fun, supportive, and engaging companion, while her unpredictable nature keeps things from getting dull and routine. However, she has extremely high ideals, and if her partner doesn't live up to them, she can be disappointed and angry and rarely forgets a perceived slip on their part. Some Aquarius women may explore alternative paths to relationships that don't fit societal norms, and there are those who simply choose not to "do relationships" at all during phases in their life.

Aquarius women are just as fascinating sexually as they are in every other area of life. Because her biggest erogenous zone is her mind, she often has a unique take on sex. Sometimes that means she is drawn to the experimental, but other times it's all just a thought experiment. Aquarius can be one of the most uninhibited signs, and some women embrace new sexual experiences with few holds barred. She may also define her sexual orientation in a variety of ways: heterosexual, homosexual, bisexual, pansexual, and anyplace in between. Some Aquarians reject the binary gender model, and others resist labeling their sexual orientation or identity altogether. On the other hand, there are those Aquarians for whom sex is not a main focus, and they may identify primarily as asexual, although they may use additional labels to define their orientation.

The Aquarius woman's keen intelligence, authentic individuality, and friendly nature open a host of career possibilities. She's not usually drawn to a traditional career, and many Aquarius women design their own career paths based on their personal interests and ideals. Because of her dislike for rules and authority, she often does well as an entrepreneur, although she's also a valuable asset in any group setting or team environment. Whatever she does, she needs freedom to express her individuality and a certain ability to come and go as she likes. Freelance work can be especially suited to her for this reason.

Aquarius specializes in coming up with original ideas and would make a cutting-edge social media maven, creative director, copywriter, or graphic designer. Her brilliant imagination and creative genius would also make her a natural in any of the arts, especially if she can channel her ideals through her work. She can also be a cutting-edge, avant-garde trendsetter who inspires new direction in fashion and photography and would also shine as an innovative hairstylist or makeup artist. With her ability to tune in to the collective and shine the light on controversial subjects, she would make a thought-provoking author, blogger, commentator, or independent filmmaker. She may turn her high intelligence to any of the sciences and make an important breakthrough or discovery that creates change. The tech world is especially suited to Aquarius, and a career in web or software development, programming, or data science could catch her interest. Yet another direction for the Aquarius woman is in social justice and activism. Social work, counseling, education, environmental protection, nonprofit work, or a career in politics may call. She can also put her ideals to work in reforming everything from government policies to community structure. Her friendly disposition also makes her a natural in the hospitality industry or sales. On the other hand, Aquarius is often drawn to the unusual, and she can be most happy on a career path that not many tread. Astrology itself is under the domain of Aquarius, and I've met many Aquarian astrologers bringing their brilliant insight into the field. She may also resonate with various New Age modalities and create a career based on her specific interests.

## Guiding Goddess Archetype: Brigit

Brigit is a multifaceted goddess whose stories trace a spiral path through several traditions. She is variously known as Brighid, Bride, Brigantia, Brigantu, and Ffraid and is a widely known central goddess of the Celtic lands whose name means "high one." [48] Epithets for Brigit are "bright one" and "fiery arrow," which highlight her connection with creative inspiration as well as embody a protective aspect. In *The White Goddess,* scholar Robert Graves states that not only was she cognate with poetic inspiration, but poets were under her protection: "In Cormac's *Glossary* it was necessary to explain her as: 'the goddess worshipped by the poets on account of the great and illustrious protection afforded them by her.' It was in her honor that the ollave carried a golden branch with tinkling bells when he went abroad." [49]

Brigit is a triple goddess and in her three aspects is connected to healing, poetry, and smithcraft. She is the patron goddess of *filidhact* (Bardic lore and poetry), and as such, poets, storytellers, writers, and artists of all kinds petitioned her to ignite the fires of their imaginations and enchant their work while awakening their creativity with her divine inspiration. Brigit is also associated with midwifery, medicine, the hearth fire, and divination, and she presides over sacred wells and springs. She was the goddess of the forge and was loved and petitioned by artists and craftspeople. The forge is associated with transformation, of shaping metal through the elements of fire and water to become something new.

When Christianity came to Ireland, the people loved their goddess Brigit so much that she was transformed into a saint, Saint Brigid, and she is venerated to this day as one of the three main religious figures in Ireland. Through Christianity, she became known as the midwife to the

48. Patricia Monaghan, *Encyclopedia of Goddesses and Heroines* (Novato, CA: New World Library, 2014), 181.

49. Graves, *The White Goddess*, 390.

Virgin Mary and subsequently the foster mother of Christ.[50] Her main center of worship is in Kildare, in the province of Leinster. The name *Kildare* originated from *Cill Dara,* which means the "church of the oak tree." It's said that the site of her abbey at Kildare was overlaid on Druid sacred ground. One of the mysteries associated with Saint Brigid was her perpetual fire at her shrine at Kildare. This sacred fire was tended by nineteen sisters and never burned out nor left any trace of ash. The fire was said to be surrounded by a protective hedge and that no men were permitted to enter. However, if any man was foolish enough to attempt to enter the circle, he could expect divine vengeance.[51] The fire was put out during the reformation because it was too Pagan but was relit in 1993, as many women have been drawn once again to the light of Brigit. To me, this suggests that not only is Brigit associated with inspiration, but she *is* inspiration, and her fire cannot ever truly be put out, as it dwells in the hearts of the people who experience her. Each year, pilgrims visit her shrine in the village of Kildare for ritual contemplation and to pay homage to Saint Brigid. Here they pray for healing, collect holy water from the spring, and tie small ribbons or pieces of cloth called *clooties* on the nearby wishing tree as offerings.

Brigit's sacred day is Imbolc, the beginning of lambing season and the harbinger of spring. By February 2, the increasing sunlight has begun to warm the earth once again, and this time does indeed herald the return of the waxing light, along with the illumination and optimism that accompany the longer days. The rekindling of hope inherent at this time of year cannot be overstated. Without electricity or refrigeration, the ancients never knew how long their food supplies would last. Lactating ewes and cows were a welcome sign that spring was on its way. There are many folk customs that take place around Imbolc to honor Saint Brigit that suggest her ancient Pagan roots. In *The Language of the*

---

50. Gimbutas, *The Language of the Goddess,* 110.

51. Giraldus Cambrensis, *The Topography of Ireland,* ed. Thomas Wright, trans. Thomas Forester (Cambridge, ON: In Parentheses, 2000), PDF e-book, 54.

*Goddess,* Dr. Marija Gimbutas describes some of Brigit's enduring rituals, which echo her Pagan origins:

> *Special cakes were baked on her day, and dolls in her image were carried by girls in procession through the town. At each household they would stop while the householder made a present to Bride and paid homage to her, the gift could be a pebble shell, or flower. The mother of each household baked a special cake for her. Finally the girls ended up at one house where they locked all the doors and windows, setting the doll in the window where she might be seen. Then the dancing began which continued until dawn, when they formed a circle to sing the hymn "Beauteous Bride, Choice Foster-Mother of Christ."* [52]

On Imbolc, Brigit is celebrated in her maiden aspect, and the dolls that Gimbutas mentions were usually made of corn sheaves. I made one such doll several years ago, and she still has pride of place on my altar every February. Women would also weave Brigit's crosses, small crosses with four arms and a square center, typically made of rushes or corn sheaves. These were hung over doorways for protection around Imbolc.

Not only does Brigit's sacred day occur in the middle of Aquarius season, but there are many other correlations that align this beloved Celtic goddess with the Aquarius archetype. Both are aligned with the sudden spark of creative inspiration, and they are each a catalyst of hope for the future. The glyph for Aquarius has been described as the waves of the water of consciousness but also as the lightning bolts of inspiration, which align with Brigit's epithet "fiery arrow."

As all creatives know, inspiration can be evasive when we most need it. It can be capricious and evanescent: you almost have it, and then it disappears. One thing for certain is that inspiration cannot be forced, only invited. We must make space for it, prepare the ground so the seeds can sprout. We must remember to fill our own well and tend our inner flame by feeding the fire with those things that nourish it.

---

52. Gimbutas, *The Language of the Goddess,* 110.

A year ago my husband and I bought our dream house on a tiny island in the Salish Sea. It is the first time I've lived in the country, and we are blessed to have a well on our property that supplies all our water for our every need. Being a city girl, this was a revelation for me. Crystal clear, sweet water magically bubbles up out of the earth so I can take a bath, wash my clothes, and water my garden! During our first summer here, we heard tales of neighbors whose wells had run dry. At first, I was incredulous. I had no idea that a well could actually run dry. What do people do without water? I've learned a lot since then. During a drought, you need to be mindful about how much water you use. You just can't keep pumping it up and expect your well not to run dry. But then, miraculously, the rain comes, the water table rises, and your well is refilled. I think in all of this there is a lesson. As with an actual well, we cannot expect that our own creative or spiritual wells will never run dry. We must learn to trust the cycles and know that if we are in a creative dry spell, the life-giving rain will return and we will once again be overflowing with creative inspiration. Brigit is a goddess who resonates through the elements of both fire and water. When fire and water are combined, they create steam. This is the steam that powers our creativity, the mist that rises when sunlight warms the dew on the ground, gifting us with startling and mysterious visions—if we only remain still enough to see.

## Pathworking: Rekindle Your Flame, Refill Your Well

*You've been feeling stuck for some time, and try as you might to bring up something new, something fresh, something inspired, it seems as if your well has run dry. For every seed of a thought you have, an inner voice whispers, "Someone's already done it. Someone's done it better. Why even bother trying?" And even worse, a comparative, self-pitying thought sneaks in: "Why am I not original and gifted and brave like …?"*

*You begin to walk up the winding green path that leads to the top of the hill, with these thoughts clattering uncomfortably in your head. It is an unseasonably warm February afternoon. Flashes of white snowdrops and deep purple crocus are peeking through the first of the new green* growth, and you hear the gentle sound of sheep bleating in the distance. The path splits into two, and you pause for a moment as you decide which direction you'll take. One path is well traveled and goes straight to the top, but the one on your right curves around the back of the hill. You choose the less trodden path and soon find yourself in a sun-dappled oak grove.

You walk for a time and come upon a crumbling stone wellhead. The wellhead is dressed in colorful flowers, and you count eighteen flickering votive candles tucked in amongst the greenery. There are nineteen candles altogether, but one is unlit. A gnarled old hawthorn tree stands to the left of the well, and clooties decorate its ancient limbs. You stand in silent contemplation for some time, spellbound by the beauty and mystery before you.

Suddenly, you realize you are no longer alone. A tall red-haired woman crowned with a garland of snowdrops emerges quietly from the shade of the oaks and stands beside you. She is barefoot and dressed in white and there is an incandescence about her that glows like a flame in the approaching twilight. Elegant Celtic knots and spirals delicately pattern her forearms. You realize this is the goddess Brigit at your side.

She turns to you. "There is yet one candle not lit. Will you light it?"

You walk to the wellhead and kneel before the altar of flowers and candles. You see offerings amongst the flowers, including a chalice of fresh milk, but you see nothing with which to light the nineteenth candle. You lean forward, entranced by the twinkling reflection of the candlelight on the dark surface of the well water. Your vision blurs, and the light becomes little pinpoints like stars in the night sky. The stars become a galaxy and then dance into spirals and symbols, swirling in images that rise and take shape and then dissolve and rise again into another. You lose track of time, allowing the visions to rise and transform one into the next.

From far away comes the voice of Brigit, clear and musical as a bell: "What is it you see?" Although at first you find it difficult to answer, you name aloud the things you can. In time, the visions clear, and once again you are looking at the reflection of simple candlelight flickering on the dark water. You realize Brigit is beside you.

*"Will you light the nineteenth candle?" She touches three fingers to her luminous brow and transfers the gossamer light into your hand. Tentatively, you reach toward the unlit candle and pass your hand over its wick, and instantly a tiny flame is kindled into being. You sit back on your heels and gaze at the newborn flame. You are completely transfixed and lost for words. You turn to thank Brigit, but find yourself alone at the edge of the well. A waxing Moon has risen in the sky, and far off to the west you see a faint golden glow where the Sun has set, suffusing the deep blue of the fading twilight. Spring is just another turn of the Wheel away.*

## Ritual: The Wishing Tree

Two of my most treasured memories involve a wishing tree. The first was at a baby-naming ceremony when I lived in Glastonbury, England. It was summer solstice eve, and the golden early evening light guided our merry procession up the back of the Tor. Two by two, we climbed an old hawthorn and tied ribbons in the branches to make our personal wish for the baby's future. Then we celebrated on blankets in the warm grass and ate bread and cheese washed down with elderflower wine and mead. Many years later, when my husband and I were handfasted in our backyard at Lughnasadh, we had our friends and family write wishes for us on organic paper and then tie them into the branches of our favorite apple tree with red silk ribbon. The seasons came and went, and the paper dissolved, becoming part of the nutrients for the tree, but the red ribbons survived the winter storms. Sometimes I would go out and gaze up at them, marveling at how each person had tied their ribbon on with their own personal signature: some were fancy bows, some simple knots. When we moved three years ago, it was one thing I knew I'd miss about our old home. Tying a ribbon or clootie in a tree has a similar function to the Tibetan prayer flag. Prayer flags fly in the wind, carrying their blessings out to all. Although clooties are usually of a more personal nature, the wind passes over them, carrying blessings, hopes for healing, and wishes out into the world of form.

Wishing trees have long been a symbolic marking of a rite of passage, making a wish, or asking for healing. Many sacred wells in the British Isles have a wishing tree or faery tree nearby, and hundreds if not thousands of sacred wells in Ireland are dedicated to the goddess Brigit. Your ritual can be simple or elaborate, and you can be alone or with loved ones. It can be on a tree on your property or a special tree in the woods. You can purchase ribbon from a fabric store or use shreds of an old garment that has special meaning for you.

### Brigit's Inspiration Incense

Invoke Brigit's gift of inspiration any time you need to connect with her. Brigit's Incense is especially helpful when doing creative work or studying. This incense is most potent when made while the Moon is in its phase of waxing to full.

**You Will Need:**

1 part each:

    Dried blackberry leaves

    Honey

    Lavender

    Dried rosemary

1 drop peppermint essential oil

1 pinch cinnamon

The incense can be used immediately or stored to be used later. Mix the ingredients and place the incense in a small sealable plastic bag. As always, experiment with making a very small batch at a time, and adjust to your preference.

### The Wishing Tree

Brigit's Inspiration Incense

Incense burner or heatproof container

Lighter or matches (be very careful if it's dry or windy)

Charcoal for the incense

A length of ribbon or cloth long enough to tie onto a branch (natural fibers are best: cotton, silk, wool, etc.)

Tree: Choose a tree you are drawn to. Hawthorn and rowan are both associated with the Fae and have been used widely in ritual work with wishing trees, but you may use any tree that suits your purpose.

Offering for Brigit: Milk, cheese, honey, wool, Brigit corn dolly, Brigit's cross, shell, flower, special stone. Preferably, only leave something biodegradable that will not harm the tree or any animals in any way (e.g., nothing plastic or toxic).

Ground and center in your preferred way. Light the incense and smudge yourself and any other participants. Pass your ribbon or cloth through the incense smoke and consecrate it to Brigit.

Take your ribbon and go to the tree you have chosen. Carry the ribbon and walk clockwise around the tree three times. Ask permission from the tree to tie your cloth to one of its branches. Place your palms on the tree's trunk and listen for a message. It may be very subtle. Thank the spirit of tree and make your offering to the goddess Brigit. Close your eyes for a few moments, and make your wish or ask for a blessing. When you are ready, tie your ribbon onto a branch. Give thanks to the goddess and to the tree spirit. Visualize your intent growing with the tree and moving out into the world on the wind. Close the circle if you have cast one, and celebrate with food and libations.

## Aquarius Correspondences

*Astrological Dates:* January 20 through February 18

*Sabbat:* Imbolc

*Aquarius Goddess Archetypes:* Brigit, Hebe, Adoma, Ara, Nut, Tanit, Lilith, Eve, Sophia, Athena, Tien-Mu

*House:* Eleventh

*Element:* Air

*Mode:* Fixed

*Planets:* Saturn (traditional), Uranus (modern)

*Colors:* Electric blue, violet

*Crystals:* Astrophyllite, cavansite, celestite, kunzite, petalite, phenakite, sugilite

*Essential Oils:* Peppermint, benzoin, lavender, cypress

*Parts of the Body:* Ankles, circulatory system

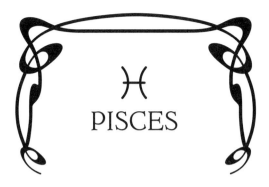

# PISCES

Although we come to the end of the cycle, as we move into Pisces season there are signs of renewal everywhere. In the space of one day, or even one hour, the last of the winter storms rage and then magically give way to elf rain dazzling through sunlight. Rainbows arch across the sky and prisms sparkle in each drop of water. Pisces is a mutable water sign. It is the last of the threshold signs, taking us from winter's end to the gateway of spring equinox. In Pisces, we have come full circle. The last sign resonates through the element of water—oceanic, flowing, and connected to Source.

Pisces season is liminal space. Between the worlds. Dreamtime. Pisces illuminates the most sacred of all Mysteries: the promise of rebirth inherent in all endings. Its archetype encompasses both resurrection and redemption. In the tarot, Pisces is the Mystery hidden behind the veil of the High Priestess. Pisces is Neptune ruled, embodying the archetypes of the Mystic, the Poet, and the Dreamer, as well as the Martyr and the Victim. As Pisces is the last sign on the wheel, it has been often said that it contains every lesson on the path. Pisces has gone down all roads before and comes into this lifetime knowing what it is to walk in the shoes of another. Pisces brings with it the wisdom of every face of the Goddess.

In *The Hero with a Thousand Faces*, Joseph Campbell writes about the hero's crossing of the return threshold, which I think perfectly illuminates the central life task of Pisces. After the soul has made its archetypal journey from first sign Aries to last sign Pisces, it has seen it all.

It has seen wonders and fought battles and known every experience of the human condition, from the dizzying heights of ecstasy to the depths of sorrow. Although it has much wisdom to bring back to the every-day world, it is also understandably exhausted. Campbell writes of the hero's occasional reluctance to return to the world of ego and mundane life, of the desire to escape into a state of rest and unending bliss, which has some interesting parallels with Pisces.[53]

Pisces's penchant for escapism is well known, and we will touch on that soon enough. But Pisces, like Campbell's Hero, has a job to do, and even though it's tempting to curl up and drift off indefinitely, we are reminded that the nature of life is cyclical. As Campbell explains, "The boon brought from the transcendent deep becomes quickly ratio-nalized into nonentity, and the need becomes great for another hero to refresh the word."[54] Pisces is symbolized by two fish swimming in op-posite directions, meaning one part of the psyche is ever swimming up-stream, striving for transcendence, to bring wisdom from the deep and remind us of the Mysteries, while the other would prefer to rest, to take the path of least resistance, and be swept along by the current. Which direction to swim is a decision Pisces must make for herself.

## The Pisces Woman

Enigmatic and enchanting, the Pisces woman embodies the quintessen-tial creative muse. There is often a subtle glamour about Pisces, a kind of otherworldly vibe that many find beguiling and seductive. She has often been compared to a siren or mermaid, and although she's often perceived as a romantic figure, she possesses uncanny wisdom and is of-ten a creative visionary in her own right. Perhaps because of her innate receptivity, she seems to have an unconscious predisposition to reflect the projections of others. Sometimes these projections are unwelcome, and she is often baffled at the way others see her. But other times she

---

53. Joseph Campbell, *The Hero with a Thousand Faces*, 3rd ed. (Novato, CA: New World Library, 2008), 189.

54. Campbell, *The Hero with a Thousand Faces*, 188.

is quite aware of her ability to cloak herself in glamour and plays tricks with light and shadow to make people see what she wants them to see. There is a bit of the Enchantress in the Pisces woman, a natural ability to shift shape. She certainly does have a talent for conjuring and enchantment, which can be an incredible asset for anyone working in the creative fields.

Her fertile imagination usually gives rise to inspired creative talent. She is a true romantic with the heart of a poet and is entranced by the stories, myths, and legends of old. Her connection to the boundless ocean of the collective unconscious allows her to travel inner realms and draw on the treasures of the deep, and she has the innate gift of understanding the archetypal and the numinous more readily than mundane reality. She is at home in the dreamtime, with the ability to translate the symbols found therein, channeling the inspiration from the intuitive realm into sublime forms of art, music, poetry, and dance. Of course, her creative expression is not limited to the fine arts, and she can be creative in myriad ways according to her interests. Whatever medium calls her, her work almost always has a touch of the enigmatic. It is usually dreamy, flowing, and graceful, featuring organic forms and ethereal or mystical elements. Many Pisces women also incorporate the spiritual into their art, and some are inspired by the mythology of the Goddess in their work. Art nouveau, particularly the works of Alphonse Mucha, bring to mind what I think of as the Pisces esthetic. Sensual, feminine, otherworldly and enchanting, his images have an intangible quality that are infused with the sacred.

Because of her acute receptivity and awareness of the interconnectivity of life, the Pisces woman is often highly intuitive, even psychic. Some are aware of their extra sensitivity from an early age, and if they are fortunate enough to have open-minded, supportive families that can help them develop their gifts, they can develop their intuition as naturally as any other sense. Many Pisces women are drawn to the intuitive arts and have a natural aptitude for tarot and other types of divination. They may also have an interest in astrology, channeling, magick, and spiritual healing of all kinds. Some incorporate these arts as part of their own private spiritual path, while others may choose to make a career out of their esoteric interests.

Whether she is embracing her intuition consciously or not, Pisces soaks up impressions without trying and sometimes is at a loss to explain her sudden mood shifts or the strange thoughts that come to her unbidden. She may be what in recent times has been termed an *empath*—a person who unconsciously experiences the feelings of others whether she wants to or not. And while this can be an asset for those working in the helping professions, when it isn't managed skillfully, it can also be emotionally exhausting and unproductive, which can lead to burnout. Because she is at heart a kind and compassionate soul, Pisces must take care not to confuse compassion with codependence.

One of Pisces's greatest life lessons is to learn healthy boundaries, and despite her desire to help and serve, she needs to practice self-care so that she does not become subsumed by the unconscious agendas of others. Pisces has a trusting nature, and her compassion is one of her greatest gifts. Unfortunately, these very qualities can also lead her to be gullible, and she needs to learn that not everyone has her best interests at heart. There are those out there who would take advantage of her trusting nature and use it to their own ends. She wants to believe the best in people, and if she's not grounded, she can be taken in by charlatans or self-styled gurus.

Although service is a concept central to Pisces, there is another current that can run through the shadow of this sign. She may identify unconsciously with the Victim archetype and find herself either as someone's doormat or trapped in ego identification as the Savior. On one hand, if she finds herself repeatedly aligned with the Victim or Martyr archetypes, she may be getting secondary gains by receiving attention or sympathy for her long suffering and stoicism. And, while life happens and people do sometimes end up being a victim through no fault of their own, we are talking here of something that is more of an ongoing pattern. People in her life may start wondering why no matter the circumstance she always ends up in the same predicaments. If she recognizes that she's caught in this self-defeating pattern, she would do well to seek therapy to break the cycle and move forward with new tools for self-awareness. On the other hand, Pisces sometimes ends up on the opposite end of the spectrum and identifies with the Savior archetype. Through what appears to be selfless altruism (usually quite plainly at a cost to her), she takes on the guise as the self-sacrificing Savior, garnering a sense of specialness, or ego inflation, in the process. Although helping others is a noble aspiration, she must become aware of her underlying motives, particularly if she is giving at the expense of her own mental, physical, or emotional health. She must also accept that as much as she might like to, she cannot fix everyone.

While Pisces is still learning the importance of creating healthy boundaries, she may develop unhealthy coping mechanisms that do not serve her (or anyone else's) greatest good. She may occasionally feel engulfed or flooded by her intense feelings and attempt to escape them by softening their edges through substance misuse. Of course, this is just one way to evade feelings, and she may try and escape through a variety of means, including compulsive romantic or sexual distractions, which may lead to indiscriminate or risky behavior. She can be highly impressionable and therefore drawn to people or circumstances that are emotionally unhealthy or dangerous. Or she may retreat into a fantasy world, withdrawing from responsibility, and becoming deceptive and evasive in a misguided attempt at self-protection. The world can be a difficult place for the ungrounded or wounded Pisces woman. She is, after all, a gentle, sensitive creature, and she may have learned early on either to self-soothe or harden herself, lest she be swallowed up by the sorrows and chaos that are a part of life.

One of the ways Pisces can recharge her psychic batteries is by seeking solitude. Walks in nature, meditation, and intentional me time are mandatory for her psychological health. She can balance too much emotional receptivity by developing the qualities of her opposite sign, Virgo, and may benefit from taking a workshop on boundary setting. Pisces is associated with spiritual healing, but before she can offer healing to others, she must start with herself. She needs to learn the basics of self-care and develop a strong sense of self as well as healthy personal boundaries so that she can serve in a way that is for the good of all.

Nowhere is the reminder of good boundaries more important than when talking about Pisces and love. This is the cult of romantic love at its most sublime. When Pisces finds the magical Other that matches her inner ideal, she is swept away on a tide of romantic bliss, losing herself in an otherworldly paradise painted with the color of dreams. And, although a great part of this is often projection, Pisces can easily find herself over her head. Love is a drug that conjures images of her and her beloved as the protagonists in a tale that rivals the great love stories of the world. When she falls in love, she may indeed feel like she has strayed into the Otherworld, embodying the elemental stories of the Goddess and the Greenman, Arwen and Aragorn, Lancelot and Guinevere. In her urge to merge with her beloved, she yearns to dissolve the boundaries that keep them from being one, to experience that meeting of souls described by poets. She may experience an overwhelming certainty that she and her loved one have known each other before and that their love transcends this lifetime.

If her love is unrequited or for some reason she cannot enter into unending bliss with the object of her affection, Pisces steps into the archetypal cult of longing. And, while there may be no condition more excruciatingly torturous, for Pisces the exquisite ache that accompanies her intense longing makes it all the more romantic. No matter the circumstance, she will convince herself that this magical Other is the one. The only one. No one on earth could be more beautiful, deep, artistic, or amazing. He or she may be married, unavailable, or have some serious personality flaws, but that won't matter. She'll defend them and the situation to anyone who will listen, particularly herself. She'll intentionally turn a blind eye to the fact that he hasn't called her in weeks, is dating other people, or is cheating on his wife. She will rationalize almost anything in light of her projection. She will not hear when someone tells her that she's wearing rose-tinted glasses. He or she may somewhat resemble her inner ideal, but no human person can ever live up to the pedestal Pisces has fashioned for her beloved. Usually, the projection will eventually dissolve when she finally begins to see things for what they are. She may find herself terribly disillusioned, washed up on the shore of morning, wondering how things can look so different in the light of day. Or enough time will pass that she moves on, but until then, she may use the intensity of her feelings to create some of her life's finest and most inspired creative work. Then there is the Pisces woman who does move on and create a full life with another partner, but for years she may keep a secret place in her heart where the moments she shared with her magical Other live on. She will retreat here from time to time, as if stepping into a waking dream, and escape between the worlds.

Although most Pisces are incurable romantics, not all Pisces dive into the deep end and abandon all reason when it comes to love. In fact, some are so afraid of the overwhelming feelings it produces and the potential loss of control associated with "falling" in love, that they do everything possible to avoid it. They may be evasive and vague about their feelings and slow to commit. They may be feeling all the feels but slip away when it comes to declaring them. With emotional maturity and self-awareness, Pisces can be a loyal, committed partner, affectionate, sentimental, and generous. She is not afraid of her partner's feelings, or her own, and she will always keep the romance alive.

Sex is usually tied up with romance and intimacy for Pisces, and sex that is devoid of either usually fails to do a thing for her. Although she is very much given to fantasy, her fantasies usually are more romantic than purely of a sexual nature. If sex is involved in her fantasies, it's a part of a bigger romantic picture. The Pisces woman is sensual and dreamy and can also be deeply passionate in the right circumstances. At its best, sex for her is a transcendent, mystical experience, with a poetry of desire and longing that dissolves the boundaries between her and her partner. She may be moved to tears by the depths of her feelings and overwhelmed by the magical dimensions that may open for her during intimacy. She will appreciate a romantic and mysterious atmosphere, with candlelight and music. Evoking the spiritual or mystic can also help to transport her to a place of enchantment and imagination, while connecting her to a sense of the sacred.

Because Pisces is a mutable sign, she is adaptable and versatile and can go with the flow. She is a multifaceted woman with many talents. She is ideally suited to work in an area that provides flexibility in terms of schedule. Although she can work equally well on her own or with others, a career in which she can have a balance of both would suit her. She is warm and personable and is usually quite popular in the workplace for being a good listener. However, she usually does not do well in a highly structured or harsh environment. Pisces is known to change careers at different stages of her life and may have a challenge choosing what she wants to focus on, especially when young. But later in life, usually coinciding with her midlife transits (approximately between ages thirty-nine and forty-five), she may begin to want a more creative career and will aspire to do what she can to manifest it.

If she's drawn to a creative career, her choices are virtually limitless, depending on her interests. She would excel in any of the arts, from music to dance to writing and all points in between. She is a consummate storyteller and may be an aspiring novelist, creating mythic worlds and landscapes for her readers to immerse themselves in. She also has a special affinity for creating glamour and may do well working as a photographer or in the film and television industry. Although the long hours of film and TV could be a potential challenge, she should aim for a job in the creative end of film rather than in the production office or on set; anything in the art department, photography direction, set design, makeup, hair, script writing, and acting would all be good choices. Pisces brings a creative flair to whatever she does.

With her generous heart and desire to serve, the helping professions are another natural fit for Pisces. She would make a brilliant therapist, especially a depth psychologist, archetypal psychologist, or Jungian analyst. Her connection to the subconscious could lead her to a career in dream work or she could blend her love of creativity with the therapeutic process and become an expressive arts therapist. With her inborn sense of compassion, she might choose a career in social work or in the nonprofit sector or turn her compassionate nature to working with mistreated animals.

Given her connection to the intuitive realm, the spiritual is another direction Pisces would shine in. She could cast a wide net here depending on her aptitude and interests: she could be a member of the clergy, priestess, celebrant, ceremonialist, intuitive healer, Reiki practitioner, energy healer, professional tarot reader, or medium. She may be a retreat facilitator, providing a container for others to heal, create, and step into the flow. And finally, with her passion for story, she would shine as a mythologist, folklorist, or a teacher or professor of poetry, creative writing, literature, art history, or spiritual studies.

## Guiding Goddess Archetype: Kwan Yin

Kwan Yin is the goddess of mercy and compassion, a female *bodhisattva* who is one of the most important and beloved of all Buddhist deities. Kwan Yin's name means "she who hears all the prayers of the world," and after she became enlightened, she made the choice to stay in human form until every other sentient being on earth also received enlightenment. She has often been compared with the Tibetan goddess Tara and Mother Mary, two other figures known for their compassion.

In her iconography, Kwan Yin is usually depicted as wearing flowing white robes and the necklaces and bracelets that signify her status as bodhisattva. In her hands, she is often shown carrying a vase, a willow branch, and sometimes a lotus flower. The vase contains the healing water of life (or dew of compassion) used to cleanse away suffering and to purify body and mind. The willow branch is used for healing and to grant requests. Other representations show her riding on the back of a tiger, suggesting her fierce, protective aspect, while some depict her with a child in her arms, underlining her connection to fertility; mothers would pray to Kwan Yin to bring them children. She is also sometimes portrayed with her hands in symbolic postures of benevolence or banishing negativity. It is said that chanting or even saying Kwan Yin's name is enough to protect one from physical or spiritual harm, and people pray to Kwan Yin to relieve sorrow, heal sickness, and transcend worry and strife. Her most devout followers are vegetarian and dedicate themselves to living a life of peace and nonviolence.

There are differing accounts of how Kwan Yin came into being. Some say her first incarnation is in India as the male bodhisattva named Avalokiteshvara, who vows to stay on earth to relieve the suffering of other beings rather than ascend to Nirvana. It is said that he has the ability to transform himself into any form so he can best impart the teachings of the dharma. He can appear as a male, female, adult, child, or god.[55] However, because of his deep compassion for all sentient beings, he eventually becomes overwhelmed by the endless cycle of suffering and, in his sorrow, shatters into pieces. From these pieces, Kwan Yin is formed as woman; it may have been thought that in female form she could best offer comfort and attend to the suffering of the world.

Kwan Yin herself has many regional aspects and is known in different Asian countries by various names, making her accessible to all who call on her by appearing in the guise which will most resonate with the seeker. She also is depicted in her iconography in many aspects: as Dragonhead Kwan Yin, as a goddess of fertility, as a mother goddess, and as a healer, to name just a few. I encountered Kwan Yin in Nagoya, Japan, as Kannon-sama at a moment when I most needed her. Working in Japan, far from home, missing my family, and needing to return home to deal with a situation that had arisen, I was feeling very much alone and isolated. I still had another two months left on my contract when I stumbled upon her temple, Osu Kannon. Kneeling before her wooden statue, surrounded by an altar holding candles and offerings of fruit, I silently asked her to comfort me in my state of wretched homesickness. I thanked her and left the temple.

From that moment, a strange series of events unfolded. First, I became utterly and completely lost in the streets of Nagoya. I found myself going in circles, returning again and again to the same landmarks, no matter what direction I set off in. My Japanese was limited, and it

---

55. *The Lotus Sutra*, trans. Tsugunari Kubo and Akira Yuyama, 2nd ed. (Berkeley, CA: Numata Center for Buddhist Translation and Research, 2007), PDF e-book, 297–98.

was getting dark. Eventually, in a state of absolute despair, I walked into a shop on the edge of tears to ask yet another person if they could help me find my way. The young woman working in the shop spoke a little English and together we pieced out where I was and where I wanted to go. As I thanked her profusely for her help, I noticed a small altar to Kannon tucked into a shelf on the wall. In my very broken Japanese, I tried to convey to her that I had just been at the temple that afternoon. She smiled at me graciously and bowed. With her help, I got into a cab and found my way back to my apartment. The next day, a most unexpected turn of events occurred, and I was offered the opportunity to end my contract earlier than expected. It was like a miracle. I took the chance and was on a plane home within a few days. Since then, I have always kept a special place of honor and gratitude in my heart for Kwan Yin, goddess of mercy.

In another of Kwan Yin's origin stories, she begins existence as a princess named Miao Shan, whose name means "wonderful virtue." When she is born, blossoms fall from the sky and a beautiful fragrance fills the air, which the people agree signifies a sacred incarnation. Her parents care nothing for her virtue and pure heart, as they are materialistic and concerned only that Miao Shan had not been born a boy. When Miao Shan comes of age, her father expects to marry her off, but all she wants is to become a nun and help all sentient beings end their suffering. The king of course is frustrated with his young daughter and sends her to live in a monastery, where he instructs the nuns to give her the hardest of tasks, hoping she would see the futility of her efforts and do his bidding. Amongst her many difficult tasks is to create a kitchen garden out of barren soil, as well as the backbreaking job of carrying firewood and water.

However, because of her devotion and kindness, she is soon helped by the creatures near the monastery and is able to turn the garden into a fertile oasis that blooms year-round. When her father learns of her success, he orders the monastery to be burnt to the ground. Miao Shan miraculously saves herself as well as the other inhabitants, but her father doesn't stop there. He orders her execution. In one of many versions of the tale, the executioner is unable to kill Miao Shan, as she is protected by higher forces. She is rescued by a magickal white tiger and transported to the realms of hell, where she hears the weeping and suffering of all the souls trapped in *samsara*. Her heart spills over with compassion for these lost souls, which frees them from their bondage and causes the hells to become places of music, light, and fragrance while she is there.

At the end of the tale, her father becomes very ill, and in an act of supreme self-sacrifice, Miao Shan not only forgives him but willingly gives her eyes and arms to him as medicine, as the only cure for his malady is the eyes and arms of one who has never experienced anger. When the king and queen go to thank the bodhisattva who has offered this cure and realize it is their own daughter who has made this sacrifice, they are deeply humbled and cry for forgiveness. The air fills with the scent of a thousand blossoms, and flowers rain down from the heavens. Miao Shan is restored. With their eyes now open, Miao Shan's parents dedicate themselves to a spiritual life and build a shrine to their daughter on Fragrant Mountain, what is now known as Mount Putuo, an important Buddhist sanctuary southeast of Shanghai.[56]

There are many correspondences with Kwan Yin and Pisces. As a bodhisattva, Kwan Yin has experienced much suffering, but instead of leaving this world for the unending bliss of Nirvana, she selflessly chooses to offer compassion to all sentient beings. Similarly, the Pisces archetype is the soul that has embodied every earthly experience and, when coming from its highest vibration, chooses not to slip off into a place of rest but to step up and be of ultimate service in some way in the world. Pisces and Kwan Yin are also aligned with the idea of transformation: in Kwan Yin's earlier incarnation as Avalokiteshvara, he could transform himself into the best guise to teach someone. Pisces too, as a mutable sign, has the gift of adaptability, the ability to go with the flow and transform consciousness with her creativity. And like Princess Miao Shan, Pisces is often devoted to the higher spiritual principles of devotion, self-sacrifice,

56. Daniela Schenker, *Kuan Yin: Accessing the Power of the Divine Feminine* (Boulder: Sounds True, 2007), 18–20.

and forgiveness. Kwan Yin also resonates with the water element, carrying the vase containing the dew of compassion. However, the most powerful connection between Pisces and Kwan Yin is a shared deep and powerful compassion for the suffering of the world.

## Pathworking: The Beauty of Impermanence

*A gentle rain is falling, and the sky is gray. A fine-spun mist gracefully shrouds the top of the nearby mountain. Water droplets collect on the petals of early cherry blossoms, and the ground is carpeted in pink snow. You inhale deeply, the scent of a thousand falling petals reminding you of the impermanence of all things but also the beauty and renewal that come with the cusp of spring. You bend down to pick up a slender sprig that has fallen to the ground. Your heart has been weighed down lately, and you are ready for some guidance. You catch the delicate fragrance of temple incense in the air and stop and close your eyes for a moment to ascertain what direction it's coming from. You turn, follow the scent, and find yourself on a path leading up the mountainside.*

*Soon, it is as though you are walking through a cloud. You cannot see behind you or in front of you, and even your feet have become nebulous in the gossamer swirl of mist. Somehow you stay on the path, putting one foot in front of the other, intuitively feeling your way forward. You realize the fog is clearing, and ahead of you a beautiful temple emerges. The Sun shines brightly here at the top, and gray cloud gives way to blue sky. Shimmering drops of water glisten in an explosion of countless rainbows. You cross a small bridge and look down to see koi swimming in the water.*

*You come to the foot of the temple and ascend the stairs to the top. All is still, but from far off the sound of Buddhist chanting comes to you. A fierce lion statue guards the entry to the temple, and beside it is a large bronze incense burner. You pick up three sticks of incense and light them, holding them between your palms, at your heart. You feel compelled to bow, and you make a silent wish or request for help. What comes to your mind? Where can you most use compassion in your life at this time? You put your incense sticks in the sand, inside the large*

*burner, where they accompany hundreds of other incense sticks. You*
*take a deep breath and step over the threshold. You see that others have*
*neatly placed their shoes out here, and you stop to take yours off too.*

*You enter the hushed stillness of the sanctuary, and at the far end,*
*you see an elaborate altar with a large statue of Kwan Yin, surrounded*
*by offerings of flowers, fruit, and flickering candles. You walk toward*
*her and kneel in respect. You look up at the goddess, and her expression*
*is one of such gentle serenity and benevolence that you are suddenly*
*filled with a deep, enveloping sense of calm. It's as if all your worries,*
*sadness, and confusion have been lifted from you. You realize that noth-*
*ing is permanent, and spring always comes again. In gratitude, you*
*press your forehead to the floor, with your arms stretched over your*
*head, and silently thank Kwan Yin for her comfort and compassion.*
*You place the cherry blossoms into a container on the altar and turn to*
*leave, feeling lighter and more optimistic than you have in a long time.*

## Ritual: Calling on the Goddess of Compassion

### Kwan Yin's Incense

1 pinch sandalwood powder
1 pinch danshen dried root or powder
1–2 drops lotus oil
1 pinch five spice powder

Mix the ingredients and place in a small sealable plastic bag. The incense can be used immediately or stored for later use. As always, experiment with making a very small batch at a time, and adjust to your
preference.

### Calling on the Goddess of Compassion

Charcoal
Bell
Iconography of Kwan Yin, a statue or image in any of her aspects you
    are drawn to

Offering to the goddess: fruit, flowers, cakes, organic green tea or high
    mountain tea, Kwan Yin's Incense
White altar cloth, preferably silk
White candle
Paper
Pen
Container of clear, pure water
Small ceramic container filled with uncooked rice or fine sand

Cleanse your space and ground and center in your preferred way. Light the charcoal (it will take about ten to fifteen minutes to be whitish and ready for the incense). Ring the bell three times. Let the bell tone ring until it has completely dissipated before ringing again.

Prepare your altar to Kwan Yin, placing the statue or image in the center or, if she is tall, at the back of the altar and centered. Place your offerings respectfully around her. Light the small white candle in her honor and set it before her. Take your paper and either write a wish or ask for compassion from Kwan Yin. Carefully fold it and place it at her feet. Take the bowl of water and drink from it. This is the dew of compassion, clearing away and purifying unhelpful thoughts and emotions. Take as long as you wish to connect with Kwan Yin. Breathe deeply and slowly, aligning yourself with her qualities of compassion and serenity.

When you're ready and the charcoal is hot, take a tiny pinch of Kwan Yin's Incense and touch it to your heart and to your forehead, and then drop it onto the charcoal as an offering to her. Visualize your wish or request floating to her on the smoke of the incense. Silently ask Kwan Yin for what you need, or quietly speak the words aloud. Ring the bell three times. Thank Kwan Yin and trust that she will give you what you seek. You may wish to show your gratitude and respect by bowing three times with your palms pressed together at your third eye.

Do not blow out the candle. Either allow it to burn out safely or wave the flame out with your hand. Allow the incense to burn out safely, or if you must, quench it with the rice or sand.

# Pisces Correspondences

*Astrological Dates:* February 19 through March 20

*Sabbat:* Threshold sign between Imbolc and spring equinox (Ostara)

*Pisces Goddess Archetypes:* White Tara, Kwan Yin, Sedna, Persephone, the Andrianas, Idemili, Oshun, Yemaya, Nisaba, Brizo, the *leanan sidhe*, Mami Wata, Melusine, Morgan le Fay, Aufruvva

*House:* Twelfth

*Element:* Water

*Mode:* Mutable

*Planets:* Jupiter (traditional), Neptune (modern)

*Colors:* Soft gray, lilac, lavender, pastel ocean shades, silver green

*Crystals:* Ajoite, amethyst, aquamarine, chrysoprase, opal, pink tourmaline, smithsonite

*Essential Oils:* Jasmine, sandalwood, lemon balm, ylang-ylang, spearmint, lotus, lavender

*Parts of the Body:* Feet, lymphatic system

# CONCLUSION

We are at a time in history when the world needs the sacred feminine more than ever. It is the responsibility of each and every one of us to show up as our authentic selves, speak with our unique voices, and reclaim our connection to the Goddess. We are each the heroine of our own story, and it is our soul's mission to awaken the magick and mystery in our lives and, in the process, illuminate our own personal myth. As we walk our path, we will each embody the many faces of the Goddess at different junctures on our journey. There may be times we need to stand our ground and show up with the fierce face of Macha, ready to fight for what we believe in. We may find ourselves in a personal descent, and it is the face of Inanna we wear for a time. Perhaps we come to a place where it is the face of Kwan Yin we identify with, as we realize that compassion not only for others but also for ourselves is what is required. It is my sincere hope that you continue your path of seeking self-knowledge, kindling the sacred flame that illuminates new horizons and brings you a life of authenticity, passion, and purpose.

Blessings on your Quest!

# BIBLIOGRAPHY

Blundell, Sue, and Margaret Williamson, eds. *The Sacred and the Feminine in Ancient Greece*. New York: Routledge, 1998.

Cambrensis, Giraldus. *The Topography of Ireland*. Edited by Thomas Wright. Translated by Thomas Forester. Cambridge, ON: In Parentheses, 2000. PDF e-book.

Campbell, Joseph. *The Hero with a Thousand Faces*. 3rd ed. Novato, CA: New World Library, 2008.

Frazer, James George. *The Golden Bough: A Study in Magic and Religion*. Old Saybrook, CT: Konecky & Konecky, 2010. First published 1890 by Macmillan.

Gimbutas, Marija. *The Language of the Goddess*. New York: Harper Collins, 1989.

Graves, Robert. *The Greek Myths*. Rev. ed. Harmondsworth, UK: Penguin, 1960. PDF e-book.

———. *The White Goddess: A Historical Grammar of Poetic Myth*. 1948. Reprint, New York: Farrar, Straus & Giroux, 1999.

Green, Miranda. *Symbol and Image in Celtic Religous Art*. London: Routledge, 1992.

Greene, Liz. *Astrology for Lovers*. York Beach, MA: Weiser, 1989. First published 1980 by Stein & Day (New York) as *Star Signs for Lovers*.

Gregory, Augusta. *Gods and Fighting Men: The Story of the Tuatha de Danaan and of the Fianna of Ireland*. 1905. Reprint, Aukland, NZ: Floating Press, 2012. PDF e-book.

Guest, Charlotte, trans. *The Mabinogian*. New York: Dover, 1997. First published 1906 by J. M. Dent & Sons.

Gwynn, Edward, trans. *The Metrical Dindshenchas*. 4 vols. Electronic reproduction by Dublin Institute for Advanced Studies, 1991. First published 1903–06 by The Royal Irish Academy. http://www.ucc.ie/celt/published/T106500A/index.html.

Hamel, Debra. *Trying Neaira: The True Story of a Courtesan's Scandalous Life in Ancient Greece*. New Haven, CT: Yale University Press, 2003.

Hughes, J. Donald. "Artemis: Goddess of Conservation." *Forest and Conservation History* 34, no. 4 (Oct 1990): 191–97. doi:10.2307/3983705.

Jung, C. G. *Collected Works of C.G. Jung, Volume 5: Symbols of Transformation*. Princeton, NJ: Princeton University Press, 2014.

———. *Collected Works of C.G. Jung, Volume 8: Structure & Dynamics of the Psyche*. Princeton, NJ: Princeton University Press, 2014.

*The Lotus Sutra*. Translated by Tsugunari Kubo and Akira Yuyama. 2nd ed. Berkeley, CA: Numata Center for Buddhist Translation and Research, 2007. PDF e-book.

Macalister, R. A. Stewart, trans. *Lebor Gabála Érenn: The Book of the Taking of Ireland*. Dublin: Irish Text Society, 1956. https://archive.org/details/leborgablare00macauoft.

Monaghan, Patricia. *Encyclopedia of Goddesses and Heroines*. Novato, CA: New World Library, 2014.

———. *The New Book of Goddesses and Heriones*. St. Paul, MN: Llewellyn, 1981. Reprint, 1997.

Pinkola Estés, Clarissa. *Women Who Run with the Wolves: Myths and Stories of the Wild Woman Archetype*. New York. Ballentine Books: 1992.

Rayor, Diane J., trans. *The Homeric Hymns*. Berkeley: University of California Press, 2004.

Rhodes, Constantina. *Invoking Lakshmi: The Goddess of Wealth in Song and Ceremony*. Albany: SUNY Press, 2010.

———. "Lakshmi: Hindu Goddess of Abundance." In *Goddesses in World Culture*. Vol. 1, edited by Patricia Monaghan. Santa Barbara, CA: Praeger, 2011.

Rosen, Steve. *Essential Hinduism*. Santa Barbara, CA: Praeger, 2006.

Rosenzweig, Rachel. *Worshipping Aphrodite: Art and Culture in Classical Athens*. Ann Arbor: University of Michigan Press, 2004.

Schenker, Daniela. *Kuan Yin: Accessing the Power of the Divine Feminine*. Boulder, CO: Sounds True, 2007.

Shinoda Bolen, Jean. *Goddesses in Everywoman*: *A New Psychology of Women*. New York: Harper & Row, 1984.

———. *Goddesses in Older Women: Archetypes in Women over Fifty*. New York: Harper Collins, 2001.

Wolkstein, Diane, and Samuel Noah Kramer. *Inanna: Queen of Heaven and Earth*. New York: Harper Collins, 1983.

# ACKNOWLEDGMENTS

Deepest heartfelt gratitude to my husband and best friend, Jamie, who believed in me from the first day we met and I showed him my goddess-inspired paintings. Thank you for supporting me throughout all the incarnations that this work has moved through and for gifting me the time to concentrate on writing this book. Goddess only knows if this book would ever have been completed without your ministrations of tea and massages, red wine and chocolate.

Thank you to my son, Jesse. From the day they put you into my arms, I knew you for the questing visionary Sagittarius you were born to be. You have taught me what it is to know the nurturing face of Demeter, as well as the protective and fierce face of Macha. Thank you for your patience as I learned the ropes, went back to school, and did my best to figure it all out. Everything I do is for you.

Thank you to my family for your encouragement along the way to completing this book: Mom, Vaysha, and Andre. Thank you to all my clients over the years who taught me more about astrology and archetypes than all the books I've read. Special gratitude to all the amazing souls who read my manuscript and gifted me with your support and blessings. More than once I was brought to tears by your kindness and gracious generosity. In the order in which these wonderful words came through, thanks to Anne Newkirk Niven, Ashleen O'Gaea, Adam Elenbaas, Steven Forrest, Stephanie Woodfield, Lisa Tenzin-Dolma, Jhenah

Telendru, Mickie Mueller, Kris Waldherr, Deborah Blake, Jen McConnel, Brandi Auset, Ellen Dugan, and Donna Henes. And, of course, special gratitude to my Teacher, astrologer and author Erin Sullivan.

Thank you to my dear friend Michelle Carlson of Solstice Stones for your wisdom in choosing crystals that resonate with each astrological archetype. Thanks to Rebecca Coates for your patience and editorial insight in the earliest stages of this book. A shout-out to my good friend and colleague Kelly Benson for years of near-daily conversations about astrology, as well as listening to my occasional fiery rants and chalking it up to my double Aries, Scorpio rising. And of course, a special thank-you to my editors at Llewellyn: Senior Acquisitions Editor Elysia Gallo, for giving me the chance to see a lifelong dream fulfilled, and for all your encouragement and wisdom along the way; and to my production editor, Lauryn Heineman, for your keen editorial eye, and for talking this first-time author off the ledge more than once. Thank you, all.

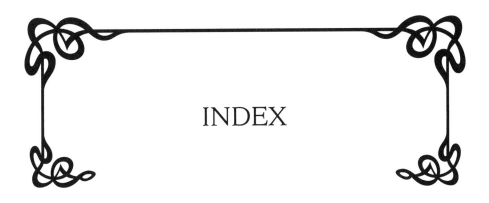

# INDEX

# To Write to the Author

If you wish to contact the author or would like more information about this book, please write to the author in care of Llewellyn Worldwide Ltd. and we will forward your request. Both the author and publisher appreciate hearing from you and learning of your enjoyment of this book and how it has helped you. Llewellyn Worldwide Ltd. cannot guarantee that every letter written to the author can be answered, but all will be forwarded. Please write to:

Danielle Blackwood
℅ Llewellyn Worldwide
2143 Wooddale Drive
Woodbury, MN 55125-2989
Please enclose a self-addressed stamped envelope for reply,
or $1.00 to cover costs. If outside the U.S.A., enclose
an international postal reply coupon.

Many of Llewellyn's authors have websites with additional information and resources. For more information, please visit our website at http://www.llewellyn.com.